The
Common Sense
of Politics

Books by Mortimer J. Adler

The
Common Sense
of Politics

MORTIMER J. ADLER

HOLT, RINEHART AND WINSTON

New York   Chicago

San Francisco

Published simultaneously in Canada by Holt, Rinehart
and Winston of Canada, Limited.

Library of Congress Catalog Card Number: 72-138870
SBN: 03-085966-2

First Edition

Designer: Ernst Reichl

Printed in the United States of America

TO

ROBERT MAYNARD HUTCHINS

Lawyer, Constitutionalist,
Philosopher, Revolutionary

Contents

Part Four

The Goal of Progress and the End of Revolution

Preface

In my Preface to *The Time of Our Lives,* which undertook to expound the ethics of common sense, I announced my intention to write this companion volume on the common sense of politics. The two books dovetail as reciprocally interdependent parts of a single whole—moral philosophy, of which the part that is ethics deals with the problems of the good life, and the part that is politics deals with the problems of the good society. Distinct in substance by virtue of the quite different problems with which they deal, they are alike in method and approach: both offer themselves as philosophical refinements of common-sense wisdom, and both are normative rather than descriptive—both attempt to prescribe ideals that ought to be pursued and the steps that ought to be taken toward their realization.

In *The Time of Our Lives,* I commented on the decline of moral philosophy in the twentieth century and painstakingly answered objections to discourse that is not embarrassed to affirm and defend the truth of moral principles. So far as the problems of ethics are concerned, some positive efforts have been made in this century to propose solutions that have the look of novelty and that claim to establish normative truths concerning what is good and bad, or right and wrong. In my judgment, all of these efforts have failed: their appearance of novelty derives from ignorance of traditional thought, especially that of antiquity and the Middle Ages; and their claims are vitiated by errors that have been overlooked.

When we turn from ethics by politics, we find that the decay of moral philosophy has gone even further. There have been almost no positive efforts, on the part of leading twentieth-century writers, to address themselves to the problems of politics in a normative manner. Normative political philosophy has almost ceased to exist and has been supplanted, in the literature and teaching of the subject, by historical studies and descriptive discourse. If I were asked to list twentieth-century writings that, on the basis of clearly formulated normative truths, project political ideals which, reflecting conditions, problems, and trends new in this century, look to the future for their realization, I could name only a few: Bertrand Russell's *Roads to Freedom,* Jacques Maritain's *Man and the State,* Yves Simon's *Philosophy of Democratic Government,* and John Strachey's *Challenge of Democracy.*

If one restricts himself, as I have attempted, to purely normative considerations and to the exposition of principles that have the certainty and universality appropriate to political wisdom, much that usually fills the pages of books on politics will be omitted. The reader should be forewarned that he will not find lengthy discussions of historical or contemporary institutions, nor will he find panaceas, jeremiads, activist programs, political polemics, or shibboleths. For such omissions he will be compensated, I hope, by the fact that this book tries to provide him with the standards for judging political institutions, past and present, and for assessing the conflicting appeals made by the major political movements of the day. It should certainly protect him against the inflammatory rhetoric that exhorts or denounces without defined objectives, defensible standards, factual basis, or rational argument.

If the political theory here set forth is rejected, as I think it will be, by both the old right and the new left, that will confirm my judgment of its soundness. To the professed or unwitting anarchist of the new left, its controlling principles will appear to bespeak reactionary conservatism. To the reactionary conservative of the old right, the ideal of the classless establishment that it projects will appear to be revolutionary, and may even evoke such epithets as "anarchistic" or "communistic." That is, perhaps, as it should be, for the doctrine of this book is both conservative and revolutionary—conservative without being reactionary, and revolutionary without being either anarchistic or communistic.

So far as this book does relate directly to the cross currents of opinion and action on the contemporary political scene, the one tendency or trend that it explicitly challenges is the recently revived anti-political philosophy of anarchism, which underlies or pervades the various revolutionary movements that are united, if by nothing else, at least by their opposition to "the Establishment." My aim is not merely to expose the fallacies and utopian illusions of the anarchist doctrine, but to restore faith in politics —faith in the reform and improvement of our institutions as the only way to perfect society and better the conditions of man on earth. That is why I have thought it appropriate to dedicate this book to my old and good friend, Robert M. Hutchins, who, as administrator and educator, as conservative and reformer, has been the staunchest and ablest defender of that faith in both thought and action.

The Common Sense of Politics has been elaborated from the fourth series of Encyclopaedia Britannica Lectures delivered at the University of Chicago, under the same title, in the spring of 1970. I am once more grateful to the University of Chicago for the auspices it has provided, and to Encyclopaedia Britannica, Inc. for its initiation and support of this lectureship at the University.

Like the three earlier books that were developed from Encyclopaedia Britannica Lectures at the University of Chicago, this one has also profited greatly from the collaboration of my colleagues at the Institute for Philosophical Research, of which I am Director. I am especially grateful to Charles Van Doren, Otto Bird, George Ducas, John Van Doren, and Arthur L. H. Rubin for their critical comments on the lecture outlines and on the manuscript of this book at various stages in its development, and for the emendations and improvements that they suggested. I also wish to thank other members of the Institute staff for bibliographical research, for the preparation of the index, and for the typing and editing of the manuscript. I cannot leave unspoken my debt of gratitude to my wife for the lively dialogue, generous patience, and sustaining encouragement that have helped me immeasurably in producing this book and its three predecessors.

Mortimer J. Adler

Chicago
November, 1970

Part One

Ethics, Politics, and History

CHAPTER I

Introduction:
Common Sense and Politics

(1)

I N every country of the Western world, three flags are flying —the national emblem of the establishment and two revolutionary flags, one the red flag of communism, the other the black flag of anarchy. If the repressive forces of the police state were not operative in countries that have adopted the red flag for the emblem of their establishments, counter-revolutionary flags might be flying there too.

The present age is revolutionary the world over. But this does not distinguish it from earlier centuries, certainly not the nineteenth, or even the eighteenth. Because of almost instant global communication, we may be more conscious than earlier centuries that revolution is in the air everywhere, but in one form or another revolution has always been pervasive, just as establishments of one kind or another have always prevailed—from the very beginning of organized society. In fact, it might almost be said that establishment and revolution have been inseparable and reciprocating features of organized social life; government and opposition thereto, or institutions and the change thereof, are everywhere found together in the pages of history.

That this has been the case does not by itself warrant the conclusion that it must always be the case. The facts of history, even when they are without exceptions, do not demonstrate universal laws and should not mislead us into thinking that the past shows us what the future must necessarily be like. One of the questions with which we shall be concerned, especially in the concluding chapters of this book, is the question about the future of revolution; or to put it another way, whether revolution must always be, as it has so far been, an inseparable feature of man's political life on earth.

Both the red flag of communism and the black flag of anarchy represent opposition to the establishment, but they also stand for tendencies or impulses that are themselves opposed. It is one thing to seek to overthrow the existing establishment in order to replace it by another that is thought to be better, and it is quite another thing to call for the demolition of all establishments in order to usher in a totally new state of affairs in the social life of man on earth—a state of affairs in which men will live together in peace and with justice but without any form of dominion of man over man or any exercise of organized force. The proponent of anarchy, if we consider only his opposition to an existing establishment, can be regarded as a revolutionist, since the revolutionary impulse is characterized by such opposition. But the proponent of anarchy is misunderstood if he is classed as just another revolutionist. His opposition is not to this or that establishment, but to all establishments—to government itself and to all the other institutions of organized society that he lumps together under the name "state."

To keep this significant difference clear, I propose to call the revolutionist who wishes to overthrow an existing establishment in order to replace it by another a "political revolutionist," in contradistinction to the "anarchistic revolutionist," who seeks to overthrow all establishments and replace them by none.

I will presently comment on the various meanings of the word "political," but for the moment I would like to use it to cover all the institutions of organized society—that total ensemble of established arrangements and practices that the anarchist lumps together under the name "state." Employing the word "political" in that sense, we can say that the political revolutionist is one who seeks to improve human life or society by institutional changes of one sort or another—through supplanting one set of institutions by another. In contrast, the anarchistic revolutionist—or, for short, the anarchist—is one who seeks to improve human life or society by non-institutional means or, what is the same, by emancipating mankind from the trammels of the state.

I pointed out a moment ago that revolutionary movements, activities, or impulses cannot be regarded as a distinctive characteristic of the present age. But I think that it can be said with historical accuracy that anarchism is. I do not mean that it is the dominant tendency of the present age, that it enlists the support of a substantial or numerous following, or that it is in the foreground rather than in the wings of the stage on which the conflicts of our day are being acted out. What I have in mind is that the doctrine of anarchism—sometimes called "philosophical anarchism"—was born in the last two hundred years and has gained a certain currency in our own day. Its first appearance can be dated with the publication of William Godwin's *Inquiry Concerning Political Justice* in 1793. There are traces of it in the writings of Thoreau, as an implication of his doctrine of civil disobedience, and a very special form of it appears in the Marxist theory of the withering away of the state—as the ultimate, not the proximate, objective of the revolutionary program. But it is not until the latter half of the nineteenth century and the first quarter of the twentieth that revolutionary anarchism receives its first full dress promulgation in the writings of Bakunin and Kropotkin in Russia and of Proudhon and Sorel in France. It is only with them that the annihilation of the state becomes an uncompromising and immediate objective of revolutionary action. [1]

While it cannot be said that these writings have been widely read or carefully studied by large numbers in the present century, no more than it can be said that many of those who sympathize with Marxism have been close readers or careful students of the major treatises of Marx, Engels, or Lenin, anarchistic sympathies are nevertheless widespread in the world today, especially among the younger generation and most especially among those who are in the forefront of the opposition to the present state of affairs, both in the United States and abroad. There may not be many in this group who are full-fledged anarchists—committed followers of the doctrines of a Bakunin or a Sorel. Nevertheless, among those who express profound dissatisfaction with the way that things are set up and being run, we find a manifest and growing loss of faith in institutional change as the way to remedy the trouble.

What is new in the world today and distinctive of our time is the conflict between those who think that, where our institutions are defective, the defects can be removed by institutional changes of one sort or another and those who despair of institutional change itself and who turn, in their desperation, to noninstitutional means of reaching the promised land of a better day.

(2)

Preeminent among the motives responsible for the writing of this book is the desire on my part to do what I can to restore faith in politics—to combat the current hopelessness about improving the condition of mankind by improving our institutions.

Before I mention another of my controlling motives, I cannot refrain from referring to a recent paper by Robert M. Hutchins. He proposed "five possibilities that [might] brighten the prospects of this scientific and technological age." The first four are the redefinition and restoration of liberal education; the redefinition of the university; the redefinition and restoration of the idea of a profession; and the revival of philosophy. The fifth, he wrote, "is the restoration of and the resort to politics." Antecedent thereto, I would add, is the restoration of our faith in politics; and that, as this book will suggest, is dependent both on the restoration of liberal education and the revival of philosophy.

"The decay of political philosophy," Mr. Hutchins went on to say, "means that politics is nothing but the exercise of power. . . . Politics so conceived cannot help us find the means of guiding and controlling science and technology. On the contrary, the conception of politics as power has produced and will continue to reproduce the situation we have today, in which science and technology are being exploited for the purposes of power in such a way as to threaten the existence of the race.

"Politics," Mr. Hutchins continued, "is and ought to be the architectonic science. It is the science of the common good. Good is a moral term. The common good is a good that accrues to every member of the community because he belongs to it; he would not have it if he did not belong to it. The task of politics," he concluded, "is to define the common good and to organize the community to achieve it." [2]

I will shortly attempt to expand on these remarks of Mr. Hutchins by a fuller explanation of the approach that will be made in this book to a conception of politics and to a statement of the principles of political philosophy—an approach that is motivated by a desire to restore faith in political or institutional means for achieving progress. But first I would like to dwell for a moment on the other consideration that motivates my approach to the subject. It is my sense that the present generation of the students in our colleges and universities not only manifest a growing loss of faith in politics, but also reveal a massive ignorance of history and, worse, a rejection of what can be learned from the past as totally irrelevant to present-day concerns. [3]

The two phenomena are hardly disconnected. I draw my faith in politics from my reading of history. I think this is true of others who find in history not only the record of institutional progress, but also the promise of further progress to be made by further institutional changes. Only ignorance of history could lead to the mistaken impression, mentioned earlier, that a revolutionary spirit or revolutionary activity distinctively characterizes the present age. Ignorance of history might also generate the false supposition that anarchism has always been one of the revolutionary forces at work in the efforts of men to improve their condition. It is not just ignorance of history that matters, though the gravity of such ignorance can hardly be overestimated. What is even more serious is the dismissal of the past as irrelevant—even so recent a past as the opening decades of the present century up to the end of the Second World War.

Let me concede at once, lest I be misunderstood, that the past is not of critical relevance to all our human concerns. There are speculative and scientific questions that can be fruitfully investigated without recourse to history. This is even true of the basic questions concerning the good life for man. But it is not true of the basic questions concerning the good society. Here we have a fundamental difference between ethics and politics as the two main branches of moral philosophy. I will have more to say on this point presently, when I discuss the ways in which these two branches of moral philosophy are related to one another. For the moment, I wish only to stress the fact that historic changes in the institutions of society have occasioned seminal political insights and have led to the general acknowledgment of political truths. The historic changes did not establish the truth of the political principles thus discovered; but they did make these truths discoverable and make them generally known.

All who are concerned with the improvement of human life on earth, and especially with the improvement of human society, must ultimately choose between two views of the main source of progress in human affairs. One looks to meliorative changes in human nature; the other to meliorative changes in human institutions. Let me declare at once my commitment to the second view, postponing until later my reasons for thinking it the only sound view of the matter. I am asserting, in short, that all the progress that has so far been made in the social life of man has been accomplished by cumulative improvements in man's social institutions, without any improvement—indeed, without any significant change—in the nature of man. Those who have lost faith in politics and who brand the past as irrelevant should be able to show that this proposition is factually false if they wish to defend the position that they take on more than emotional grounds.

(3)

So far I have concerned myself with the state of mind of those who may need a corrective for their tendency to turn away from politics and from the past. But such considerations do not define the scope and subject-matter of this book, which, I hope, will be instructive as well as therapeutic. Its title contains two words that I must comment on if I am going to make clear what it is about and, just as important, what it is not about. One is the word "politics"; the other, "common sense."

That second term has played a pivotal role in two earlier books of mine which, like this one, were based on the Britannica Lectures that I delivered at the University of Chicago. In the book based on the first series of Britannica Lectures, common-sense opinions, formed in the light of common experience, were shown to be the rudiments out of which philosophy develops by critical reflection. [4] The sub-title of the book based on the third series of Britannica Lectures was "The Ethics of Common Sense."[5]

The shift in the phrasing—from the ethics of common sense to the common sense of politics—does not portend a change of intention. In both cases, my aim is identical: to expound the truths of moral philosophy—in the first case those of ethics, in the second case those of politics—which are known to the reflective man of common sense in the light of common experience. The moral philosopher, concerned with the problems of ethics or of politics, shares these truths with the man of common sense. In both fields, common sense, consisting of the insights that men develop by reflection on the facts of common experience, is the point of departure and the occasion for philosophizing. In both fields, such philosophizing as we can do is nothing but the rational development of common sense—by definitions, distinctions, analyses, and arguments. Such wisdom as we can attain in either ethics or politics is common sense philosophically defended and philosophically developed.

In politics, as in ethics, the attempt to expound such philosophical wisdom as we possess should set forth principles that a reasonable man of common sense would recognize as true, in the light of his common experience (without the need of anything to be learned by specialized research or additional investigation), by bringing to bear, on that common experience, his intellectual resources—his ability to think clearly, cogently, and critically; in short, his capacity for being reasonable and rational.

However, the word "ethics" used in connection with "common sense" does not give rise to as many possible misunderstandings as the word "politics" used in the same connection, largely because the latter word has such diverse connotations in everyday discourse and in academic parlance. The word "ethics" in everyday discourse usually connotes the consideration of what is good and bad, or right and wrong, for the individual in the conduct of his life. The word "politics" is rarely used in a parallel fashion, to connote the consideration of what is good and bad, or right and wrong, in the institutions of society. On the contrary, it is for the most part used in a variety of other senses.

Most frequently, in ordinary speech, it is used to refer to engagement in the affairs of government. Thus, we speak of men going into politics or getting out of politics. With almost equal frequency, it is used even more broadly to refer to any kind of maneuvering or machination aimed at getting and holding power —any form of power play. Not only in the sphere of government but in all forms of corporate enterprise—in universities, hospitals, museums, and businesses—we describe men as engaged in politics when they vie with one another for power. It was in this sense of the term that many years ago Professor Harold Lasswell wrote a book entitled *Politics: Who Gets What, When, How.* [6] And it is in this sense that politics is thought of as the art for which Machiavelli wrote the rules.

This book is not concerned with politics so conceived. Nor is it concerned with politics as a branch of descriptive behavioral science. Here once again we find that the words "ethics" and "politics" are no longer used, as they once were, in a parallel fashion. For the most part, ethics is still regarded as a branch of philosophy, and it is usually so taught, not as a behavioral science. But unless one specifically names the subject of one's interest as political philosophy or political thought, a reference to politics in academic circles will usually be understood as signifying political science. What is at stake here in insisting on the distinction between political philosophy and political science—

or politics as a branch of philosophy and politics as a behavioral science—is the importance of maintaining the line that separates the evaluative or normative from the purely descriptive approach to politics.

With regard to human conduct, there is a clear difference between questions concerning how men do in fact behave and questions concerning how they ought to behave—what end they ought to seek and what means they should employ in seeking it. So with regard to human society, there is an equally clear difference between questions concerning how in fact society is organized, how its institutions are formed, and how they are operated, and questions concerning the ends that organized society should serve and the institutional means that should be employed to achieve those goals.

Questions of the first type are questions of fact, to be answered by empirical investigations productive of scientific knowledge. Such questions are beyond the competence of common sense to answer in a reliable fashion. More than common experience is needed to answer them. Questions of the second type are, in contradistinction, usually called questions of value—questions about what is good and bad, right and wrong. Here common sense, based on common experience and enlightened by rational reflection, can provide the rudimentary answers that philosophical analysis and argument is then able to perfect and defend.

Hence it should be clear that a book concerned with the common sense of politics is concerned with politics as a branch of practical philosophy and as a normative discipline, not with politics as a branch of descriptive behavioral science and as an empirical or investigative inquiry. [7]

(4)

I trust that I have now roughly indicated the scope and subject-matter of this book—what it will try to do and what it will not attempt. I know, of course, that full clarity about this cannot be achieved at the outset; I can only hope that it will develop.

Nevertheless, it may be useful to call attention here to three additional points that will prepare for what is to follow.

First of all, let me say that unless I specifically indicate some other meaning, I will always use the word "politics" to stand for political philosophy—a branch of practical or moral philosophy. Philosophy is practical rather than speculative when it is concerned with *what ought to be* rather than *what is or happens*—with the norms or standards of action rather than with the modes of being or becoming. And practical philosophy is, in my conception of it, identical with moral philosophy. Questions about what is good and bad, or right and wrong, whether with regard to individual conduct or with regard to the institutions and operations of society, are moral questions. The word "ethics" is sometimes used as if it were identical in meaning with "moral philosophy." But, clearly, ethics does not exhaust moral philosophy when the latter is understood as covering questions about the good society as well as questions about the good life. I will presently discuss ethics and politics as the twin branches of moral philosophy—how they are related to each other and how they differ. For the moment, the only point that I wish to reiterate is that moral philosophy is not to be identified with ethics exclusively, for it includes politics as well.

Second, let me comment briefly on the two meanings that I will attach to the adjective "political." One is the narrow meaning that we employ when we distinguish the political from the economic or the social. In this narrow meaning, political institutions are the institutions of government—its framework, its constitution, its offices, its laws. Used narrowly, "political" does not apply to all the aspects of society; it does not cover social arrangements, customs, or practises that lie outside the sphere of government and law, though they may be affected by it; nor does it cover the economic institutions and processes of society, though these too may be affected by government and law. We have this narrow meaning in mind when we speak of political as contrasted with economic or social justice, or distinguish between political and economic or social revolutions.

The other and broader meaning with which I will use the word "political" covers all aspects of society—not only the institutions of government, but social and economic institutions as well, *insofar as the latter are in any way affected by the institutions of government.* Please note the proviso that I have just mentioned: "insofar as social and economic institutions are in any way affected by the institutions of government." According to this stipulation, whatever social or economic arrangements or practices are *in no way affected* by the institutions of government lie outside the sphere of the political, even in the broad sense of that term.

The term "political economy" was once used to signify the consideration of the economic aspects of society insofar as these are affected by the institutions of government. The parallel term, "political sociology," might have been invented to signify the consideration of social arrangements and practices that are similarly conditioned or affected. If one were to add the further stipulation that political economy and political sociology, thus conceived, are, like politics itself, normative disciplines and parts of moral philosophy, there would be little danger of confusing them with scientific economics and sociology as these are now pursued in our universities. The latter are descriptive, not normative disciplines; they are branches of behavioral science; and they do not limit themselves to the study of those economic and social phenomena that are affected by the institutions of government. In what follows, I will always indicate whether I am using the term "political" in the narrow or the broad sense whenever, for clarity, it becomes necessary to do so.

Third, and most important of all, I must call attention to the strict limitation that I will observe in this treatment of the problems of political philosophy. Not only will it deal with normative questions exclusively, but it will also limit itself to such answers as can be found on the level of universal principles, applicable to every variety of circumstance. It will not go below that level to questions of policy or to matters that call for decisions in particular cases. Let me explain this threefold division of the levels of normative or practical thought—thought aimed at action and concerned with what goals should be sought and what means should be chosen to achieve them. [8]

The highest level is the level of universal principles. In the sphere of ethics, this is the level on which we deal with the conception of the good life as the ultimate end that men should seek and with the means that they should employ in seeking it. Statements about the end and the means constitute the universal principles of ethics, applicable to men at all times and places, without regard to the vast range of individual differences among men and the wide variety of external circumstances under which men live at different times and places. Politics, on this highest level of practical thought, deals with the ideal of the good society as a means to the good life and with the shape that its institutions must take in order to realize the ideal thus conceived. Here, as in the case of ethics, statements about the end and the means constitute the principles of politics, having a universality that is comparable to that of the principles of ethics, even though historic circumstances critically condition our discovery and acknowledgment of them. I will have more to say on this last point, for it represents a major difference between ethics and politics as related branches of practical or moral philosophy.

The second or intermediate level of practical thought is the level of rules or policies, which have a generality that is relative to a given set of circumstances. In the sphere of ethics, this is the level of practical thinking on which a certain type of man formulates general rules or policies for applying universal principles to his own life, different from that of other men by virtue of the type of man he is and also, perhaps, by reference to the type of circumstances beyond his control that condition his life. On this level, practical thinking in politics is concerned with adapting universal principles to the contingent circumstances of a particular historic society. Thus, for example, the institution of political liberty may be an indispensable means for realizing the ideal of a good society, but understanding and acknowledging the truth of this universal principle leaves open many difficult and complex questions about the establishment and operation of political liberty in a given society under its special set of historic circumstances—questions of policy about which reasonable men can disagree.

The third and lowest level of practical thought is the level of decisions, the level at which the thinking we do is proximate to action. It is the level on which we make a judgment about what is to be done here and now in this singular case that confronts us and calls for action on our part. In the sphere of ethics, this is the level on which universal principles, mediated and adapted by general rules or policies, are applied by the deliberation in which we engage when we have to decide how we should act here and now in our effort to make a good life for ourselves. It is on this level that political decisions are made, whether by the officials or by the constituents of government. The members of a legislature enacting a law, the judge deciding a case, the executive determining for or against a particular administrative act, and the citizen voting for this candidate and the policy he stands for rather than for his opponent—all are operating on this level, and they do so more or less wisely to the extent that their decision is reached by deliberations that involve the consideration of the universally applicable principles of politics and the relevant general policies which makes those principles applicable to a particular society.

In the strict sense in which practical philosophy consists of such wisdom as men can achieve about the problems of action, practical philosophy is necessarily limited to the first or highest level—the level of universal principles. At its very best, it consists of no more than a slim body of fundamental truths. This is not a limitation that I am imposing arbitrarily or as a matter of convenience. It is a limitation that philosophy must impose upon itself if it wishes to make good its claim that its formulations have the character of practical wisdom.

I am not saying that philosophers have always observed this limitation. On the contrary, they have usually transgressed it, especially in the sphere of politics. From Aristotle to Mill, the great political philosophers or theorists have not restricted themselves to questions of principle at the highest level; they have also dealt in detail and at length with problems that occur at the two lower levels. The solutions of such problems do not have the universality and cannot be demonstrated with the degree of certitude that is requisite for wisdom. In consequence, they have also introduced into their writings matters that belong to descriptive political science rather than to normative political philosophy. [9]

I am going to try scrupulously to observe the limitation that I think a political philosopher should impose upon himself. If I succeed, one consequence will be the omission of many matters that are traditionally discussed in treatises on political theory. I hope that I can retain the reader's interest even though I will not touch on many of the issues or deal with many of the problems that occur to him when he thinks about politics—problems that are genuine, important, and urgent on the second and third level, but which are, in my judgment, beyond the special competence of philosophy as such.

(5)

May I anticipate the objection or protest that will probably occur to the reader? Does not such purism prevent political philosophy from being practically useful? And from being of vital interest? How can it be said that political philosophy is practical when the universal principles that exclusively occupy its attention, even if they constitute the best wisdom we can achieve, are obviously inadequate by themselves for the solution of the practical problems of society and social life?

The answer to that question must begin by admitting—more than that, by emphasizing—the inadequacy of practical philosophy, be it ethics or politics, to solve the difficult, complex practical problems that arise for men living in a particular society, under the special circumstances prevailing at a given historic time and place. Universal principles do not by themselves decide what is to be done in particular cases; nor do they automatically determine our choice of the best among conflicting policies, all reasonable, and all applicable to a particular set of circumstances. Failing in these two respects, the universal principles of political philosophy are woefully inadequate for the solution of practical problems.

However, though ethical or political wisdom is inadequate for the solution of the practical problems that confront us, it is nevertheless indispensable for achieving sound solutions to them. Universal principles constitute the framework—the broad outline or plan—within which sound solutions can be and must be developed. They point us in the right direction. The framework they provide is like a map that helps us to find our way to our destination, even though it does not tell us everything that we need to know in order to get there. This framework of universal principles cannot tell us which of two sound policies to adopt or which of two reasonable courses of action to take, but it does provide us with the basis for discriminating between sound and unsound policies and between reasonable and unreasonable courses—those that fall within the framework of principles and so are wise decisions and those that do not and so are unwise.

Thus it is political wisdom, achieved only at the level of universal principles, that safeguards against making fundamental errors and keeps us from going in the wrong direction. As I have written elsewhere, "without it we would have no assured guidance at all, even though the guidance it does provide does not suffice at every turn of the road." [10] Hence when we confess that political wisdom is by itself inadequate for practical purposes, we should be quick to add that it is also practically indispensable.

CHAPTER 2

The Good Life
and the Good Society

(1)

POLITICS is sometimes regarded as the sovereign or controlling discipline in the practical order—the order of action. It was called the architectonic discipline by Aristole many centuries ago, and it was so called by Robert Hutchins in the recent essay I quoted earlier.

Mr. Hutchins explained why he regarded politics as architectonic. Politics, he said, aims at the common good. The common good is the end to be served by political action and political institutions. The common good—the good that is somehow shared or participated in by a number of individuals—would seem to be a greater good than the good of any one individual. John Stuart Mill and the utilitarians have argued in a similar manner. The general happiness, sometimes referred to as "the greatest good for the greatest number," takes precedence over the happiness of any one individual.

Hence if ethics is the discipline that is concerned with the good life for the single individual and politics the discipline that is concerned with the common good, the general happiness, or the general walfare, politics would seem to be architectonic, by virtue of having a superior end in view.

Though the argument appears to be clear and cogent as thus stated, it needs further clarification with regard to its basic terms. The truth of the matter is more complicated. Without denying the sense in which politics is architectonic, I will try to show that ethics is architectonic in another and more fundamental sense.

We have already observed that ethics and politics are related branches of practical or moral philosophy—both are practical in that they are concerned with action; and both are moral or normative in that they deal prescriptively with ends and means: with what ends ought to be sought or aimed at, and with what means should be devised or chosen to achieve those ends. To distinguish them as related branches of moral philosophy, I would like to repeat an earlier statement that I made about the end or ultimate good with which each is concerned.

The sphere of ethics is the good human life. Its primary and controlling question is: *What ought a man do in order to make his life really good?* And its primary normative principle is that every man ought to try to make a really good life for himself. The sphere of politics is the good society. Its primary question is: *What institutions should be devised and how should they be organized and operated in order to produce a good society?* But what is the primary normative principle of politics? Is there one comparable to the first principle of ethics—that one ought to seek everything that is really good for oneself and nothing but that which is really good?

When one understands the distinction between real and apparent goods, it is immediately evident that real goods ought to be desired; and hence that a good life, consisting in the possession of all real goods, ought to be sought. That principle is self-evident; it is the one and only self-evident principle in ethics. The comparable first princple of politics would appear to be that a good society ought to be aimed at. But here we can give a reason for the *ought;* and since we can, that principle is not self-evident as is the first principle of ethics. [1]

The reason, which will become clearer as we proceed, is that the good society is itself an indispensable or necessary means to the achievement of a really good life by the human beings who comprise it. Thus we see that the ultimate end at which politics aims, the good society, is itself a means to the ultimate end with which ethics is concerned, the good human life. This being so, politics is subordinate to ethics. The ordering of the good society to the good life, as means to end, makes ethics architectonic.

Now let me return to the other way of looking at the same picture, in which it still remains true that politics is architectonic. When it stays strictly within its own sphere, ethics considers only the means that the individual—a single human being—ought to employ in order to achieve the really good life that he ought to make for himself. Politics enters the picture, even with regard to the good life for a single individual, because there are certain goods involved that are not within the individual's power. He depends upon the existence, institutions, and actions of organized society for certain of the things that he needs in order to make a good life for himself.

However, in providing the individual with the conditions or means that are not wholly within his own power or mastery, organized society does not restrict itself to any one single individual. The institutions and operations of organized society always affect a number of individuals—in fact, *all* the individuals who comprise it. In saying this, I do not mean that society always provides the conditions of a good life for *all* its members. On the contrary, it never has done so in the course of history so far. Up to the present, organized society, at its best, has always favored some and disfavored others. The numbers of those whom it has benefited, by helping them to lead good lives for themselves, has varied from the few to the many, but it has never been *all*.

Nevertheless, it remains true that insofar as organized society has been good to any degree whatsoever, its goodness has consisted in its promoting the pursuit of happiness (i.e., the effort to make a really good life) for some number of individuals: whether the *few* or the *many*, but always *more than one*, even if never *all*. Hence politics, in being concerned with the good society, which is a means to the good life of its members (few, many, or all), has as its ultimate concern the good life or happiness of a number of individuals. Since the ultimate good of a number of individuals is greater than the ultimate good of a single individual, politics aims at a greater good, and is in this sense architectonic. The truth that politics is architectonic in this sense remains quite compatible with the truth that ethics is architectonic in the sense that the good society, at which politics aims, is itself a means to the good life, with which ethics is concerned.

Let me restate the point another way. The good life provides the standard or measure for judging the goodness of organized society; in this respect, politics presupposes ethics, and ethics is architectonic or primary. The good society is indispensable as a means to the good life, and in providing the conditions that the individual cannot provide for himself, it serves the general happiness rather than the happiness of a single individual. In this sense, and only in this sense, is politics architectonic. [2]

(2)

The term "common good" has played a critical role in the preceding discussion. It has a number of meanings that we must distinguish and keep clear.

One of its meanings derives from that sense of "common" that refers to what is the same in a number of individuals. Thus, all real goods, which satisfy the natural needs of man, are common goods. Human nature being the same in all individual members of the human species, natural needs are the same in all individuals. Real goods being the goods that satisfy natural needs, they, too, are the same for all individuals. Consisting in the possession of all real goods, a really good life or happiness is the same for all men. Happiness or the good life is, therefore, a common good in this sense of the word "common."

But there is another sense in which something can be common to a number of individuals, not through their being the same in this or that respect, but through their participating or sharing in that one thing. Thus, for example, a tract of land is called a "common" when it is not exclusively owned by anyone and is shared by a number of individuals. In this sense, the good of an organized community is a common good, in which some (few, many, or all) of its members share. When we speak of the good society, the good we are referring to is the goodness of the organized community as such, and this goodness is a common good, one that is shared by or participated in by its members.

Two Latin phrases may help us to remember this distinction of senses. *Bonum commune hominis* signifies the good that is common to a number of men simply because as men they are all the same; *bonum commune communitatis* signifies the good that is common to a number of individuals because they are members of one and the same organized community. It should now be clear that the common good enters into the considerations of politics in both senses of the term. Since it aims at the good society, politics is concerned directly with the *bonum commune communitatis*, the good or goods of the organized community in which its members share—some at least, if not all. And since the good society is itself a means to the good life, politics is concerned indirectly with the *bonum commune hominis*—the ultimate good or happiness that is the same for all men because they are men.

(3)

Because ethics and politics are related in the ways that have been indicated, it is almost impossible for an exposition of either subject to avoid crossing the line that separates them. But the reason why a treatise on ethics as a branch of moral philosophy must deal with certain matters that belong to politics is not the same as the reason why a treatise on politics—again as a branch of moral philosophy—must advert to ethical considerations.

If all the conditions requisite for or all the means involved in making a really good life were wholly within the individual's control, it would not be at all necessary for a treatise on ethics to discuss the institutions of society, for they would play no significant role in the pursuit of happiness. But this is not the case. On the contrary, such things as war, slavery, poverty, unhealthy conditions of life, lack of educational opportunity, deprivation of liberty, lack of free time, and so on, clearly affect the pursuit of happiness; and it is equally clear that whether such conditions or their opposites exist lies beyond the power of the single individual to control. Whether or not these adverse conditions or their opposites prevail lies within the power of the organized community, to whatever extent they are subject to human control at a given time in history.

Hence in expounding the truths of ethics, the moral philosopher cannot avoid discussing the role that the institutions of organized society play in the pursuit of happiness. But his incursion into politics need go no further than the making of the following three points.

(1) That men have natural rights, among which the primary right is the right to the pursuit of happiness, all subsidiary rights being rights to whatever means are indispensable for the pursuit of happiness. [3]

(2) That the goodness of an organized society is measured by the degree to which it secures the natural rights of its members, the best society being one that secures *all* natural rights for *all* its members. [4]

(3) That so far as, at any time, it succeeds in doing this, the good society does it in two ways: *negatively*, by preventing one individual or one group of individuals from injuring others by violating their natural rights; *positively*, by promoting the general welfare—that is, by aiding and abetting the individual's pursuit of happiness with regard to those conditions of its pursuit that he cannot provide for himself. [5]

A treatise on ethics need not deal with political matters, beyond these few simple points. To go beyond this is the task of political philosophy, which it discharges when it defines and delineates the institutional means by which organized society serves the pursuit of happiness on the part of more and more men.

(4)

While it is the main business of political philosophy to deal in detail with matters that need only be mentioned in ethics for their bearing on the good life, politics in thus going beyond ethics cannot leave ethics behind. Since the good life for the individual (one, some, or all) constitutes the normative standard by which we judge the relative goodness of one set of social institutions as compared with another, the formulations of the political philosopher must at all critical points be controlled by his understanding of the good life and of its necessary conditions. It is for this reason that a treatise on politics cannot avoid an exposition of matters that belong properly to ethics.

A few ethical principles have been mentioned in the preceeding pages. The remainder that are of relevance to politics can be briefly summarized, for no more is needed than the bare statement—without analysis or argument—of truths that constitute the ethical presuppositions of the political philosopher. [6] The summary follows.

As the ultimate good to be sought by the individual, the good life consists in the possession and enjoyment of all the real goods that satisfy a man's natural needs. I will from time to time use the word "happiness" as a strict synonym for "a whole life that is really good." And I will use the phrase "the pursuit of happiness" as equivalent in meaning to "the effort to make one's life really good." This usage of the word "happiness" is strictly ethical and excludes all the psychological and hedonic connotations of the word in ordinary speech, in which it refers to an experienced pleasurable state of contentment or satisfaction. In its ethical as opposed to its psychological connotation, happiness as a whole life that is really good cannot be experienced or enjoyed at any moment or period of one's life. To understand this is to understand that happiness or a good life is strictly a normative, not a terminal end. It is not something that can be achieved, possessed, and enjoyed at a given moment in time. Happiness thus conceived is not the *summum bonum* or highest good, but the *totum bonum*, the whole of goods. The happy or good life is one in which all real goods are present—one that suffers no deprivation of any of the real goods that a man needs. [7]

The real goods that constitute the *totum bonum* or whole of goods can be exhaustively enumerated under the following seven headings.

(1) *Goods of the body*, such as health, vigor, and the pleasures of sense.

(2) *Goods of the mind*, such as knowledge, understanding, a

modicum of wisdom, together with such goods of the mind's activity as skills of inquiry and of critical judgment, and the arts of creative production.

(3) *Goods of character,* such aspects of moral virtue as temperance and fortitude, together with justice in relation to the rights of others and the goods of the community.

(4) *Goods of personal association,* such as family relationships, friendships, and loves.

(5) *Political goods,* such as peace, both civil and external, and political liberty, together with the protection of individual freedom by the prevention of violence, aggression, coercion, or intimidation

(6) *Economic goods,* such as a decent supply of the means of subsistence; living and working conditions conducive to health; medical care; opportunities for access to the pleasures of sense, the pleasures of play, and aesthetic pleasures; opportunities for access to the goods of the mind through educational facilities in youth and adult life; and enough free time from subsistence-work, both in youth and in adult life, to take full advantage of these opportunities.

(7) *Social goods,* such as equality of status, of opportunity, and of treatment in all matters affecting the dignity of the human person.

Of these seven classes or categories of goods, the first four belong to the inner or private life of the individual. Whether or not he acquires and accumulates them in the course of his life depends mainly on him. With regard to these goods, the actions of government can do no more than abet the pursuit of happiness *indirectly,* by the actions it takes in the sphere of political, economic, and social goods. The last three classes of goods are environmental or external in the sense that the individual's possession of them is mainly dependent on the outer or public conditions of his life. It is with respect to these three types of goods that the institutions of society and the actions of government exert a *direct* effect, favorable or adverse, on the individual's pursuit of happiness. [8]

The fact that all men have the same natural rights stems from the fact that all men have the same natural needs. Therefore, what is really good for any man is really good for all men. Let me spend a moment more on the significance of this. My natural needs make certain things really good for me. The things that are really good for me impose moral obligations on me in the conduct of my private life. These, in turn, give me certain moral or natural rights, and my having such rights imposes moral obligations on other individuals and on the organized community with respect to me. Hence, as my primary moral obligation is to make a really good life for myself, so my primary natural right is my right to the pursuit of happiness.

All of my subsidiary natural rights—rights to life, security and life and limb, a decent livelihood, freedom from coercion, political liberty, educational opportunities, medical care, sufficient free time for the pursuits of leisure, and so on—derive from my right to the pursuit of happiness and from my obligation to make a good life for myself. They are rights to the things that I need in order to achieve that end and to discharge that obligation. If I did not have that one basic natural right, I would not have any subsidiary natural rights, because all other natural rights relate to the elements of individual happiness or to the parts of a good life—the diverse real goods that, taken together, constitute the whole that is the sum of all these parts. [9]

An individual's obligations toward his fellow men derive from the natural rights that are theirs as well as his. His *direct* obligations in justice to other individuals are all *negative*. They require him, as far as that is possible, to do nothing that inflicts injury on them by depriving them of the things they need in order to make good lives for themselves. Hence these obligations are based on the rights involved in their making good lives for themselves. They are all duties not to *prevent* others form doing so.

The individual's one *positive* obligation in justice to his fellowmen is *indirect* in the sense that it is an obligation to act for rather than against the good of the community (the *bonum communitatis*) and for rather than against all institutional changes that favor the pursuit of happiness by more and more individual members of the community in which he lives. Since the *bonum communitatis* is itself one of the real goods and a good that each individual needs in making a good life for himself, acting for the good of the community indirectly helps others in their pursuit of happiness. Since the institutions of society can either help or hinder an individual with regard to certain goods that he cannot obtain wholly by his own efforts, acting for institutional changes that help rather than hinder his acquirement of such goods indirectly aids others in their pursuit of happiness. [10]

Not all the things that a man desires are really good for him in the sense of satisfying natural needs. Some are merely apparent goods—things that he consciously wants without needing them. Seeking such apparent goods may or may not interfere with the individual's acquirement of all the real goods that he needs. If they do not interfere with or impair his possession of real goods, these apparent goods are innocuous rather than detrimental.

In contrast to real goods, which are all common goods—the same for all men because they are the objects of natural desire, apparent goods are individual, not common goods, for they answer to the idiosyncratic desires or conscious wants of this or that individual. Since the good of the community (*bonum commune communitatis*) is a real good and an element in the total common good of the individual (*totum bonum commune*), no disorder results when the state requires the individual to sacrifice or give up individual goods (*bonum individuale*) that come into conflict with the good of the community. On the contrary, the state is then only requiring the individual to give up individual goods that are detrimental to his own ultimate good. Since the good of the community (*bonum commune communitatis*) is good only as a means to the happiness of its individual members (*bonum commune hominis*), society is never justified in subordinating to its own good the ultimate good of its human members. [11]

(5)

It is necessary to add one critical qualification that must be placed upon the obligations of justice. No one—neither the individual nor society—can be expected to do what, at the time, is impossible; failure to do the impossible is not morally culpable.

Men are morally responsible only for what it is within their power to do or not to do; similarly, societies and governments are morally accountable only within the limits of the possible. This, of course, raises a crucial question of fact about what is possible or impossible at a given time in history, under the circumstances that exist at that time. The familiar saying that politics is the art of the possible epigrammatically expresses the point that the application of moral criteria—especially the criteria of justice and injustice—to political action is limited by the consideration of what is feasible at a given time and under given circumstances. This limitation is removed only by *ideal conditions*—conditions under which doing complete justice is possible, when no injustice can be condoned on the grounds that it is unavoidable.

Herein lies the crucial difference between practicable and utopian ideals in the sphere of politics. The good society as a practicable ideal is one that is intrinsically possible, even though it has not yet existed so far under any set of historic circumstances. In contrast, a utopian ideal not only is one that has no historic reality so far, but also one that, in the very nature of the case, lies beyond the bounds of possibility.

We will look more closely, in Chapter 4, at the relation of politics to history. We shall see that history has a bearing on political thought, and especially on the growth of political wisdom, that it does not have on ethics. This, as we shall see, arises from the fact that politics is the art of the possible, as ethics is not; and that the political philosopher depends upon historical developments for his changing demarcation of the possible from the impossible. The three great revolutions with which we shall be concerned in Chapter 5 have opened our eyes to realizable possibilities that were not imaginable to our ancestors—to those who lived long before these revolutions occurred.

With these preliminaries covered, I will then, in Parts Two and Three, attempt to set forth the basic principles of political wisdom, so far as such wisdom is available to us *at this time in history*. The exposition of these universal principles will, in effect, delineate the shape of the good society as a practicable, not a utopian ideal—one not yet achieved, but genuinely achieveable. Finally, in Part Four, I will consider the steps that remain to be taken in order to bring into existence the best society that is now seen to be practically possible. And I will there deal with the question whether there can and must be an end to political progress and a cessation of political revolution—in a future which lies beyond that point in time when the best society that we can now conceive of is fully realized in the institutions that men have devised and perfected.

CHAPTER 3

The Political Animal

(1)

SINCE political philosophy should be controlled by the conception of happiness or the good life as the ultimate end to be served by the good society, the truths about human nature that constitute the factual basis for the ethics of happiness also provide, in part at least, the factual basis for the politics of the good society. In addition, they help us to understand the meaning and truth of the proposition that man is by nature a political animal.

I have elsewhere stated four propositions about the nature of man upon the factual truth or probability of which the normative truth of the ethics of happiness rests. [1] Briefly summarized, they are as follows:

(1) That man, like any other animal, has a certain limited number of natural needs, and that the natural needs which are specifically human differ from those of other animals as man differs specifically from them; to wit, by virtue of his having the related powers of propositional speech and conceptual thought, powers totally lacking in other animals.

(2) That man, because he has the power of conceptual thought, is the only animal whose consciousness embraces an extensive past and a far-reaching future, without which he could neither make plans for the conduct

of his whole life nor extrapolate from the historic past of society projections concerning its future.

(3) That man does not have any genetically pre-formed patterns of species-specific behavior—no definite instincts of the sort to be found in the insects and other lower animals. While man does have instinctual drives or needs, each man, when he is in control of himself, determines how he responds to or satisfies them.

(4) That man, having the power of conceptual thought, also has freedom of choice—a freedom that enables him to choose this or that course of action without being determined to do so by his past experience, the habits he has formed, or the character he has developed up to that moment. He has, in short, the power of self-determination, the power of creating or forming himself and his life according to his own decisions.

The truth or probability of these propositions is, of course, relative to the present state of the empirical evidence. The scientific evidence now available and the evidence of common experience overwhelmingly favor the first three propositions. None has been falsified by critical negative instances. While the fourth proposition about freedom of choice is still subject to philosophical dispute, there is as yet no decisive evidence to the contrary, and there is good reason to believe that its truth will be progressively confirmed by future empirical evidence. [2] In any case, what must be said about freedom of choice in relation to a normative ethics must be said with equal force about it in relation to a normative politics.

A categorical ought is practically void unless the individual it obligates is free to obey it. Unless the individual has freedom of choice, he is not morally responsible for his acts; he cannot be held responsible for making or failing to make a good life for himself. Similarly, there is no point in saying what institutions men ought to devise and support in order to improve society and work toward the goal of the best society that is possible, unless they have freedom of choice with respect to the political decisions they make and the political programs they support or oppose.

If all the institutional changes that have taken place in the past and that will take place in the future were inexorably determined or necessitated, then programs of political reform or revolution would be nothing but wishful predictions, for they could not then meaningfully declare what ought or ought not to be done for the improvement of society. Without freedom of choice on the part of individual men as social agents, the effort to create the best society is as meaningless as the effort to make a good life for one's self. Unless men have freedom of choice, they have no genuine moral problems, either ethical or political.

(2)

What further consequences do these basic psychological presuppositions of the ethics of happiness have for the politics of the good society? There are three to which I would like to call attention.

First, our consideration of the good society is based on a set of values that is relative only to human nature, not to the *mores* or value-system of a particular historic society or culture. [3] The sociologists and cultural anthropologists tell us that we cannot transcend what they call the "ethnocentric predicament." Any judgment we make about a society or culture other than our own will assume the soundness or validity of the mores or value-system of our own society or culture. This would, of course, be true *if all* value-systems were relative and had validity —or acceptance—only for the society in which they were inherent. But the value-system involved in the scale of real goods that constitute the means to a good human life are relative *only* to human nature and not to the particular circumstances of any historic society or culture. It provides, therefore, a standard for judging one society or set of social institutions as better than another, a standard by which we can measure the degree to which any society approximates the ideal of the best society that is possible. Transcending the *mores* and diverse value-systems of particular societies, it is a universally applicable standard precisely because it is based on what is universally present in all societies—human beings, always and everywhere the same in their specific nature.

Second, the proposition about man that denies the existence of human instincts (i.e., denies genetically determined patterns of species-specific behavior) excludes aggression as an instinct to be reckoned with in political thought or in any other thinking we do about man's social life. Though the ethics of happiness and the politics of the good society would become questionable if a human *instinct* of aggression were a fact, their truth, especially that of politics, involves the acknowledgment of aggressive *tendencies* present in varying degrees in human beings. Let me explain.

If aggression were an instinct in the sense that it constituted a natural human need, then all men—all without exception, not just some—would naturally desire to dominate other men or to inflict injury upon them. If that were the case, then the pursuit of happiness would be competitive, not cooperative. If domination over other men or injuring them were a real good, because it satisfied a natural desire, and as such were a component part of an individual's happiness, then the success of some individuals in making good lives for themselves would necessarily deprive others of real goods that they needed and so defeat their pursuit of happiness. [4]

Furthermore, if real goods make natural rights, and if the best society is one that secures to every individual all of his natural rights, the existence of a natural need to dominate or inflict injury would make it impossible for any society to secure for everyone all his natural rights. On the one hand, to make laws that prohibit one man from injuring or dominating another would act to deprive all men of one of their natural rights. On the other hand, to permit some men to injure or dominate others in order to secure to them one of their natural rights would result in depriving others of their rights to freedom and to security of life and limb. Hence if aggression were an instinct which created a natural need that had to be satisfied in order to give men possession of something that is really good for them, then the ideal of the best society as one which promotes the pursuit of happiness by all its members would become, in the very nature of the case, impossible to realize. It would be a utopian rather than a practicable ideal.

However, to deny the presence in human beings of any tendency whatsoever to dominate or to inflict injury on their fellow-men would also have serious consequences for political philosophy.

If men were totally devoid of aggressive tendencies, if they were in all things pacific and always motivated by impulses of benevolent love toward all their fellow-men, the maintenance of civil peace, the preservation of individual freedom from coercion and intimidation, and security of life and limb would not need the operation of such institutions as the criminal law and the police force; nor would the sanctions of constitutional government be needed to protect men from being dominated by one individual or group of individuals whose appetite for power makes them seek despotic domination over all the rest.

One of the fundamental principles of politics, to which we will devote considerable attention in Chapter 6, is the proposition that society cannot exist without government and without the exercise of coercive force by government. The truth of this proposition is crucial to the issue between the political philosopher and the philosophical anarchist. But the truth of this proposition rests—in part at least—on the fact that aggressive tendencies are present in some, if not all, members of society, varying in degree from individual to individual.

How can we resolve the apparent contradiction that confronts us, made by the denial, on the one hand, that aggression is a human instinct that creates a natural need which must be satisfied for the sake of the good life; and by the affirmation, on the other hand, that aggressive tendencies are present in the members of society to an extent which necessitates the exercise of coercive force by government in order to maintain civil peace and to protect the natural rights of all? I propose the following answer.

Whatever properties or tendencies are present in all men without exception are species-specific, and by this criterion they are instinctive or natural. Any property or tendency that is found in some men, but not in others, whether the number in whom it is found is small or large, cannot be species-specific. It is a product of nurture or at most an endowment of individual nature, but in no case an endowment of specific nature. The scientists who deny the existence of an instinct of aggression in man offer as critical evidence in support of their view the absence of aggression in a certain number of men in any society and its absence from a substantially large number of men or even all in certain societies. [5] The very same evidence supports the proposition that aggressive tendencies on the part of some individuals are largely a product of nurture, though perhaps with some basis in innate temperamental disposition. It is unlike the instinctive sexual drive which, being present in all members of the human species, is inherent in man's specific nature.

The apparent contradiction is thus resolved, but the resolution leaves us with other difficulties that must be faced. If aggressive tendencies are largely a product of nurture, then it would seem as if, in principle at least, they are eliminable from human life, since a reformation of the conditions that cultivate aggression is a conceivable possibility. The critical question here is whether the institutions of society, as we have known them so far in the course of history, are solely responsible for fomenting aggressive tendencies in a certain number of human beings; or whether, in contradistinction, aggression develops in the cauldron of the emotional conflicts that are inexpungable from family life. If the former, then institutional reforms might conceivably result in the elimination of aggression. But if, in a certain number of cases, aggression is nurtured by the irremediable tensions and conflicts of family life, then unless the family is itself a dispensable institution, no alteration in our other institutions would result in the complete elimination of aggression.

Third, underlying the four propositions about human nature that are presupposed by the ethics of happiness is the even more important proposition that there is a specific human nature—that man *is* a species of animal and that, like any other species of organism, he has a specific nature which, in regard to its species-specific properties, is the same in all members of the species. [6]

The affirmation of the sameness of the specific nature in which all human beings participate as individual members of the species has many consequences for ethics and one consequence of particular importance for politics. In ethics, it supports the proposition that all men have the same natural needs; that real goods, corresponding to natural needs, are the same for all; and that all men have the same natural rights, based on the real goods that satisfy their natural needs. In politics, it supports the proposition that all men are equal as men, equal in their humanity, in their dignity as persons, and in their natural rights.

I will postpone until Chapter 11 the consideration of the political consequences that flow from affirming or denying the proposition that all men are equal as men. [7] We shall see that a sound resolution of the basic issues about equality of treatment, equality of status, and equality of opportunity involves not only an understanding of the human equality that is rooted in man's specific nature, but also an understanding of its relation to all the personal inequalities among men that are rooted in their individual differences, whether differences in natural endowment or differences in personal attainments and possessions. But I cannot leave the matter here without one further comment.

The judgment that all men should be treated equally in certain fundamental respects, and similar normative judgments concerning equality of status and equality of opportunity, would not be tenable if it were not factually as well as normatively true that all men are by nature equal. I mention this point because it is so insistently denied by many today who, on the one hand, uphold the prescription of equal treatment, or call for an equality of conditions, and, on the other, deny that it has or need have any basis in the fact of man's specific human nature. [8]

(3)

Are there any other psychological presuppositions of sufficient importance to deserve explicit statement? I think there is at least one more, which has special significance for political philosophy. It is the fact that man is by nature a political animal. To understand what is meant by that statement, it is necessary to understand the difference between saying that man is a social animal and saying that man is a political animal; and also to understand what is involved in saying that man is by nature both social and political.

Animals other than men are social or gregarious; only man is political in addition to being social or gregarious. In contradistinction to solitary or non-gregarious animals, gregarious animals, such as the social insects and many vertebrate species, exhibit in diverse ways and varying degrees patterns of organized social life. To say that these animals are by nature social or gregarious is to say that their natures are such that they need to associate with other members of the species for the exigencies of their organic life and for the perpetuation of the species. How is this need satisfied? In each case, by a particular pattern of association, a particular mode of social organization, that is distinctively characteristic of a particular animal species or population. The fact that a particular pattern of association or mode of social organization is uniformly and universally exhibited by the members of a particular animal species or population warrants the inference that it is a species-specific property of that animal population or, in other words, that it is instinctively determined.

This is tantamount to saying, *negatively*, that the members of a particular animal species do *not* determine for themselves the precise way in which they will associate to satisfy their need for social life, a need that is inherent in all animals that are, by nature, gregarious. Not only is their need for social life something that is genetically determined by the inheritable nature of a given animal group or population. It is also the case that genetic determination produces the manner or mode of their association (as, for example, the organization of the beehive or ant-mound, the wolf pack or walrus herd); and it is in this sense that a particular form of animal association is instinctive—a consequence of the inheritable nature of a particular animal population, not a choice made by the members of that population at a given time and place.

While man is by nature social or gregarious in the sense of being so constituted that he needs to associate with his fellow-men for the exigencies of organic life and for the perpetuation of the species, he is not instinctively social in the further sense that the way in which men associate is genetically determined. There is no one pattern of human association or one mode of social organization uniformly and universally found wherever men live together, either in families or in larger communities, as there would be if the manner of human association and mode of social organization were instinctive, i.e., were a genetically determined, inheritable, and species-specific property of the human race. The variety of forms manifested by human association is the incontrovertible factual basis for the denial that the diverse forms of human association are instinctively determined.

If they are not instinctively determined, how are they to be explained or accounted for? There is only one tenable answer to this question: *by human institution and by choice*. Naturally needing to associate with their fellow-men in families or in larger communities, men determine for themselves how they will associate and how they will organize the communities in which they live. They invent or devise the institutions and arrangements of social life, institutions and arrangements which, taken together, produce this or that particular form of human association; and when they are able to envisage alternative forms of association, they are also able to choose one mode of social organization rather than another.

We can now understand the sense in which man, in addition to being a social or gregarious organism, is also uniquely a political animal. In this characterization of man, the negative meaning of "political" consists in denying that human social organization is genetically determined, i.e., instinctive. To say that man is *politically social* is to say that he is *not instinctively social* in the manner of his association. The positive meaning of "political" consists in affirming that the diverse forms of human association are *instituted* by men and subject to *choice* on their part. The invention of social institutions and the adoption of one set of institutions rather than another by choice are the marks of a political animal. [9]

That, among social or gregarious organisms, man and man alone is a political animal in the sense just indicated is to be accounted for by the basic properties that distinguish man from all other living organisms; namely, his unique possession of the powers of propositional speech and of conceptual thought, together with the freedom of choice that is a consequence of his intellectual powers. Without the power of conceptual thought, man could not invent or devise social institutions before their existence becomes an enacted reality; nor could he choose among the diverse institutions that he is able to conceive and project in advance of their adoption. Without the power of propositional speech, man could not engage with his fellow-men in the public consideration of social arrangements. The development of human communities, in their myriad forms, involves speech about social institutions in the same way that the development and improvement of tools by the human species is conditioned by speech about technological devices and inventions.

Hence when we say that man is by nature social, we mean that, like other gregarious animals, he needs to associate with his fellow-men for his own good; and when we say that he is by nature political, we mean that, unlike other gregarious animals, he is, by virtue of powers that are uniquely human, able to devise and adopt one or another set of social institutions to produce the various forms of social organization in which he lives. Wherever we find a natural need, we also find a natural capacity, and conversely. Thus gregarious animals not only need to associate, but also have the capacity for doing so, not present in non-gregarious animals. Man's natural ability to devise and adopt social institutions must bespeak a natural need on his part.

What is the need that corresponds to man's political capacity? It is the need to participate, by speech, thought, choice, and action, in public affairs. Stated another way, man's political capacity carries with it a need to act politically—to exercise a voice or have a say about the organization of the community in which he lives. The full significance of this will not become apparent until, in later chapters, we come to understand that political liberty and equality are requirements of a good society because they are indispensable components of the good human life that a good society must seek to promote. Because man is by nature political, he has natural needs that make political liberty and equality the real human goods they are.

CHAPTER 4

The Historical Enlargement of Our Vision of the Possible

(1)

THE most striking difference between ethics and politics is that the development of political wisdom is dependent on history, as ethics is not.

I pointed out in *The Time of Our Lives* that the ethics of common sense is as old as the Greeks; Aristotle first expounded it. [1] We may be able to improve on his exposition a little, by adding philosophical refinement here and there, but its essential outlines remain unaltered 2500 years later. The extraordinary changes in the human environment that have taken place in that time—the myriad changes in the social institutions and in the technological conditions of human life—do not affect the answer that common sense, based on common experience, gives to the question, *How can I make a good life for myself?* In other words, what is really good for a man is the same yesterday, today, and tomorrow, because man is the same. Only a basic change in the nature of man, amounting to the emergence of another species, would call for fundamentally different answers to the question about the good life.

In contrast to ethics, political thought is conditioned by the shape of existing institutions at a given historic moment and by the limited vision that such institutions give us of the possibility for further changes in the future. Revolution and progress operate in the sphere of politics as they do not operate in the sphere of ethics. What I have just said includes technological as well as institutional changes. Because it is so relevant here, let me recall a fundamental thesis advanced in Chapter 1, namely, that all the progress which has so far been made in the social life of man has been accomplished by cumulative improvements in technology and in social institutions, without any improvement in the nature of man. [2]

The familiar remark that politics is the art of the possible is also relevant here. We are concerned in political philosophy with the ideal—with the best society that is possible. The best society that is possible is a practicable or realizable ideal, as opposed to utopian ideals, which go beyond the bounds of possibility. The species-specific properties of human nature set limits to what is possible for man as he is specifically constituted; but this is purely *negative* in its effect. It tells us only what is *impossible* and so helps us to dismiss utopian dreams as impractical and unrealizable ideals. A knowledge and understanding of historical developments is needed to open our eyes to what lies within the bounds of possibility. Institutional and technological changes alter the positive content of our vision of the *possible*. Hence with such changes, advances can be made in political philosophy, as they are not made in ethics. [3]

(2)

We observed earlier the apparent contradiction between maintaining, on the one hand, that political wisdom is a philosophical refinement of common-sense insights based on common human experience and holding, on the other hand, that political philosophy is dependent for its development on historical developments or changes in the institutions of society.

The paradox with which we are confronted cannot be bypassed. Even the most superficial study of the great works in political theory would help us to discern significant advances in political thought as one passes from antiquity to the present day. A closer study of political theory in relation to the events of

political history will find that the discovery or general acknowledgment of new truths that enlarge our fund of political wisdom
has been occasioned by radical changes in the actual institutions
of society.

How can there be such signal advances in political thought,
productive of a growth or development of political wisdom, and
how can such advances be conditioned by the basic institutional
changes that history records, if the political wisdom available to
men at any time is nothing but a refinement of common sense
insights drawn from the common experience of mankind? That
question, I repeat, cannot be avoided. Can it be answered?

To lay a basis for the answer I am about to give, I must first
repeat what I have said elsewhere about the two distinct senses
in which we refer to experience as *common* rather than special.
Employing that distinction, I think I can show a basic difference
between the way in which common sense and common experience operate in ethics and in politics. This will caution us
to impose certain qualifications on the best formulation of political wisdom that may be attainable in the present century.

In *The Conditions of Philosophy*, I distinguished in the following manner between the negative and the positive senses
of the term "common experience." [4] The negative sense relates to the clear difference between common and special experience. Special experience always depends upon deliberate
and planned investigation in response to the explicit formulation
of a question to be answered. All the observational data of the
investigative or experimental sciences are, accordingly, elements
of special experience. The scientist would not have obtained such
data if he did not have a question in mind and had not deliberately
tried to answer it by one or another act of observation. Common experience is the experience we have *without* asking a single
question that calls for steps of observation especially contrived
for the purpose. It is non-investigative in its origin; it is the experience we have during the hours when we are conscious
and yet are not consciously trying to answer some specific question by making observations for that purpose; i.e., when we
are not engaged in laboratory experiments or field research.

The positive sense in which one can speak of experience as common focuses on that small body of experience that is the *same* for all men everywhere at all times. Not everything that belongs to the common experience of a particular man is shared by all the rest of his fellow-men. The ordinary non-investigative day-to-day experiences of a twentieth-century Eskimo, New Yorker, and Hottentot are certainly not the same in all respects. The same must be said of an Athenian in the fifth century B.C., a Parisian of the eighteenth century, and a Muscovite of the twentieth. In other words, much of the experience that is common in the purely negative sense that it is non-investigative in origin does not satisfy the criterion for being common in the positive sense; namely, that it is the same for all men at all times and places, as is our experience of the shift from day to night, living and dying, eating and sleeping, losing and finding, giving and getting, standing still and moving about in space, and so on.

That small body of common experience which is universally the same, I shall refer to as "the core of common experience." When I speak of experience as common *without reference to the core of it*, I will have in mind only the negative sense of "common," whereby we understand that the experience does *not* result from any special effort of investigation on the part of the individual having it.

One further point must be added. The common (i.e., *non-investigative*) experience of an individual living under a particular set of conditions and in a particular physical and social environment at a given time and place will be shared to a great extent by many other individuals or even by all who share the same physical and social environment. Thus, while the common experience of an Athenian in the fifth century B.C. will differ from that of an eighteenth-century Parisian or that of a twentieth-century Muscovite, there will be much that is common or the same in the experiences of many or all fifth-century Athenians, eighteenth-century Parisians, and twentieth-century Muscovites. The extent to which the non-investigative experience of a fifth-century Athenian, an eighteenth-century Parisian,

4 · OUR VISION OF THE POSSIBLE   45

or a twentieth-century Muscovite is shared by others living at the same time and place, or the number of those sharing in such elements of experience, does not affect the character of that experience as common or non-investigative rather than special or investigative.

(3)

With these distinctions before us, I can now make clear the difference between the way that common experience functions in ethics and the way that it functions in politics.

For the most part, the common-sense approach to the problems of ethics can rely on the *core of common experience*, the non-investigative experience that is the same for all men by virtue of their all having the same specific nature and living in the same world. This is not to say that the differences between the common or non-investigative experience of a fifth-century Athenian and of a twentieth-century New Yorker have no effect on the details of the common-sense answer each would give to the question about how to make a good life for himself. Nevertheless, it remains the case that the common-sense answer as developed philosophically in fifth-century Greece and in twentieth-century America preserves the same general outlines, especially in its fundamental insights and its controlling wisdom. That is why it can be said that a common-sense ethics, based on common experience in both the positive and the negative sense of that term, is for the most part unaffected by historical changes or developments.

What I have just said is not true of the common-sense approach to politics precisely because, with regard to the problems of the good society, the common experience on which common sense must rely and to which philosophy must appeal is common *only in the negative sense:* it is the non-investigative experience of men living under certain social conditions at a given time and place, experience that may be shared by many who live in the same environment, but certainly not experience that will be universally the same for all men—for the fifth-century Greek, the nineteenth-century American, and the twentieth-century Russian. [5]

Consequently, both the common-sense wisdom and the philosophical development of it that is attainable under one set of historic conditions will differ from the common-sense wisdom and the philosophical development of it that is attainable under a radically different set of historic conditions. At any given historic moment, the political wisdom that is available derives from the common or non-investigative experience of men living at the time in the social environment that is then a reality—a limited realization of the possible. The existing institutions at the time and the existing technology determine the content of that common experience and set certain limits to man's vision of the possible, relative to which political ideals can then be formulated.

In the course of history, with radical changes in social institutions and in technology, common experience changes and with it the vision of what is possible. Hence there can be advances in political thought and accretions of political wisdom, even though the power of common sense and of philosophical reflection to draw wisdom from common experience remains the same at all times. The increment of wisdom that is added with each advance in political thought is as much a development of common sense as was the deposit of wisdom to which it is added. The difference between the new wisdom and the old is not to be attributed to a more discerning or perceptive power of common sense or to a greater skill in philosophical analysis, but rather to a change in the common experience on which both must rely—a change that results from alterations in the external circumstances, both institutional and technological, which condition political experience and thought at that time.

(4)

This difference between politics and ethics—the dependence of the one on historical developments and the independence of the other—can, perhaps, be illuminated by a parallel difference between sciences that depend on elaborate instruments of observation, such as telescopes and microscopes, and sciences that employ the unaided senses in their observational procedures.

Thus, for example, the gross anatomy of the human body known to Hippocrates, Galen, and Vesalius is still largely correct in its general outlines, though additions and corrections in certain details have been made by later observers. In sharp contrast, our histological knowledge of cell structure originates with the invention of the microscope and improves radically with increases in its power of magnification and even more remarkably with the invention of the electron microscope. What is to be known about cell-structure was always in the domain of the knowable. It was only made known, not knowable, by the microscope; just as the motions and properties of the celestial bodies were what they now are, before we had telescopes to observe them. They were observable or knowable at the time when, lacking the instruments, we could not observe or know them. In such sciences as histology and astronomy, the increase and improvement in our scientific knowledge is a function of technological advances in our instruments of observation, but such increments of knowledge must always be viewed as an enlargement of that portion of the knowable that has become actually known.

I would like to suggest that the great historic developments in man's social life, both institutional and technological, function for political thought as the microscope and the telescope do for histology and astronomy. By altering man's common experience of the social environment, these historical developments enable him to enlarge the common-sense and philosophical wisdom that he can derive from such experience. They do so mainly by enlarging his vision of the possible. Things that were not thought feasible at an earlier time, or were not even thought about at all, become at a later time and under radically altered social conditions, aspects of the experienced reality of social life. Man's altered vision of what is politically possible in the light of what has been actually achieved gives rise to new increments of political wisdom in the formulation of the political ideal, involving possibilities still to be realized. In political philosophy, as in histology and in astronomy, the improvement in our knowledge does not imply any enlargement of the knowable, but only an enlargement of that portion of the knowable which, at a given time, has become actually known. [6]

If at the dawn of history, one could have known enough of the nature of man—his natural needs and his natural rights—and could have imagined the institutional and technological inventions required for the realization of the social possibilities involved in satisfying all of man's natural needs and securing to all men all of their natural rights, it would have been possible to predict the great revolutions that have occurred in human affairs and that are still to occur. The great political changes that have occurred so far, including changes in social and economic arrangements, as well as changes in the institutions of government, are revolutionary improvements that should have occurred. While it cannot be asserted with confidence that what *should* happen always *will* happen, the course of political history so far does give us some reasonable basis for the prediction that the vision which we now have of the best society that is possible will be realized by radical changes or revolutions still to come.

The hypothesis that I proposed a moment ago is, of course, contrary to fact. At the dawn of history, we could not have imagined the institutional and technological inventions required for the fulfillment of man's natural needs and the protection of all his natural rights, even if we could have had an adequate understanding of human nature at that time. Historical developments, both institutional and technological, have given us an experience of emergent social realities in the light of which our vision of the possible has been altered and enlarged.

(5)

The dependence of political thought on historical development, as I have tried to explain it, has obvious consequences for the formulation of political philosophy at a particular time. Through the experience that our present position in history affords us, our vantage point for engaging in political philosophy is superior to that of our ancestors, just as the vantage point of political theorists in the eighteenth and nineteenth centuries was superior to that of Plato, Aristotle, and Cicero in the ancient world. [7]

Failure to understand and acknowledge this has led some of our predecessors to regard their formulations as final or good for all time, as if nothing more would be learned as a result of historical developments beyond their own day. Not only did most of the great political philosophers of the past fail to limit themselves to the level of universal principles, on which alone wisdom is attainable; they also failed to recognize the unavoidable limitation that history itself imposes on the best formulation which they could make of the wisdom then attainable. They could only see a little beyond the historic realities of their own time to possibilities then imaginable; they could not see the full range of possibilities, for it included those not imaginable or conceivable in their day because of the limited range of social realities then experienceable.

I hope that I have said enough to make clear that while I think that we, living in the twentieth century, are in a position to attain a richer and more mature political wisdom than our ancestors, we are far from standing at the end of time or history, and so the best formulations we can achieve are not the last or the complete word on the subject. Our knowledge of human nature, so far as it goes, will enable us to make highly probable, yet seldom certain, judgments about utopian schemes that lie beyond the pale of the practically possible in the sphere of our social arrangements and institutions. Our knowledge of historic developments so far, and our experience of the social realities that now exist, will enable us to project a number of possibilities still to be realized, but hardly *all* the possiblities that the future holds in store. A common-sense approach to politics that properly acknowledges these limitations will refrain from claiming completeness or adequacy for the political wisdom it is able to formulate; but such restraint should not prevent it from offering its formulations as the fullest wisdom that is now attainable.

CHAPTER 5

Three Great Revolutions That Have Increased Our Political Wisdom

(1)

To illustrate the thesis advanced in the preceding chapter, I would call attention to three great advances in political thought that were occasioned or conditioned by radical, progressive, and revolutionary changes in the organization and institutions of society. But, first, let me explain what I mean by characterizing these changes as radical, progressive, and revolutionary. After that I will attempt to give a brief description of these three steps forward in political life and political thought.

The changes that I have in mind can be characterized and named in a number of different ways. In calling them *radical* changes, I mean to say that they involved a change in kind, not just in degree: something new was added, not just more of the same. In calling them *progressive*, I am stressing the fact that improvement was accomplished—a whole step forward was taken toward the best society that is possible. (I have already indicated the standards by which such progress is to be measured. It involves an increase in the justice of society's institutions and arrangements. That, in turn, means that the conditions needed for living a good human life—for the pursuit of happiness—have been extended to a larger proportion of society's members.)

In one widely accepted sense of the word "revolutionary," a change that is radical and progressive is, *ipso facto*, also a revolutionary change—one that turns a corner in human affairs. A change that is revolutionary, in this sense of the word, may or may not be brought about by the kind of armed insurrection or violent action that is called a revolt or rebellion. The three great changes that I have in mind were accompanied by revolutionary action, either at their outset, or in their defense against reactionary movements, or in their spread and development. When, in what follows, I refer to them as three great revolutions, I will be stressing both points—that the changes were revolutionary turning points and that they were initiated, defended, or consolidated by revolutionary action.

For brevity of reference and also for the symbolic value that is involved in the designation, I am going to name each of the three revolutions by identifying it with the time and place of its first institutional fulfillment—*first*, please note, *not final or fullest* institutional accomplishment. Each of these revolutions is still going on and, in my judgment, will continue to go on until the ideal at which it aims is completely realized in securely established institutions and realized for all mankind. In other words, each of these revolutions has a history, longer or shorter according to the length of time that has elapsed since its first inception. And that history is, for the most part, a checkered career, in which the advance that was made at one time or place is lost at another, regained and lost again, over and over, until the institutions involved in the change have become sufficiently well established to resist corruption or reaction.

Permit me to add two further preliminary observations. Each of these revolutions was a social experiment, in the sense in which we speak of experimenting as trying something new. For those who engaged in the experiment, it was an experience, a new experience that men had not had before. Each also involved an idea, an idea that may have been expressed and formulated in advance of the revolutionary action or the institutional change, but the general acknowledgment of which almost always followed it and reflected its accomplishment. Hence, in connection with each of these revolutions, I shall be able to name the writings in which the revolutionary idea was set forth, either by way of anticipation or by way of summation. [1]

(2)

The three great institutional changes that have been accompanied by signal advances in political thought are, *first*, the Greek revolution, which began in the seventh century B.C. and has been going on ever since; *second*, the American revolution, which began in the first part of the nineteenth century, is still going on and still spreading; and, *third*, the Russian revolution, which began in the twentieth century and which, taken together with its two predecessors, is now effecting changes that are almost global in their extent.

The Greek revolution marks the advent of constitutional government and of citizenship—the two most fundamental political inventions and innovations ever achieved. Until the Greek cities set up and adopted constitutions under which some men, never all, enjoyed the status of citizens exercising a voice in their own government, all men living in cities were subject to the arbitrary and absolute rule of despots. This was clearly a radical and progressive change in social arrangements.

The passage from a state of affairs in which no men had political liberty to a state of affairs in which some men, *even if only a few*, became free men politically through being citizens and having a share in the sovereignty, was a change in kind; something that did not exist before came into being for the first time. The change thus accomplished was progressive; it was a step toward recognizing a basic natural right that had never been acknowledged before.

What was in its inception a Greek experiment and, for the relatively short duration of a little less than four hundred years, a Greek experience, became in subsequent centuries an experiment performed in other places and an experience enjoyed by other peoples. Two hundred years after its initiation in Greece, constitutional government was instituted in Rome, with the expulsion of the Tarquins, and endured with varying vicissitudes until the retrogression of Rome to despotism under the Caesars. It made its next appearance in the constitutional provisions of the mixed regimes that developed during the feudal Middle Ages in Western Europe. The revolt of the barons that led to the signing of Magna Carta in 1215 marked the introduction of the mixed regime in England. Another manifestation of mediaeval constitutionalism is to be found in the wording of the pledge entered into by the Spanish nobles at the coronation of the kings of Aragon: "We who are as good as you, swear to you who are no better than we, to accept you as our king, provided you observe all our liberties and laws; but if not, not." [2]

When, with the recurrence and rise of absolute monarchies, the mixed regime dissolved in favor of its despotic component, the Greek revolution had to be fought and won again and again in modern Europe: in England in 1688 at the time of the so-called "bloodless revolution"; in the rebellion of the American colonies against the despotism of Parliament; in the overthrow of the Bourbons in France and the setting up of the first French republic; in the revolutionary uprisings that occurred in Europe and in Central and South America in the middle of the nineteenth century and that struggled for some vestige of representative government; and right down to the present century in Russia in 1905 and 1917 and in the spread of efforts to set up republics in the Far East and in Africa. Thus, from the seventeenth century on, the republican ideal that was first realized in the Greek experiment and experience has acted as a powerful leaven to bring about the radical and progressive advent of constitutionalism in all parts of the modern world.

Though it can be said with a certain degree of assurance that constitutionalism has been well developed and securely established in the United States, in Great Britain and its associated self-ruling commonwealths, in most of Western Europe, in Japan, and even, perhaps, in India and Pakistan, one cannot speak in the same vein of the Soviet Socialist Republics, of the Arab republics, of the recently established new national regimes in Africa, or of most of the Latin American governments. In all essentials, these are republics in name or in aspiration rather than in fact and in operation. Hence not only in these areas and for these populations, but also in other regions and for other peoples, the Greek experiment is still either to be initiated or carried out more fully, so that societies everywhere on earth will have, in some measure, the experience of constitutional government—rule of law, citizenship, and suffrage.

The idea of constitutional government, together with the republican ideal that it generates, did not make its appearance as an expressly formulated doctrine in political philosophy until the Greek experiment had been tried and the Greek experience had matured. Not until the fifth and fourth centuries B.C. did Plato's *Statesman* and Aristotle's *Politics* distill the Greek experience into the formulations of political thought. Cicero's *Republic* performed the same service for the Roman experience, as did the writings of Bracton and Fortescue for the mediaeval experience of the mixed regime—the rule that was both royal and constitutional. In the modern world, Montesquieu's *The Spirit of Laws*, Locke's *Second Essay on Civil Government*, and Rousseau's *Social Contract* argued the case for constitutionalism and the republican ideal in advance of the revolutions in England and in France that began to take the steps forward that these documents recommend. Schooled in these writings as well as in those of antiquity, the writers of the *Federalist Papers* concerned themselves mainly with the specific provisions of the American consitution, for they no longer regarded the replacement of despotism by constitutional government as needing elaborate defense.

In the realm of political action, the Greek revolution has not yet been fully won nor the Greek experiment and experience fully universalized, but the fundamental normative truths involved in the Greek idea have, in the domain of political thought, now become almost universally acknowledged. No major or respected political philosopher in the twentieth century has argued or would argue for the abolition of citizenship and the overthrow of constitutional government in order to re-establish an absolute or despotic regime.

(3)

The American revolution, *not* the rebellion of the colonies in 1776, *but* the gradual emergence of a democratic republic, is the second radical turning point and step of progress in political institutions and political thought.

In this case, the idea of political equality—the equal enjoyment of political freedom by all men as citizens with suffrage—and the democratic ideal that it projects were envisioned or proclaimed in advance of the institutional changes that constitute the revolutionary experiment and experience. One of the first intimations of the doctrine occurs as early as the first half of the seventeenth century, in the arguments for suffrage reforms advanced by the Levellers in a debate which took place in Cromwell's army in 1647. [3] Early proclamations of the democratic ideal are to be found in pre-revolutionary American writings, in the Declaration of Independence, in the suffrage debate in New York State in 1820, [4] and in the Gettysburg Address. These statements cannot be read as descriptive of existing institutions; they are rather pledges to the future; they call for revolutionary changes still to be made.

Throughout the nineteenth century and right down to the present, the gradual achievement of an equality of political conditions through the broadening of the franchise in the direction of universal suffrage did not occur only in the United States. It was concurrently happening in Great Britain and its associated commonwealths, in many of the states of Western Europe, and elsewhere. Nevertheless, there is good reason for speaking of the democratic revolution as American in origin. It lies in Tocqueville's insight about America as the first republic to be born in a land without a feudal past, without a feudal tradition of ranks and privileges, and so without the persistence of feudal class distinctions. [5] American society was, therefore, peculiarly hospitable to the idea of political equality and inclined to take the steps necessary for a progressive realization of the democratic ideal. [6]

Though the ideal is not yet fully realized in practice anywhere, the democratic experiment has been carried further and the democratic experience has been more widely enjoyed in the United States and in a small number of other countries that, either concurrently or subsequently, have moved in the same direction. In large areas of the world, the democratic ideal, even where it is nominally acknowledged, still remains no more than a pledge to the future; and there are many places where it is not operative even as an acknowledged ideal.

In the sphere of political thought, the first great book in political philosophy to argue for constitutional democracy as the ideal polity was as recent as John Stuart Mill's *Representative Government*, published in 1861. With the exception of Plato's *Republic*, twenty-four centuries earlier, it is also the first great book in political philosophy to argue explicitly for the political equality of men and women. Of the two, Plato's is the more radical statement of the case for the equality of the sexes. Between Plato and Mill, there is little or no discussion of the issue; the disfranchisement of women is either tacitly assumed or explicitly asserted without argument. And it was not until the twentieth century that the democratic revolution really matured with the success of the woman's suffrage movement in such countries as the United States and England. Until that point was reached, political democracy—with half the adult human population disfranchised—did not really begin to exist. [7]

What I said earlier about the almost universal acceptance of constitutional goverement, as preferable to despotism, does not apply to political democracy. The issues about political democracy are still moot questions in political theory. While political equality through universal suffrage has able defenders, it also has able opponents, as we shall see in Chapter 11. And this is likely to continue until the democratic experience has become more widely diffused and until the democratic experiment has succeeded in surmounting the difficulties that are inherent in so radical a change.

That the change involved in the American revolution is both radical and progressive should be clear. The transition from republics in which only some men are enfranchised citizens and in which there still remains a sharp distinction between a ruling and a subject class, to republics in which all men have suffrage and all belong to the ruling class, consists in passing from a politically class-divided society to a politically classless society.

That is a change in kind, not in degree; and it is clearly progressive. It carries forward the advance first made when the right to political liberty was acknowledged in the early republics, but acknowledged with qualifications and restrictions that granted citizenship to the few or to the many, but always to less than all.

(4)

The Russian revolution is difficult to describe in a fashion that parallels the account just given of the Greek and the American revolutions for two reasons.

In the first place, the Greek and the American revolutions can be described as cumulatively progressive. As I just pointed out, the democratic experiment carries forward to fuller realization an ideal that is only partially realized in the republican experiment. While there can be constitutional government without political democracy, political democracy is impossible without constitutional government. Such phases as "constitutional democracy" and "democratic republic" indicate not only that the republican and democratic ideals are compatible, but also that democracy is a form of constitutional government. When it is understood that democracy is superior to oligarchy as the other basic form of constitutional government, by virtue of the greater justice that results from the extension of the franchise from some to all, it is seen that the transition from oligarchical to democratic republics is progressive.

Can the Russian revolution be similarly described as cumulatively progressive, conserving the radical gains made by the Greek and the American revolutions, and yet adding thereto a further step of progress toward the fullest realization of the best society that is possible? I think it can be if we are willing to distinguish between the socialist ideal (i.e., the end aimed at by the socialist revolution or experiment) and the socialist program (i.e., the means proposed or employed for achieving the end in view).

The end of socialism is the establishment of social and economic equality, brought about by the abolition of privileged classes and by the participation of all in the general social and economic welfare. As thus defined, the socialist ideal is definitely cumulative with regard to the ideals aimed at by the two preceding revolutions. Social and economic equality are not merely compatible with the political equality of universal suffrage, but, upon closer examination, they will be seen to be indispensable to the fullest realization of political democracy. The socialist democratic republic is an advance over the republic that is democratic only in the narrowly political sense, by going still further in the direction of achieving the truly classless society—the society in which an equality of all conditions obtains, not just an equality of political status and opportunity, but also an equality of economic and of social conditions. [8]

One might replace the word "socialism" by speaking of economic and social democracy, as additions to or extensions of what, in the narrow sense of the term, we call political democracy; but to do so might involve a loss of some of the historic connotations of the word, which remind us of the fundamental changes in the economic system and in social institutions that are required for the achievement of the socialist ideal.

While there is no question that the socialist ideal is compatible with the republican and democratic ideals of the two earlier revolutions and additive thereto, the same cannot be said for certain features of the socialist program. Let me mention only two.

First, in the program of Marxist communism, the abolition of the private ownership of all means of production and their transfer to the state, together with the dictatorship of the proletariat in the first stage of the communist revolution, would appear to be destructive of constitutional democracy. In the program of anarchistic communism or of syndicalism, as outlined, for example, by Bakunin or Kropotkin, or by Sorel, the abolition of the private ownership of all means of production is to be accompanied by the abolition of the state itself, at least in any of its known historic forms; and this would also appear to be destructive of constitutional democracy. I say "appears" in order not to foreclose or beg the question, but to postpone for later consideration a question that we shall have to deal with at some length; namely, what measures or means for realizing the socialist ideal would not only sustain but also consolidate the gains made by the earlier revolutions, rather than wipe them out. [9]

My second difficulty with regard to the Russian revolution concerns the propriety of letting the great institutional changes that began to take place in Russia in 1917 stand for or symbolize the whole socialist movement in all its many forms. As the *Communist Manifesto* itself makes clear, socialism either as a revolutionary ideal or as a revolutionary program, did not begin with that document in 1848. It is not necessary to enumerate the writings of the many economic and social reformers of the nineteenth and early twentieth century—in England, in France, in Germany, in the United States, as well as in Russia—in order to point out that the socialist ideal and one or another socialist program were under discussion and debate for almost a full century before the Russian revolution occurred. [10]

Why, then, should we regard the Russian revolution as symbolizing the third great institutional change which has occasioned or conditioned an advance in political thought? My answer is that, with the Russian revolution, we have, for the first time, the emergence of the welfare state—a society concerned with the economic and social welfare of its whole population. It was only after the Russian experiment had begun that other technologically advanced nations in the West or in the East undertook experiments in the socialization of the economy that created other versions of the welfare state. It therefore seems justifiable to say that, although the socialist ideal had been in the air for a hundred years or more, the Russian revolution resulted in the adoption of the socialist ideal by many societies that gradually transformed themselves into welfare states without fully adopting the socialist program of either Marxist or anarchistic communism.

In a sense, the Russian revolution has been more successful than the American revolution in gaining acceptance for its ideal. In the world as it is today, both East and West, South and North, the socialist ideal of the welfare state, separated from the specifically communist programs for realizing that ideal, has won a more impressive victory. Not only can it claim, in the world of action, the allegiance of more peoples than the ideal of constitutional democracy. In addition, in the domain of thought or theory, it has fewer able and respected opponents than democracy—fewer who question the practicability of the ideal, fewer who doubt that the ideal can be fully realized by one or another set of practicable measures.

It remains to be said, of course, that the tripartite ideal which sums up the cumulative advances made by the three great revolutions—the tripartite ideal of the socialist democratic republic—is still far from realization anywhere in the world today. Recognizing this to be the case is quite consistent with recognizing that the three revolutions—the three experiments in institutional reform and the three alterations in social experience—have produced significant advances in political thought that would not have been possible without them. The point is not that without them the new truths or insights might not have been discovered. In the case of the American and the Russian experiments, the seminal insights were present and the truths dimly seen even before the revolutionary action began and developed. But the acknowledgment of these insights and truths as matters of common-sense wisdom, together with a sound philosophical elaboration of them, sprang from the common experience of men living in societies the institutions of which had been radically altered by these revolutions.

(5)

The description of each of these revolutions as an advance—as a step of progress—in political life as well as in political thought involved an expressed or implied normative judgment: that one state of affairs or one set of opinions is better than another. Let me make quite explicit the three normative judgments which have thus emerged.

The first was that the transition from despotic to constitutional government is an improvement by virtue of the fact that with the creation of citizenship at least some men—the few who were citizens in the republics of antiquity—enjoyed political liberty and exercised the right to participate in the government of their community.

The second normative judgment was that a further advance along the same line is made when citizenship or suffrage is universalized and the right to participate in government is recognized as one that all men have by virtue of their equality as men. As the constitutionalism of a republic is an improvement over the despotism of absolute rule, so the democratization of the republic is an improvement over the oligarchical constitution that restricted suffrage to a privileged political class, whether on the grounds of wealth, birth, race, sex, or nationality.

In describing the second great advance as the democratic revolution, I am using the term "democracy" in the narrowly political sense in which it encompasses no more than the achievement of political equality—the accession of all men to the equal political status of citizenship with suffrage. Thus used, democracy does not mean equality in all respects, but equality only with respect to participation in government and in the possession of political rights. The term democracy has been and can properly be used in the broader sense of referring to all the conditions of communal life—social and economic as well as political. The recognition of this broader sense involves what I have denominated the socialist revolution—the revolution that calls for social and economic democracy to supplement political democracy and render it efficacious.

This brings us to the third normative judgment, the one involved in regarding the socialist revolution as a still further advance along the same line, which begins with the acknowledgment that political liberty and equality are right and good for at least some men and moves forward to the judgment that they are not only right and good for all men, but also that their full achievement for all men requires that they be extended from participation in government to the social and economic aspects of communal life as well.

To say that liberty and equality with respect to the political, economic, and social conditions of communal life are right for all men is to say that men have a natural right to them, a right that is common to all men because of their sameness as human beings. And to say this is to say that these things are really good for men—that all men ought to have them—because they are needed by every man in his pursuit of happiness, his effort to live well. They are not ultimate goods, but indispensable means to the ultimate good that every man is morally obliged to seek—the happiness which consists in a whole life lived well.

While the meaning of justice is not exhausted by reference to natural rights, one measure of the justice of a community is the extent to which it secures the natural rights of man and secures them not merely for some members of society but for all. Hence the three normative judgments can be expressed in terms of justice as well as in terms of liberty and equality. The transition from despotic regimes to the constitutional government of republics is an advance in justice; the democratization of republics marks a further increase in justice; and the socialization of democracies enlarges justice still further.

The readers of this book—or at least a substantial number of them—may not question the normative judgments that I have just expressed or the values in terms of which they are formulated. Concurring in these judgments, they may ask who would deny that liberty and equality—social and economic as well as political—are goods that all men have a right to demand. Who would hesitate to admit that one society is better than another in proportion as its institutions and arrangements are more just? And, therefore, who could challenge or dispute the judgment that republics are better than despotisms, that democracies are better than oligarchies, and that socialized democracies are better than those in which economic and social inequalities still persist?

Those who think this way may, therefore, question the necessity of defending these basic normative judgments by further argument; and they may even wonder what tasks are left to political philosophy once these judgments are accepted as normative truths. Let me address myself to the state of mind that I have just delineated.

It is necessary, first, to remember that we are living at the end of the twentieth century and that the truth of these judgments was not acknowledged in earlier centuries, or even at the beginning of this century, either by men generally or by political philosophers. Second, it must be recognized that even though these truths are generally acknowledged today in certain quarters of the world, they are not yet universally acknowledged—in the West or in the East, or in the Southern Hemisphere. Third, even where they have come to be matters of common sense, they are not as well understood as they might be, their implications are not fully seen nor their relation to other basic propositions in the framework of principles that constitute an adequate political philosophy.

Hence even for those who accept, as matters of common sense, the normative judgments concerning constitutional government, democracy, and socialism, the philosopher has a service to perfrom, which involves clarifying their meaning, deepening our understanding of their truth, relating them to other truths, and solving the problems that we become aware of when we accept them as true.

(6)

The foregoing review of the revolutionary changes in the institutions of society that have occasioned or conditioned advances in political thought leaves most of the basic questions of political philosophy unanswered.

The few answers that may appear to have been given—by normative judgments concerning constitutional government, democracy, and socialism—have been advanced without the analysis and reasoning required for establishing their truth. The fact that a man of common sense may today recognize the truth of these normative judgments is no more than the point of departure for the political philosopher whose task it is to offer reasons in support of such judgments and others.

I shall try to discharge that task, in the chapters that follow, by setting forth, as briefly as possible, the controlling principles that constitute the common sense of politics and that express the political wisdom that is now available to us in the twentieth century. I will begin, in the next two chapters, by attempting to answer the two most fundamental questions—the question about the origin and nature of the state, why it is necessary, and if necessary whether it is a necessary evil or intrinsically good; and a similar question about government, its necessity, and goodness. I will then go on, in subsequent chapters, to questions about freedom, equality, and justice, ending with an attempt to project, in the light of our limited experience so far, the best society that is now seen to be possible.

Part Two

The New Confrontation:
Political Wisdom and
Anti-Political Folly

CHAPTER 6

The Necessity of Government

(1)

THE questions that I will attempt to answer in this chapter and the next are prior to any question we can ask about the shape that our political, economic, and social institutions should take in order to establish a just society. First are questions about government itself—why it is necessary and whether it is intrinsically good or a necessary evil. Then there are questions about the state—civil society, the political community, or body politic. Again our concern is with whether it is necessary and, if necessary, whether it is intrinsically good or a necessary evil.

The order in which I have placed these questions is based on the fact that the state or civil society is not the only community or association of men in which the role of government must be considered. As we shall see, the question about the necessity of government applies to any association of men living and acting together for a common purpose or a common good—a family, a village or tribe, or a private corporation of any kind, as well as to a state. Civil government is only one of the many types of government, the type that is appropriate to a civil society or state. The appropriateness of different types of government to different types of communities is a consideration posterior to the problem of understanding why government, of one type of another, is necessary for the existence of *any* community. We will subsequently see that the state—the political community

—comes into existence only with the institution of a certain type of government, but we must first understand why the existence of any community depends upon the institution of government.

I said earlier that the propositions I was going to set forth comprised the controlling principles of political philosophy *conceived as a purely normative discipline*. That remark calls for a word of further comment before I proceed with the exposition of the principles.

Because of the dependence of political thought upon political history, there is an inveterate tendency on the part of political philosophers to intertwine descriptive or historical statements with their normative judgments. They often pass insensibly from describing the way things are or have been to judgments about how they ought or ought not to be set up. In many cases, normative judgments or evaluations are implicit in statements that, on the surface, have the character of statements of fact; and they are left implicit, masked or concealed by appeals to historical evidence, rather than expressed explicitly in normative terms and defended as such.

I am going to try, in what follows, to concentrate on propositions that are clearly and plainly normative in their intent and that have the universality proper to controlling principles. This does not mean that I will abstain from references to historical fact or to current experience, but, where the discussion of such matters is required or helpful, I will try to treat them in a manner that is appropriate to questions of fact and not as if they were subjects about which a political philosopher has or can have special wisdom. I will try to exercise the same kind of restraint with regard to political problems that call for normative judgments which fall below the level of universality appropriate to principles. For purposes of illustration or amplification, I will from time to time deal with such problems and comment on alternative solutions to them; but I will reserve philosophical judgment about such alternatives at the level of policy, except in those rare instances in which the controlling principles require their endorsement or rejection.

(2)

Proceeding now to the question about the necessity of government, we must begin by distinguishing two senses of the term "necessity"—practical or pragmatic necessity, on the one hand, and logical and natural necessity, on the other.

We say that something happens necessarily in the very nature of the case when, given the operation of a cause, its effect cannot not occur. The causal laws discovered and formulated by natural sciences are, in this sense, statements of the necessary connections between one event and another. In the sphere of logic, we say that a valid inference is one in which the conclusion necessarily follows from the premises. If the premises are affirmed, the conclusion cannot be denied without contradicting one's self. In contrast to these two related senses of necessity, we speak of a thing's being necessary in the order of human action when it is indispensable to the end that we have in view. If it is impossible to achieve the end we are aiming at without employing a certain means, then that means is necessary in a practical sense.

Unlike natural necessity, practical or pragmatic necessity is compatible with the voluntary. We cannot violate or act contrary to natural necessities. If we lose our footing or our balance, we do not have the option of obeying or disobeying the law of gravitation. But in the sphere of practical necessities, it always remains possible for us to defeat our own purposes by voluntarily refusing to do what is required in order to achieve the end we have in view. The necessity still obtains; for the end cannot be achieved without employing the indispensable or necessary means. But nothing compels us to act in such a way that we succeed: we are free to fail by not doing what is practically necessary. If taking a plane is the only way to get to a certain place at a certain time, we can defeat our own desire to attend a meeting at that time and place by refusing to fly.

Government is a human institution; it is not a natural phenomenon, but a product of human action. Hence the question of its necessity is a question about its indispensability as a means to a certain end. To answer the question we must, therefore, look to the end that government is supposed to serve and attempt to define, as precisely as possible, the way in which government functions as a means.

The definition of government—not the government of a political community or civil society, but government *per se*—involves a number of steps. First of all, let us consider the difference between being governed and being exempt from government. An individual who is subject to government in any respect whatsoever is one who, in that respect, obeys a rule of action or carries out a decision that is not entirely or wholly of his own making. Thus, for example, when I and I alone decide the place where I shall live, the food I shall eat, or the book I shall read, I am not subject to government in the actions that I take to carry out these decisions. Or if I and I alone make the rule for my own conduct that I will not smoke cigarettes, I am not subject to government when I voluntarily obey this rule of abstinence. In matters of this kind, the young child is usually subject to government. We say that the child is governed by his parents when they decide for him the place where he shall live, the food he shall eat, or the books he shall read. Or when they lay down rules of conduct for him that he is expected to obey.

It may be supposed that the distinction between being governed and being exempt from government can also be expressed as a difference between government by another and self-government. Accordingly, it would be said that the child is governed by his parents, whereas the adult in obeying a rule of his own making is subject to self-government. For reasons that will presently become clear, I propose to reserve the term "self-government" for a certain type of government in which the decision that I act on or the rule that I obey is *neither entirely of my own making nor wholly made by others*. Instead of using the term "self-government" for the condition of being exempt from government by others, I will use "autonomy" to refer to those cases in which the individual acts on decisions or obeys rules *entirely of his own making*.

Government never completely replaces autonomy and never can. Even the young child exercises autonomy in many respects, for the strictest and most supervisory parents do not and cannot regulate every aspect of the child's behavior, nor can they issue edicts that decide everything that the child does from moment to moment. What is true of the child is also true of the adult in almost every imaginable set of circumstances. Even the slave or the prisoner of war retains a certain degree of autonomy, for the simple reason that it is impossible to make the government of anyone total—covering every action that the individual engages in.

The distinction between government and autonomy—that is, between being subject to government and being autonomous—is related to, but is not identical with, the distinction between the social and the solitary condition. If man were capable of leading a solitary life, he could be autonomous in all respects. The solitary individual would decide everything for himself and obey only such rules of conduct as he laid down for himself. He could not help being autonomous in this case; government would be inapplicable. In contrast to the solitary life, the social life is one in which a number of individuals live together, each in some dependence on the others and each being affected by the actions of others as well as affecting others by his own actions. In is only in the case of social life that the question of limitations upon the individual's autonomy can arise.

In order to avoid begging the question, I will refrain from assuming, without further analysis, that social life requires some limitation of the individual's autonomy, which is just another way of saying that social life requires some degree or measure of government. I will, therefore, put the question in the most open fashion, by asking whether it is possible for the individual who lives socially—that is, in association with others—to retain the complete autonomy he would have, in fact, could not help having, in the hypothetical case of a purely solitary mode of life.

(3)

For the purpose of answering this question, I propose to consider an extremely simple model of social life. Let me warn the reader at once that the model does not represent every variety of human association and so will not provide us with all the insights we need in order to understand all the functions of government. Nevertheless, it will help us to take a first step in that direction.

Three scientists voluntarily associate for the purpose of exploring the upper reaches of the Amazon. Before they embark on this common enterprise, they realize that, at a certain point in their exploration, they will be entirely on their own in the jungle. Each of them recognizes that he could not do alone or by himself what it may be possible for the small organized group to do, and each is willing to join the group for that reason. In other words, they are associated for a common purpose and with the realization that it is only the action of the group as a group that can achieve it. If they do not stay together and act together for their common purpose, they cannot succeed.

Before they leave civilization behind and enter the jungle as an isolated group entirely on its own, the three scientists face the question of how rules or decisions will be made for the action of the group as a group, as well as for the conduct of its individual members *in so far as such conduct affects the success of the enterprise*. The qualification just stated leaves them autonomous in matters that do not affect the concerted action of the group or the success of the enterprise. But why can they not be *completely* autonomous, each regulating his own conduct and deciding *everything* for himself?

A moment's reflection will serve to discover that complete autonomy is impractical and will not work. Understanding why this is so will throw light on the function that government is needed to perform.

Though the scientists associate as equals, each needs the co-operation of the other two in order to succeed in their common enterprise. They must agree, therefore, upon some method of regulating their own conduct and of reaching decisions in a manner that will preserve their concerted efforts to achieve a common goal. There are only three alternative procedures available to them.

One is for the scientists to require unanimity as the basis for any rule or decision that they will acknowledge as having authority for them. One dissenting voice on their part would then have the effect of a nullifying veto. And that, in turn, would mean that each scientist is committed to obeying himself alone, since no rule or decision to which he does not assent has authority for him. This would leave each of the scientists completely autonomous.

A second procedure would be for the three scientists to elect one of their number the leader of the expedition and confer upon him the authority to regulate the conduct of the party and decide all matters affecting the success of the enterprise.

The third alternative—and the only one that remains—consists in an agreement on the part of the scientists to have all rules adopted and all decisions made by a majority vote of two against one.

Only the first alternative leaves the scientists completely autonomous. The second and third institute a mode of government to which they themselves submit—two of them to the personal authority of an elected leader in one case, and all three of them to the impersonal or collective authority of a majority vote in the other case.

To show that government is not merely preferable to complete autonomy on the part of the scientists, but indispensable or necessary, we must have some reason for thinking that the requirement of unanimity on the part of the scientists will not work. Only if that is the case, must one or the other of the two remaining procedures be resorted to for the sake of carrying the expedition out successfully.

In the strictest use of "impossible," it cannot be said that unanimity must be rejected as an absolutely impossible method of adopting rules or making decisions. It is entirely conceivable that the three scientists might concur in their solution of every practical problem that called for the making of a rule or a decision. Reaching his decision independently, each might, nevertheless, find himself in agreement with the other two; or even if the matter were fully discussed, the discussion might eventuate in a unanimous conclusion.

Hence unanimity cannot be rejected in principle as impossible. But that does not mean that it should not be rejected on the grounds of its probable consequences in practice. The practical problems that must be solved by our exploring scientists are not like mathematical problems or even experimental ones—problems the solutions to which can be demonstrated or for which decisive evidence can be offered. On the contrary, they are problems about which reasonable men can disagree as to their solution. The likelihood of such disagreement, even among three scientists engaged in a practical enterprise, is sufficiently great to make the requirement of unanimity impractical. In fact, it need only fail to be satisfied at one crucial turn of affairs to prevent the expedition from succeeding. Since the probability of one such failure is extremely high, that is sufficient reason to reject unanimity, together with the complete autonomy it preserves, in favor of government.

(4)

We have now discovered one reason for the necessity of government. It is necessary as an indispensable means of getting rules adopted and decisions made about matters concerning which equals engaged in a common enterprise can reasonably disagree. Stated in another way, the three scientists must set up the personal authority of a leader or the collective authority of a majority vote in order to be sure that at every crucial turn of events their expedition will be directed by a rule or a decision the authority of which each of them acknowledges even though he may disagree with it, i.e., even though he would have adopted a different rule or made a different decision if he were acting autonomously instead of submitting to government.

While unanimity will not work as a way of getting a number of equals engaged in a common enterprise to work harmoniously together for a common goal, it is the only way in which equals can institute an authority that they acknowledge or a government to which they willingly submit. Once again we must realize that a unanimous decision on the part of all, the decision of an elected leader, or the decision reached by a majority vote exhaust the alternatives; for since we are considering voluntary action on the part of the scientists who join hands as equals, we must exclude the forceful imposition of a decision by someone outside the group itself. [1]

That being the case, we can see at once that government itself cannot be instituted by a majority vote or by the decision of a leader, since the authority of a leader or of a majority is the very thing being instituted. Hence the institution of government itself, together with the delegation of authority to an elected leader or to a majority, must be accomplished by the *unanimous consent* of the parties involved—in this case, the three scientists as equals. [2]

Since the government whose authority they acknowledge is established by their unanimous consent, the scientists form a self-governing community even though each has surrendered his autonomy *with regard to all matters affecting the success of their common enterprise*. Each of the scientists is a constituent of the government that is established with his consent. If the government established takes the form of a dictatorship (i.e., decisions by a leader), self-government is minimal, being limited to the selection of the leader, whether by lottery or by a majority vote. If, however, the government established confers authority upon a majority vote, then self-government is maximal, for each of the scientists exercises a voice in the adoption of every rule and the making of every decision.

In either the minimal or the maximal case, the individual remains self-governing when the rule adopted or the decision made is contrary to one that he himself would have chosen were he autonomous. The fact that he is obliged to obey a rule or to act on a decision that is not of his own choosing must be combined with the fact that his consent was involved in setting up the authority to which he owes obedience and, in the case of maximal self-government, with the additional fact that he participated in the voting that eventuated in a decision other than his own. For him to refuse obedience in those cases in which he disagrees with an authorized rule or decision is tantamount to his insisting upon his autonomy instead of acknowledging the authority of government. [3]

(5)

We have learned three things from our limited model. (1) Acknowledging and submitting to an authority for making rules and decisions concerning the actions to be taken by a group of men associated for a common purpose is the only alternative to retaining and exercising complete autonomy. (2) Since the retention of complete autonomy is tantamount to making unanimity the condition for adopting any rule or decision, its retention will probably frustrate concerted action for a common purpose, because the matters about which rules or decisions must be made are matters about which reasonable men can disagree. Their disagreement about such matters being highly probable, individuals associated for a common purpose must surrender their complete autonomy and substitute for it an authority that they themselves set up and acknowledge. They must do this if they wish to succeed in acting together harmoniously and effectively for whatever is their common purpose. (3) Government is necessary only as a means—a means of achieving concerted action for the good commonly aimed at by a group of associated men. The necessity of government answers to the need for a commonly acknowledged authority to make rules or decisions concerning actions that affect the achievement of a common purpose.

The points just made all relate to one function of government —one reason why it is necessary as a means. But that is not the only function of government, or the only reason for its necessity. Another is the indispensability of government for the maintenance of peace. To understand this, we must go beyond the simple model we have been considering, consisting of three men alike in character and purpose. Let us now contemplate a much larger community of equals, involving individuals differing in a multitude of respects. This type of community, much larger than a single family, we usually call a civil society—a community of men living together under civil government.

The reason why our three scientists found it necessary to institute government, the authority of which they freely acknowledged by their unanimous consent, will apply without qualification and, perhaps, with even greater force in the case of civil society: the common good for which men associate in the larger community cannot be achieved if each of them insists upon retaining his complete autonomy. Some portion of it must be surrendered to establish an authority for making rules and reaching decisions binding on all by their free consent. But in the case of the more populous and humanly heterogenous community of a civil society, there is an additional reason for government, namely, its indispensability as a means to civil peace.

In any populous community comprising men of divergent interests, conflicts or disagreements will probably arise about matters of either private or public concern. The parties to such conflicts may either be private individuals or they may be private individuals arraigned against public officials. Confronted with the probability of such conflicts or disputes, what alternatives are available for settling them? Only two: one is whatever power is at the disposal of the parties in conflict; the other is the authority of government to adjudicate disputes and to enforce its judgments. Let us consider each in turn.

In the absence of government, each of the parties to a dispute, being autonomous, must operate as judge in his own case and, in defense of his *ex parte* judgment, must try to persuade his opponent or, failing in that, exercise such *de facto* force as he can bring to bear. Disputes can, of course, be settled in this way, but not peacefully, since persuasion is likely to fail and recourse to violence will be necessitated. [4] Hence if men who live together and interact in all the affairs of their daily lives retain their complete autonomy, there is no way of excluding recourse to violence as a way of settling the disputes that are likely to arise. It follows, therefore, that government with the authority to adjudicate disputes and with authorized force to implement the judgment of its tribunals is indispensable to the peace of a civil society, in which men are associated for their common good.

Peace is essential to the very existence of a community as a community; and so, if communal life is a means to the common good of those who are associated in order to live well as human beings, then the maintenance of peace among men living together is indispensable to their achieving good lives for themselves.

The peace of a community may also be breached or marred by acts of criminal violence, as well as by the violence that would arise if the parties to a dispute could not submit their differences to an authorized tribunal for adjudication or arbitration. In the absence of government, each individual would have to defend himself against aggression by others with whatever power is at his disposal. The probability is high that wholesale violence would ensue. For this reason, as well as for the reason that, without authorized tribunals to settle disputes, the settlement of them would probably involve recourse to violence, the absence of government is a state of war rather than one of peace.

The preceding discussion of government as necessary for the maintenance of civil peace has introduced the notion of authorized force and the distinction between such force and violence. In our simple model of the three scientists in the jungle, the institution of an acknowledged authority sufficed for the operation of government; but in the more complicated case of civil society, naked authority is not enough. It must be clothed with and implemented by authorized force. The reason for this rests on the probability of disobedience together with the probability that persuasion will not always succeed in winning compliance from those who tend to be recalcitrant.

The probability of disobedience is generated by the fact of human freedom. Even those who freely acknowledge the authority of government always remain free to obey or disobey its rules of law, its administrative edicts, and its judicial decisions. In a populous community, comprising men of every stripe, good and bad, the probability of disobedience is not negligible. The disobedience may or may not be justified in the particular case. Let us for the moment table the problem of justified disobedience;

I will return later to the conditions under which there is a right to disobey. For the present let us consider only the likelihood of disobedience that is *not* justified.

One way in which the constituted authority of civil government can deal with such disobedience is to attempt to persuade the recalcitrants. Since persuasion can fail and since, furthermore, it is likely to fail in a certain number of cases, some other device must be available if the authority of government is not to be rendered ineffective for the purpose for which it is instituted.

The only other device is the employment of coercive force. It is strictly an emergency measure in the sense that its use is justified *only* by the failure of efforts at persuasion. Nevertheless, the high probability that persuasion will not be effective to overcome unjustified disobedience in *every* case makes it necesary to implement the authority of government with the right to employ coercive force. [5]

The force that is used to compel obedience or compliance may either be authorized or unauthorized. It is authorized only if it is instituted to implement the authority of civil government. Only such force as is thus instituted and employed to implement the regulations and decisions that government itself has the authority to make is, strictly speaking, authorized force or force exercised *de jure*—rightfully or by right. All other force is purely *de facto* or without right, and all such unauthorized force is violence. Violence may be committed by a government as well as by the members of a society. A government commits violence when it exceeds its authorization to use force—when it uses force that it is not authorized to use, or uses it to enforce compliance with rules or decisions that it is not authorized to make. [6]

Since authorized force belongs by right to civil government and to civil government alone, government should have a *monopoly* of authorized force. This does not mean that it necessarily does have a preponderance of the force available in the community. The *de facto* force that can be marshaled by a revolutionary party or movement may surpass and overpower the authorized force of government. Again I am postponing for the time being the question of the right of revolution, which is related to the question about the conditions under which revolutionary violence is justified.

The only point that I wish to stress here is that authorized force—force used to implement authority—is, by its very nature, the exclusive property of a civil government that is duly constituted; in other words, a government that is itself *de jure* and not *de facto*. The force exercised by a *de facto* government is as unauthorized as that government itself is, and so, being *de facto* force, is a manifestation of violence. [7]

(6)

I can sum up what we have learned so far in a single, though somewhat complex proposition: government, with the authority to make laws, to adjudicate disputes, and to issue administrative decisions, and with a monopoly of authorized force to coerce where it fails to persuade, is an indispensable means, *proximately*, to the peace of communal life; and, *ultimately*, to the happiness of its individual members, to whatever extent a good human life for each of them depends on their being able to live together, work cooperatively for their common good, and interact peacefully with one another. Those who concede that government is necessary for the reasons just indicated may still wish to ask whether, being necessary, it is also a necessary evil. Or, in addition to being necessary, is it intrinsically good?

What is being asked is not whether there can be bad government. Government can obviously be bad in a variety of ways: through exceeding its authority or its right to use coercive force, through the imperfection of its institutions, through the injustice of its acts, and so on. Since no one can deny the abuses, imperfections, or injustices that everyone knows can afflict government, the question should be not whether government *can* be bad, but whether it *must* be. For if it must be bad and, in spite of that, is necessary, then and only then would it be correct to regard it as a necessary evil. [8]

I submit that there is nothing about the nature of government that makes it impossible for it to be free from abuses, imperfections, or injustices. This remains true even if one were to add that, government being what it is and men being what they are, any government instituted and carried on by men will always reflect to a certain extent the weaknesses and imperfections of its human constituents and agents. Nevertheless, the institutions of government can be so perfected and its operations so safeguarded that they can be rendered innocuous, in spite of the ever present human proclivities to the contrary. Government is, therefore, not necessarily or intrinsically evil. [9]

The only reason that might be given for thinking the contrary would be the view that complete autonomy on the part of every individual is an absolute good; for if this were the case, then government, by taking autonomy away from the individual in certain matters, while leaving it intact in others, would necessarily be evil. This line of argument can readily be shown to be self-defeating. To be a necessary evil, government has to be necessary, in the first place. But why is government necessary? Because, as we have seen, complete autonomy on the part of individuals is incompatible with their effective cooperation for a common purpose and with their peaceful interaction in communal life. Hence if the effectiveness and peace of communal life is itself something good—good as a means to the good life of human beings—then complete autonomy, not government, is to be judged intrinsically evil.

In short, the goodness of government as well as its necessity rests on the fact that human beings, in order to engage effectively in the pursuit of happiness, must associate and cooperate with their fellowmen to obtain the goods of communal life, among which peace is a principal component, and they cannot do so unless the authority and authorized force of government replace autonomy with regard to all matters affecting communal and common goods. [10]

Before I turn to the question about the nature and origin of the state, I would like to remind the reader of matters that have been postponed for later consideration or questions that have been raised but not answered. They include such considerations of critical importance as the conditions under which resistance to government is justified and the conditions that justify recourse to revolutionary violence. They also include basic questions about the limits of a government's authority and coercive force, questions about the perfection of its institutions, and questions about the justice of its acts.

My reason for postponing the consideration of these matters is twofold. First, our concern with them is mainly in the sphere of civil society and, therefore, in the sphere of civil governments. Hence we will be in a better position to deal with these matters after we understand the state or civil society as distinct from all other communities or forms of association, and understand it as having only one mode of government that is distinctively appropriate to itself. Second, these considerations are consequent upon, not antecedent to, the question about the necessity of government and its goodness. Hence no matter what resolution we are subsequently able to achieve of the difficult problems concerning dissent and revolutionary violence or concerning the abuses or injustices of government, it should in no way detract from the soundness of the conclusion that we have so far reached concerning the necessity and intrinsic goodness of government.

CHAPTER 7

Concerning the Goodness of the State

(1)

CONFRONTED with the diversity of human associations, all of which can be called communities or societies, but only some of which are called states, we are challenged to define the mode of association or society that is properly called a state.

The problem cannot be solved either by an appeal to history or by consulting the facts of current usage. In the sphere of human institutions—arrangements devised by man for a purpose or with an end in view—definitions must be teleological, for what is being defined is a means to an end; and as teleological, such definitions also tend to have a normative character. Thus, for our example, the definition of government with which we have just been concerned is both teleological and normative.

The same holds for the definition of a man-made law as an ordinance or rule made by a duly constituted authority for the good of the community. When law is thus defined, it follows that a tyrannical law made by a *de facto* ruler for his own good is a law in name only; which is another way of saying that the word "law" is used equivocally when it is applied to the self-serving ordinances imposed by tyrants and also to rules made by duly constituted authorities for the good of the community. We must be prepared for the same consequences when we formulate a teleological and normative definition of the state.

Let us begin by considering the evidence of history and the facts as they are generally known. Examining the wide variety of human associations, we find that they differ in the size and character of their populations, in the purposes for which they are formed or which they serve, in the degree of independence that they possess, and in the mode of government that obtains and that exercises some measure of control or force. These include, on the one hand, such communities as the family, the tribal or village community, and the state (whether the latter is a city-state, a feudal state, a national state, a unitary state, or a federal state); and, on the other hand, corporations of every sort, clubs, social organizations, fraternities, and so on.

It is also helpful to observe that, as a matter of usage, a number of other terms are frequently employed as synonyms for the word "state": such terms as "commonwealth," "body politic," "civil society," and "political community." The use of these other terms as synonyms for the "state" should prevent anyone from making a mistake that must be avoided; namely, the identification of state with government. While government and even a certain mode of government is an essential component of the state, the same is true of other societies or communities, such as the family or the tribe; it also holds true in the case of other associations, such as private corporations or social organizations. Hence the words "state" and "government" should not be used as if they were strict synonyms. As an essential and determining component of the state, government may be as important to the whole as the nucleus of a cell; yet it is only a part and is not to be identified with the whole. [1]

(2)

What this brings us to, stated in familiar jargon, is the recognition that the state is a species in the genus society or community. It is a certain kind of society or community, to be distinguished from other kinds by definite differentia. Let us now consider the differentia that can serve us in our effort to define the state. I would like to propose the following five considerations as of maximum relevance.

First, the members of a society or community may or may not be related by ties of blood or consanguinity. This criterion differentiates the family from all other communities; for only the family is thus constituted. Tribal communities composed of intermarrying families under a strict rule of endogamy have some measure of consanguinity, but not to the same degree as the family.

Second, an organized association of men may or may not have the status of an independent community, where "independence" means that the community is not included in another, larger, and embracing community; and also that the community has autonomy; that is, is not the subject to government by another community. [2] In an early period of human life, families existed as independent communities, though this is now only rarely and exceptionally the case. The only other independent or autonomous societies are tribal communities and states. No other types of social organization, no other corporations, have such status. The criterion of inclusion in a larger community helps us further to differentiate the state from families and tribal or village communities among all the types of society that can have autonomy or independence. While families and tribes can have autonomy or independence, this is not essential to their existence; for both of these types of society may be included in the larger community of the state. Whereas tribal or village communities include families, families include no communities smaller than themselves. Only the state is characterized by the joint criteria (i) of including other communities, such as families and tribal or village communities and (ii) of not being included in any larger community. It is only the case of that special type of community that is a state that autonomy or independence is essential to its existence. [3]

Third, considering now only independent or autonomous communities, a further point of differentiation concerns their populousness and their economic productivity. The size of a population directly effects the division of labor that is possible in a community, and indirectly its productivity of consumable wealth— the means of subsistence. But productivity is also affected by the technology available. A more populous community with a primitive technology may be less productive than a less populous community with an advanced technology. The productivity of a community determines the amount of wealth available to its members and the amount of human time that can be freed from toil or subsistence-work. The productivity may be so low that the wealth of a community consists of no more than is needed to supply the bare necessities from day to day; or it may, in ascending degrees, approach the point where it provides, beyond the bare necessities, the comforts and conveniences of life and provides them in a quantity that would make it possible totally to eliminate deprivation or poverty. Similarly, degrees of productivity range from the low end of the spectrum at which no member of the community is exempt from time-consuming toil to the other end at which either some or all members of the community have sufficient free time for the pursuits of leisure.

A *fourth* criterion is the end or purpose served by the association. The association may aim at some partial good, some good that is only a part or component of the *totum bonum*, the whole of goods that satisfy human desires—either man's natural needs or his conscious wants. Or the association may serve, or try to serve, human life as a whole and the whole of goods that human beings strive for. Only those modes of human association that have the status of autonomous or independent communities aim at the *totum bonum* or serve the purpose of human life as a whole. Associations that cannot have such status never serve or aim at more than one or another partial good. None by itself suffices to serve human life as a whole. [4]

Among associations that can have such status, two—the family and the tribal or village community—may lack it, through being included in a larger community: the family in the tribe; families and tribes in the state. When they lack it, they, like other included associations, serve some partial good rather than human life as a whole, leaving the latter to be served by the community in which they are included. Only the state, which does not exist *unless* it has independence or autonomy, always has as its end the *totum bonum*—the good of human life as a whole.

The community that aims at a certain end may or may not serve it effectively, or may serve it with varying degrees of effectiveness. When families and tribal communities have autonomy or independence, they may not be populous enough or technologically advanced enough to provide the conditions of a good human life for any of their members; or they may be able to provide it for some but not all. What is true of families and tribes, as independent communities, may also be true of the larger community that is called a "state" and deserves that name only by virtue of having autonomy and including other communities within itself.

Finally, we come to the fifth criterion that must be employed in a normative and teleological definition of the state. That is the mode of government which maintains the peace of the community and regulates or directs concerted action for a common purpose.

Two basic distinctions in modes of government are of relevance here. The first is the distinction between the government of inferiors by superiors and the government of free men and equals. The only clear and unquestionable example of the government of inferiors by superiors occurs in the community of the family; during the infancy of children, parents are their superiors in experience, knowledge, and power. Furthermore, the infant is incapable of complete autonomy and needs the tutelary or pedagogical authority of its parents for its own survival and maturation. Parental government is absolute in the sense that its authority does not derive in any way from the consent of the governed, nor does it involve any participation on the part of the governed. The consent of the governed and participation by the governed are the differentiating criteria of the government that obtains among free men and equals who are self-governing. [5]

The second distinction, closely related to the first, is that between *de facto* and *de jure* government. *De facto* government may either take the form of government the authority of which rests on the personal superiority of the governor, as in the case of the parental government of infants; or it may take the form of government imposed by force upon the governed and exercising coercive force, the authority of which is not acknowledged by the governed. *De jure* government, in contrast, is instituted by the governed and has authority and authorized force that is acknowledged by them.

The two distinctions conjoined enable us to draw the line that divides constitutional government or the rule of law from all other modes of government. Constitutional government is the *de jure* self-government of free men and equals, instituted by the governed, involving their express or tacit consent, and also their participation in varying ways and degrees. [6] Let me warn you at once that what I have just said does not claim to be an exhaustive account of the modes of government, nor does it consider all the criteria for evaluating governments as legitimate and illegitimate, just and unjust, or perfect and imperfect. Far from it. I will discuss these additional considerations in a later connection. Here I have confined myself to what is required for the definition of the state as a civil society or political community.

(3)

We are now ready to attempt the formulation of that definition. The state is an association of men—a community or society—(1) that extends its membership beyond the bounds of consanguinity; (2) that has autonomy or independence, and that includes families, may include tribal or village communities and even subordinate political communities that are sometimes called "states" but which do not have complete autonomy or independence *vis-à-vis* other states; (3) that is populous enough and sufficiently advanced in technology to provide the economic conditions of a good human life for some or all of its members; (4) that aims at or serves, in some measure of effectiveness, the good of a whole human life, again either for some or all of its members; and (5) that, through the institution of the rule of law or constitutional government, provides the status of self-governing free men and equals for some or all of its members.

Of these five notes, only the last three are decisive in a definition that is both teleological and normative. A community may extend its membership beyond the bounds of consanguinity, it may have the requisite autonomy or independence, and it may include other communities as parts of itself, and still be a state in name only if it is totally ineffective as a means to the end of a good human life for its members. It will be totally ineffective if, in its economic aspects, it does not provide the requisite wealth and free time for any of its members; and if, in its political aspect, it does not provide the status of free men and equals for any of them. It will be partially effective to some degree less than perfect if it provides these economic and political conditions *only* for some, but *not* for all. It follows, of course, that the perfect state, the one that is totally effective as a means, provides the requisite economic and political conditions *for all*.

Of the three decisive notes, the one that is primary relates to the end that the state serves as a means, namely, human happiness or a good human life. The other two—one relating to the character of the economy, the other to the character of the government—determine the effectiveness with which the state functions as a means to its appointed end. Viewed in terms of its political institutions, the state as a civil society is a community that exists under civil government, which is to say *de jure* government. As a political community, it is a society that exists under constitutional government with the consent and participation of the governed, some or all. *It is thus by definition a republic.* [7]

This teleological and normative definition of the state has a number of consequences that deserve brief comment. The first is that the state, as thus defined, comes into existence at a certain historic moment. Before the ancient Greeks invented constitutional government and lived in republics, states did not exist, though there were, contemporaneously, many independent societies that, not being republics, were *de facto* states or states in name only, just as a tyrannical law is a law in name only. Since that point in history at which the state or republic first came into existence, there have been, of course, many communities that, lacking constitutional government and the requisite economy, have also been states in name only; and there are still many such in the world today. By whatever actual steps or processes states first came into existence and have come into existence in succeeding centuries, the formal truth of the normative and teleological definition universally applies: no society is *de jure* a state unless it has the requisite economy and unless its mode of government involves constituents who are consenting equals and freely contracting parties.

A second consequence has already been intimated, but needs to be more explicitly noted. The teleological and normative definition of the state requires us to use such expressions as "*de facto* state" or "state in name only" for those communities which have the kind of population and the independence or autonomy that is characteristic of states, but which lack the economic and political institutions that are indispensable to the state as a means to the good life of some *or* all of its inhabitants.

Our definition also requires us to distinguish between imperfect and perfect realizations of the idea of the state. If we consider only the criterion of numbers—the happiness of *some* as contrasted with the happiness of *all*—then, as our earlier discussion of the three great political advances has already indicated, there are less and more perfect realizations of the idea of the state. The first and least degree of perfection is that of the oligarchical republic—the republic with restricted citizenship, in which only some men have the status of free men and equals. [8] The second degree of perfection is that of the democratic republic—the republic with universal citizenship, in which all men enjoy the status of political freedom and equality. Complete perfection is reached only with the socialist, democratic republic, in which all men enjoy the economic as well as political conditions prerequisite to human happiness or the good life.

However, if we add the consideration that peace, in the fullest sense of that term, is an essential condition of the good human life, then nothing short of the world state—a socialist, democratic republic that encompasses all mankind or a union of socialist, democratic republics—can adequately serve the end that the state, teleologically defined, aims at; and so, normatively, nothing less than the world state just described perfectly realizes the idea of the state. [9]

A third consequence to which I wish to call attention concerns the implied answer to our question about the necessity and goodness of the state. *Teleologically defined*, the state is necessary as an indispensable means to the good life—for some or all men. *Normatively considered*, the state is intrinsically good by virtue of its being necessary as a means to the ultimate good—human happiness. And one state, as we have seen, is better than another in proportion as it is more effective as a means to its appointed end. [10]

(4)

To complete what has been said so far about the nature and origin of the state, I would like to clarify and resolve the specious opposition between those who appear to maintain that the state is a creation of nature and those who appear to regard it as a product of convention or contract.

That the opposition is specious rather than real can be clearly shown by the following considerations. On the one hand, Aristotle, who is usually cited on the naturalist side of the issue because he says that the state is a creation of nature and more natural than the family, also remarks that "he who first founded the state is the greatest of benefactors." This remark is almost universally overlooked in attributing a purely naturalist view to Aristotle. On the other hand, Hobbes, Locke, Rousseau, and Kant, who are usually cited on the conventionalist side of the issue because they attribute the origin of the state to some form of social contract or compact voluntarily entered into, also argue that men are led to quit the state of nature, in which each has complete autonomy, and enter into civil society, because life in the so-called "state of nature" is *unnatural* for man—unnatural in the precise sense that it fails to satisfy his natural needs. This aspect of the social-contract theory of the state is also generally ignored in attributing a purely conventionalist view to these authors. [11]

The truth of the matter, to which all the authors mentioned agree with minor differences in detail, is that the state is *both natural and conventional.* To understand how this can be so, it is necessary to distinguish the two senses in which a society can be natural.

The first is the sense in which a society is natural as a product of genetic determination. The beehive and the ant-mound are natural in this way: they are instinctive, not voluntary, associations, arising from genetic determinations in the species of organisms that populate them. [12]

The second sense is the sense in which a society is natural only as a means of satisfying natural needs. In this sense, the family, when it is an independent community, is a natural society because it is an indispensable means to human life and answers to the need for its preservation. The tribal or village community answers more fully to these same needs; and the state even more fully, going beyond supplying the needs of life itself to providing the conditions of a good life. Since men can live without living well, and since they cannot live well unless they succeed, first, in solving the problem of subsistence, the family, as an independent community, has a prior naturalness and necessity to that of the state. On the other hand, since the state more completely fulfills the natural needs of man than either the family or the tribe, it is the most natural and necessary of the three communities that serve the purposes of human life as a whole.

When the state is said to be natural and necessary in this second sense, both its naturalness and its necessity are teleological, i.e., derived from an end that is desired as an object of natural human need. And such naturalness and necessity are compatible with voluntariness on the part of the human beings who associate to form the society in question. Hence as an association into which men enter voluntarily, not by instinctive determination, and which they devise or institute as the means to an end toward which they are impelled by natural need, the state is at once both natural and conventional. [13]

The most unnatural condition for men—in fact, so unnatural that it probably never existed—would be the hypothetical or imaginary "state of nature" posited, for analytical purposes, by the social-contract theorists. This not only would be or would soon become a state of war rather than of peace; it would also be one in which none of the other naturally needed goods of communal life could be achieved, because communal life, as well as civil peace, is itself impossible when everyone retains his complete autonomy. Being contrary to nature, it is miscalled a "state of nature" and would have been more properly named anarchy. [14]

By the same token, the family and the tribal or village community, while natural as well as conventional, are nearer to the so-called "state of nature" than civil society to whatever extent they, as independent communities, fail to provide all the goods of communal life, including peace, that man needs in order to achieve a good human life. The same conclusion also applies to those independent communities that are purely *de facto* states or states in name only. Furthest removed from the "state of nature" is that community which most fully realizes the idea of a civil society and most effectively serves natural human needs for all men, not just some.

Hence the reason that is given for man's quitting the state of nature to enter into civil society under civil government—his desire to avoid the perils, inconveniences, deprivations, and frustrations of anarchy and war, all of which add up to too high a price to pay for complete autonomy—remains operative throughout all the stages in which social life has developed from the family through the tribal community to civil society, and from less perfect to more perfect embodiments of the state.

CHAPTER 8

The Anti-Political Philosophers

(1)

THE preceding chapters were devoted to answering two
questions: *first*, the question about the necessity of government, and whether it is inherently good or evil; *second*,
the question about the nature and origin of the state, and
whether it, too, is good as an indispensable means.

The answers given, together with the reasons in support of
them, lie at the foundation of any sound political philosophy.
They are its two most fundamental principles, setting up the
framework within which, if they are to be sound, all other
principles must be formulated. These two fundamental principles have been enunciated and defended by a long line of
eminent political philosophers, from Plato and Aristotle in antiquity, through their Roman, Hellenistic, and mediaeval com-
mentators, to Hobbes, Locke, Rousseau, and Kant in modern
times. [1] The mention of these illustrious names evokes re-
membrances of all the points on which these thinkers differed
from one another. Their differences, however, were all concerned with matters subordinate to or unconnected with the
two essential points here being considered—the necessity of
government and the naturalness of the state as a duly constituted
or *de jure* commonwealth.

The solid agreement that I am calling attention to can, in my
judgment, be interpreted as a recognition of common-sense truths
by the philosophers—truths that have been in the possession of

94

common sense throughout the last 2500 years. What I have just said does not apply to certain additional insights, such as the insight concerning the perfection of the state by the democratization and socialization of the republic or the insight concerning the need for a world state and world government. These truths have but recently emerged and are only now *becoming* part of the common sense of politics.

It was only in the nineteenth century that a philosophical attack was mounted against the two fundamental principles of political theory—an attack that was, like the principles themselves, essentially normative in character, for it advanced and attempted to support the proposition that government is unnecessary and intrinsically evil, together with the proposition that the state conceived as a society requiring a government exercising coercive force is, *ipso facto*, also evil. [2] This was the position taken, again with differences in detail that are subordinate to or unconnected with the controlling propositions, by the philosophical anarchists from Godwin and Proudhon to Bakunin, Kropotkin, and Sorel, and after them Emma Goldman and Alexander Berkman. [3] It was a position shared to some extent by Marx, Engels, and Lenin, at least in their apocalyptic vision of the ultimate stage of communism that will be ushered in by the withering away of the state and of government. [4] It is also a position that has many sympathizers in the nineteenth and twentieth century, notable among them Herbert Spencer and Henry David Thoreau, Bertrand Russell and Paul Goodman. [5] What unites this diverse assortment of writers is their rejection of or their antipathy to the state and government as *irreconcilable* with the fullest realization of liberty and equality.

The fullest possible realization of liberty and equality for all men, not living in isolation but living together in society under conditions that preclude violence and preserve peace, is an ideal on which both the political philosophers—the defenders of the state and of government—and their anarchistic opponents can agree. The question at issue then is whether, given the same ideal to be aimed at, it can be achieved, as the political philosophers claim, *only* through the institutions of the state and of government or, as philosophical anarchists contend, *only* through the abolition of government and, with it, the state as we know it.

I will attempt to show that this issue can be resolved clearly in favor of the common-sense truths and against the objections of the anarchists. Such truth as is inherent in the anarchist position can then be incorporated into the common sense of politics by a philosophically correct understanding of the grounds of dissent and rebellion—the justification of civil disobedience and revolutionary violence by the unjustified excesses or defects of government.

(2)

Though philosophical anarchists differ among themselves in their specific proposals, in their revolutionary tactics, and in their apocalyptic visions of the ideal to be achieved, they are in fundamental agreement on the proposition that the maximization of liberty and equality for all men requires the abolition of government and of the state as we know it—the state in all its historical embodiments so far. That proposition defines the position of the philosophical anarchists or, as they might just as appropriately be called, the *anti-political philosophers*. We are thus confronted with an issue or dispute about political philosophy itself—an issue that is more fundamental than any of the questions about which political philosophers disagree, for it is an issue that finds all political philosophers standing together in defense of their two most basic principles against their opponents, the philosophical anarchists.

It might be supposed that I would undertake to defend traditional political philosophy against the philosophical anarchists by attempting to show that the position of the latter is completely erroneous—entirely lacking in sense and substance. So far as its two basic principles are concerned, I do not have to go beyond what has already been said to defend traditional political philosophy—and common sense—against the anarchists. The analysis presented in the two preceding chapters and the arguments there advanced can be brought to bear to show why the anarchists are wrong in thinking that men can live together cooperatively and in peace *without government* or that they can live well in some community that is *not a state*. But this does not suffice as an answer to the anarchists, for even were they to grant the necessity of the state and government, they would still contend that both are necessary evils, because they are intrinsically incompatible with the maximization of liberty and equality for all. Here we face an issue that requires us to go much further than we have gone in the consideration of the state and government; and here the kernel of truth that underlies the anarchists' attack on the state as we know it and their antipathy to government must be saved and incorporated into political philosophy.

Traditional political philosophy prior to the nineteenth century was concerned with the question of liberty and equality, but always *for some*, never *for all*. While the emergence of democratic and socialistic doctrines in the nineteenth century began the shift of attention from *for some* to *for all*, the philosophical anarchists gave further impetus to this change of focus by setting up their goal as the *maximization* of liberty and equality *for all*. Are the state and government not only compatible with the maximization of liberty and equality for all, but also indispensable to it, as well as to the maintenance of civil peace and the promotion of the good life for every human being? That is the question that must be answered affirmatively by a political philosophy that recognizes what truth there is in the anarchist position, while at the same time exposing its fundamental errors.

To accomplish this, I propose to proceed in the following order: first, I will try to state the basic tenets of the anarchist position, tenets that are common to philosophical anarchism in most, if not all, of its varieties. My aim here will be to focus on the points at which philosophical anarchism comes into conflict with traditional political philosophy and to show that, on these points, the anarchist is fundamentally in error. Second, I will try to separate what is sound in the anarchist position from the errors with which it is there associated. This will lead us to an examination of the evils or injustices of government—evils that the political philosopher, unlike the anarchist, thinks can be eradicated without eradicating government itself. Finally, I will deal with the problem of the maximization of liberty and equality for all and attempt to show that that problem can be solved only by the maximization of justice in the institutions of the state and in the operations of government.

(3)

There are a number of points about which anarchists differ among themselves. I mention these in order to eliminate them as irrelevant to the common tenets of the anarchist doctrine.

The most extreme form of anarchism calls for the abolition of organized society in any form, not just the state as we know it. [6] Opposed to this completely individualistic extreme, the other forms of anarchism affirm the social nature of man, the need for human cooperation, and the goodness of communal life. What is to be abolished, therefore, is not society as such, but the state as we know it, the state or civil society that is inseparable from the institutions of civil government exercising coercive force. Whether anarchists look forward to a society or state without government or no society or state at all, there is agreement among them that the state as we know it, the state involving a coercive government, must be destroyed.

A second point of difference among anarchists concerns the revolutionary tactics to be employed in the abolition of the state as we know it. On the one hand, we have the tactics recommended by Bakunin, Kropotkin, and Sorel. These are the tactics of direct action or the general strike, aiming at the immediate overthrow of the state with all its existing institutions, by violence if necessary, and without any intermediate or transitional stages between the state that is to be destroyed and the ideal condition to be achieved. [7] On the other hand, we have the Fabian-like tactics of the Marxists, who think that the destruction of the state must be accomplished in two stages, the first involving the violence of direct action to overthrow the bourgeois capitalist state and replace it by the proletarian socialist state, the second consisting in the gradual and peaceful process whereby the proletarian state will wither away and be replaced by a society or communal life without coercive government of any sort. This difference in tactics does not affect the ultimate goal to be achieved. It is the same for the Fabian anarchists (i.e., the Marxists) and for their direct action opponents, just as the ultimate goal of the socialist movement is the same for the Fabian socialists and their Marxist opponents. [8]

A third point of difference has to do with the way in which the means of production are to be operated or administered after the private ownership of them is abolished. Here again the Marxists differ from other anarchists, especially the syndicalists, who are opposed to the state's ownership and operation of the means of production. [9] But the difference is one of means or tactics, not one of ultimate goals. Since, for the anarchist, it is the protection of property rights that necessitates government, the abolition of property rights is conjoined with the abolition of government, whether this is to be accomplished at once by direct action or by a gradual dissolution of the state, not only as a governing body but also as owner and operator of the means of production.

(4)

What fundamental tenets are shared by those who, however else they differ, call for the abolition of government and of the state as we know it?

(1) They hold that the maximization of freedom requires the complete autonomy of the individual, each heeding only his own private judgment, each obeying himself alone. [10]

(2) They hold that the maximization of equality involves the sovereignty of the individual, no one in any way being subject to direction or dominance by anyone else. [11]

(3) Therefore, they hold that government, being incompatible with the autonomy and sovereignty of the individual, necessarily prevents the maximization of freedom and equality.

(4) Denying or dismissing the distinction between *de jure* and *de facto* governments, they regard government as nothing but an instrument of coercive force, enabling those who hold the power of government to tyrannize over or subjugate others. Since coercion, like aggression or violence, is inherently evil, government itself is inherently evil. [12]

(5) Repudiating the state which involves one or another form of centralized government, they assert on the positive side, that men can live peacefully and fruitfully together through purely voluntary and undirected acts of cooperation; and they envisage this as happening with the maximum of decentralization and fluidity, the cooperation occuring in small leaderless groups or with leaders emerging and changing from moment to moment as the occasion warrants. [13]

(6) They anticipate the objection that their vision of the anarchic society does not fit the nature of man, by denying that man has a fixed nature independent of social and cultural conditioning. They hold, on the contrary, that man as he now is and as we now know him is the product of the historic institutions of the state and government; and that, with the destruction of the state and government, a *new* man—or man as he *can* be— will emerge. [14]

This doctrine contains an admixture of truth and error. Let me try to make the separation which will eliminate the error and preserve the truth. I start with the denial of human nature.

It is true that many human traits are a product of nurture or a selective development of human potentialities by conditioning circumstances; but it is not true that man as a species has no genetically determined properties that will persist as long as the species persists, without being affected by the changing external circumstances of the physical or social environment. To suppose that, apart from a conditioning environment, man is a wholly plastic or indeterminate blank, to be given this or that determinate character by the circumstances under which he lives, is to regard man as unlike any other species of living organism. [15]

The limited power of human reason is a case in point, and one that has a direct bearing on the question about the necessity of government. No matter how free it is from the pressures and prejudices of conditioning circumstances, the finite intelligence of man does not enable him to know with infallible certitude the answers to all questions, especially not the solutions to the problems that confront him in the sphere of action. Hence even if men were to be as fully rational as they might be under the best of circumstances, disagreements would still arise among them concerning the solution of problems that confront them when they try to live together socially and act in concert to achieve any common purpose. [16]

Carry this one step further and suppose that the emotions or desires of men were completely controlled by reason or intelligence, so that men would never come into conflict except as a result of the inability of reason to reach agreement about all practical matters. It would then still remain true that the authority of government would be indispensable for social life; for, as we have seen, authority is needed to decide matters about which reasonable men can disagree. If each individual were to retain the complete autonomy of heeding no voice except that of his own reason, his being able to act cooperatively with others would come to an end the first time that the group fell short of unanimity about the solution to a problem. [17]

The situation just imagined is, of course, plainly contrafactual. Reason is not only fallible and uncertain in its judgments about practical matters; it is also severely limited by the independent and often contrary impulses of desire or emotion, which it cannot control. Man is not a purely rational being but a rational animal, with appetites and drives that can impel him to act against the counsels of reason and can even subvert or color the judgments of his intelligence. This is a species-specific property of human nature, not a product of conditioning circumstances.

Given any social environment imaginable, even one completely devoid of all the institutions within our experience so far, men would still be so constituted that they would come into conflict with one another as the result of clashing drives or desires, and not merely because reason is unable to achieve unanimity about all practical matters. This being the case, government, with the authority to adjudicate disputes and to enforce the judgment of a tribunal, is indispensable to a peaceful resolution of the conflicts that would arise in any imaginable society, man being what he is or even what he might be under the best of circumstances. [18]

It is human nature that makes government necessary, not the institution of private property as the anarchist claims. To whatever extent he agrees with the political philosopher that social life is better for man than the life of the isolated individual and that peace is better than war or violence, he has accepted premises that work against his contention that government must be abolished for the benefit of man or for the improvement of the human condition.

(5)

With his basic thesis invalidated, the anarchist can fall back to a second line of defense. Government may be necessary, but it is inherently evil—always an instrument of tyranny and oppression, instituted, maintained, and exercised by coercive force, resulting in the enslavement or exploitation of one class by another.

In saying this, the anarchist has described, with some degree of pardonable exaggeration, *de facto* government, which is imposed by force and maintained by force, government without duly constituted authority, without consenting constituents and participating citizens. The anarchist's rejoinder at this point consists in rejecting as mythical the notion of *de jure* government and in claiming that all governments are *de facto*. There have never been and can never be governments of any other kind.

Here the anarchist's contention must be resolved into two quite separate points: one, that the distinction between *de facto* and *de jure* governments is itself meaningless; the other, that, though meaningful conceptually, it is practically meaningless because inapplicable to existing institutions, past, present, or future. Let us consider each of these points separately.

The analysis of authority and of authorized force presented in Chapter 6 suffices, in my judgment, to establish the conceptual validity of the distinction between *de jure* and *de facto* government and with it the equally valid distinction between *authorized force* and *violence*. That analysis need not be repeated here in order to say that, though the anarchist may fail to understand these distinctions, they cannot be dismissed as intrinsically unintelligible or inconceivable.

Passing from the conceptual plane to the world of existing institutions, the existence of constitutional governments and of states that are republics would appear to be an undeniable historic fact. When this fact is combined with the equally undeniable fact of the existence of absolute or despotic governments, we have before us all the evidence that is needed to maintain that the distinction between *de jure* and *de facto* governments or states is not only meaningful conceptually, but also applicable to existing institutions, both past and present. [20]

To carry the argument forward, I am now going to posit an imaginary figure—an anarchist who would admit that the distinction between *de jure* and *de facto* government is conceptually meaningful, and who would also concede that its applicability is sufficiently established by the existence of republics, on the one hand, and of despotisms, on the other. What further objection would such an imaginary anarchist interpose at this point?

He could say, and rightly, in my judgment, that in all the republics of the past and the present, consent of the governed was actually only obtained from a portion of the population: only some men were consenting constituents and participating citizens, and they comprised the ruling class. The residue, subject to their rule, suffered under government that, for them, was purely *de facto*.

He could go on to say that even in the best republics that exist today—even those which, in their political arrangements, are most effectively democratic in their provisions for the operation of universal suffrage—there are still social and economic class divisions and oppressed ethnic, racial, or religious minorities, with the consequence that some portion of the population is still actually deprived of the freedom and equality that others enjoy under *de jure* government. The condition of those who are thus deprived may differ in principle but not in practice from those who suffer the oppression of *de facto* government.

If we grant, as I certainly would, the force of this objection, the only question that remains is whether the anarchist's ideal of a society with freedom and equality for all requires the abolition of the state and government or can be realized by a *de jure* state and government that is an improvement upon any that has so far existed. My response to this question is double-barreled: on the one hand, I think it can be shown that the maximization of freedom and equality for all is impossible in the absence of a *de jure* state and government; on the other hand, I think it can be shown that the improvements in the *de jure* state and government which are required for the realization of the ideal are themselves practically realizable. [20]

To do this will take the whole of Part Three; and so I must ask the reader's patience as I proceed, step by step, to make political philosophy responsive to the challenge of the philosophical anarchists and other revolutionary movements that first emerged in the nineteenth century and are current in the world today.

Part Three

The New Ideal: Classlessness

CHAPTER 9

The Injustices to Which
Government is Prone

(1)

DIVORCED from his erroneous identification of government with tyrannical despotism, the philosophical anarchist is simply a radical reformer who seeks a society that is better than any which has ever existed and than which now exists. The terms "tyrannical" and "despotic" are, of course, terms that the normative political philosopher has traditionally employed to condemn unjust government. As we shall see, they are distinct in meaning, each referring to a different way in which government can be unjust. Taken together, they designate injustice in the extreme—the almost complete injustice that produces the total corruption or perversion of government.

I say "almost complete" in order to allow for the addition of one further note of injustice—the one we have only recently come to use the term "totalitarianism" to name. Though we usually speak of the totalitarian state rather than totalitarian government, the injustice lies in the usurpation by government of functions that do not properly belong to it. This is the evil that the anarchists have in mind when they call for the opposite extreme of disorganized decentralization. As we shall see, normative political philosophers have recognized and condemned the same evil, but they propose ways of correcting it without abolishing the state itself in the process.

Since states and governments can be unjust in various ways and in varying degrees—despotism being possible without tyranny, and a tyrannically despotic government being possible in a state that is not totalitarian—it follows that states and governments can also be just in various ways and in varying degrees. As there is the total depravity of complete injustice at one extreme of the scale, so there is the perfection of complete justice at the other.

In saying "it follows," I am fully aware that it does not follow for the philosophical anarchist or for anyone else who mistakenly thinks that governments and states are all intrinsically and absolutely evil and that there is no way of eliminating injustice from human affairs without eradicating states and governments. Not making that error, the political philosopher is as concerned as the anarchist is with all the injustices that can afflict men living in states and under governments, but his concern is with their rectification or removal by every remedy short of anarchy. With each injustice that can be removed, there is a degree of justice to be established; and since each facet of injustice can be rectified, a perfectly just state and government is conceivable and attainable, even if that ideal has not yet been completely realized.

In order to lay the groundwork for a consideration of the modes and degrees of justice and injustice, I would like to make sure that we share a common understanding of what it means to say that anything is just or unjust—a man, a human act, a government, or a state. We can, then, proceed to an enumeration of the different ways in which governments and states can be just or unjust.

(2)

When the man of common sense uses the term "unjust," it has for him the connotation of a wrong done or an injury inflicted. It always involves two parties—one committing the wrong or injury, the other suffering it. Not everything that is bad or evil is an injustice, for there are evils that men suffer from their own acts or failures, where the fault is entirely their own and no one else's. But there can be no injustice that does not involve the deprivation of a good. This is the fundamental point that must be understood. As I have said in another context, "if we did not know or could not know what is really good or bad for the individual, we would not and could not know what is right and wrong in the conduct of one individual toward others"—nor in the institutions and operations of states and governments. [1]

An individual is injured when he is deprived of the things that are really good for him—the things that he needs and must obtain in order to make a really good life for himself. His fundamental moral obligation to make a whole life that is really good underlies his obligation to seek each of the partial goods that is a component part of that whole. These moral obligations are the basis of the individual's moral or natural rights. Thus, my basic obligation to make a good life for myself underlies my basic natural right to the pursuit of happiness. Since the pursuit of happiness involves such things as liberty and a decent livelihood, these goods, being components of a good life, are the basis of subsidiary natural rights. Hence to say that an individual is injured when he is deprived of the things that are really good for him is equivalent to saying that he is injured by the violation of his natural rights. If he is without rights, he cannot be wronged by another individual or by the organized community; nor can he suffer evil at the hands of others, if nothing is really good for him.

Justice and injustice in the relation of the organized community or state to its members is more complex than justice and injustice in the relation of one individual to another. In the latter case, injustice consists in injuring another by violating his natural rights—by depriving him of some real good that he needs to make a good life for himself. The organized community or state can be unjust in this way, but it can be unjust in other ways as well.

It can be unjust by *omission* as well as by *commission*—by failing to secure the natural rights of individuals; that is, by failing to aid and abet them in their efforts to make good lives for themselves by helping them to get the things they need that are not within their power to get for themselves. The obligation of the state to act justly toward its members is both positive and negative. It must not only avoid depriving them of the real goods to which they have natural rights; it must also promote their welfare by helping them to obtain goods to which they have natural rights and which they cannot attain wholly by their own efforts. If one individual positively helps another to make a good life for himself, that is an act of love or friendship, not of justice. In the relation of individuals, justice goes no further than the avoidance of injury. But the state is obligated in justice to go further—to do what it and it alone can do to promote the pursuit of happiness by its members.

Since the natural rights of individuals can be violated by other individuals as well as by the state itself, justice on the part of the state requires government and laws that protect or safeguard the rights of the individual from both sources of invasion. A just state, then, is one in which natural rights are secured, *negatively*, by safeguards against their invasion or violation by the state or by individuals or groups of individuals and in which natural rights are also secured, *positively*, by the establishment of conditions that aid and abet men in their pursuit of happiness.

Does this statement suffice as a summary of the criteria for judging the justice or injustice of the state? Not quite.

Justice on the part of the state also consists in treating equals equally. The basic equality of men, resting on the sameness of the specific nature in which they all participate, involves their equal possession of natural rights—their rights as human beings. Hence a state is unjust if it secures the natural rights of some of its members, while others have their rights violated or transgressed.

The pursuit of happiness involves the goods of communal life, among which the peaceful cooperation of men and groups is pre-eminent. Since these goods are indispensable to a good life, men have a natural right to them. Hence a just state, conceived as one that secures all natural rights, is also one in which the government and laws serve the common good in the special sense of preserving and promoting the goods of communal life. [2]

With these two specifications added, we can now see that the just state is simply one that conforms to the normative and teleological definition of the state as a community that helps men to live well by securing or providing all the external conditions of a good human life for each and every one of its human members. I say "external conditions" to exclude whatever factors involved in the pursuit of happiness are wholly and exclusively within the power of the individual.

(3)

The foregoing discussion has concentrated on the criteria of justice applicable to the state. Government is not identical with the state. It consists of only one set of institutions upon the justice of which the state depends. The justice of the state's economic and social institutions must also be considered.

One reason for the erroneous identification of the state with government is that, of all its component institutions, those of government are primary. In addition, they can do much to shape the other institutions of the state—its social arrangements and its economic system. Hence when we concern ourselves with the justice of government, we must have two questions in mind. *First*, by what criteria do we measure the justice or injustice of the institutions of government, considered in themselves? *Second*, by what criteria do we judge the justice or injustice of government by reference to its effect on the social and economic institutions of the state, in so far as these can be influenced or controlled by government?

In this chapter and the next, I am going to confine our attention to the first of these questions, reserving the second question for subsequent treatment, and also postponing for later consideration those aspects of social and economic justice that are not wholly within the power of government to establish. At that point, we will be concerned with the way in which the social and economic institutions of the state influence, in critical respects, the shape of its government, and affect its justice in principle and in practice.

We have already touched on some of the ways in which government can be unjust. After reviewing these, I will supplement them with other ways not yet mentioned, in order to complete the picture.

The most fundamental distinction among governments as good and bad, or just and unjust, is that which divides governments into *de jure* and *de facto* regimes. For men, whose right it is to be governed as free men and as equals, only *de jure* government is legitimate and appropriate. [3] When we speak of such government as duly constituted, we are calling attention to what makes such government just, namely, that its authority derives from and is acknowledged by the consent of the governed and functions with their suffrage.

In contrast, *de facto* government is totally devoid of authority. It is instituted and maintained by unauthorized force, which is another way of saying that it is government by might instead of by right. When we speak of such government as despotism, we are specifying its injustice as violation of the rights of the governed—their right to be governed as free men and their right to be governed as equals, with their consent and with their participation.

With this basic distinction between constitutional governments and despotisms in mind, and aware that justice is many-faceted, let us ask, first, whether government that is just by virtue of its being *de jure* can be unjust in other respects, and second, whether there is any respect in which government that is unjust by virtue of being *de facto* can be just. The second question being easier to answer, let us begin with it.

(4)

The right to be governed as a free man and the right to be governed as an equal do not exhaust man's natural rights. Hence, though it is unjust in its violation of these rights, despotic government may be just in its respect for other natural rights—rights to the possession of goods other than political liberty and equality, such as the right to security of life and limb, the right to a decent minimum of economic goods, or the right to the goods of communal life, such as peace. In other words, despotic government may subjugate men by force to absolute rule, but it does not necessarily enslave them. [4]

Slavery is the condition of those who are deprived of all their natural rights. Despotic government becomes tyrannical and its injustice is compounded when it reduces its subjects to the condition of slavery. To the degree to which it falls short of tyranny, which is to say to the degree to which it recognizes and respects its subjects' rights, despotism may have some tincture of justice.

The web of natural rights is so closely knit that despotism always tends toward tyranny. Violating the basic political rights, it tends to violate other rights as well. Nevertheless, the point of principle must be reiterated: despotism may involve some admixture of justice and injustice. Only when it becomes tyrannical, does it become completely unjust.

I turn now to the other question, the one concerning the ways in which constitutional government can be unjust.

Constitutional government is often called limited government, as contrasted with the absolutism of the despotic regime. It is limited in the scope and character of the authority conferred upon it and acknowledged by its consenting constituents. Hence it can become unjust by reason of exceeding its constituted authority, usurping or exercising power that is not its by right, and thus infringing on the autonomy that should be left to its citizens. Let me explain.

We have seen that the condition of being governed is incompatible with the retention of complete autonomy by the individual. We understand that when men engaged in a common enterprise acknowledge the authority of government to make rules and decide things for the common good, they must relinquish their complete autonomy, i.e., each can no longer proceed by deciding everything for himself and obeying himself alone. But the surrender of complete autonomy in order to constitute a legitimate government with lawful authority does not involve a complete surrender of autonomy. On the contrary, only as much autonomy need be relinquished as is necessary to create the authority of government for the disposition of certain matters.

What matters? Matters affecting the common good—the peace and welfare of the republic and the happiness of its citizens insofar as that is dependent on the action of the organized community; and matters concerning which reasonable men can disagree, but which must be decided one way or the other for the good of community and the ultimate good of its members.

The authority granted to a duly constituted government is, therefore, limited by the functions it is created to perform. Precisely because the authority that it created is thus delimited, the portion of autonomy that was surrendered to create it is also delimited, leaving a residual portion of autonomy in the citizens of a *de jure* government. This residual autonomy may be exercised by the citizens, either individually, or in families, or in other organized groups—all the various types of association that are formed for specific purposes or to perform specific functions other than those that define the ends which the state is created to serve.

There are many problems involved in leading a good life that the individual must be free to solve in his own way—by his own plan of life and his own decisions. The authority of government should not extend to such matters; they should be left to the residual autonomy of the citizen.

Similarly, there are many problems of family life, affecting the welfare or happiness of its members, that do not fall within the scope of the limited authority conferred upon government. The family, as included within the state, is a dependent, not an independent, community; as dependent, it is subject to the laws and decisions of government; but just as the individual citizen should have a limited autonomy with respect to matters that are entirely his own concern, so the family as a subordinate corporation should also have an autonomy that is limited to deciding matters within the sphere of the family's specific interests—the ends it seeks to serve.

What I have just said about the family applies to all other private corporations or associations, created to perform functions or to serve ends other than those specifically relegated to the state, such as preserving the peace of the all-embracing community and promoting the pursuit of happiness by its citizens, by securing and safeguarding their natural rights and by doing for them what they cannot do for themselves, either as individuals or as organized in subordinate groups. [5]

(5)

When a duly constituted *de jure* government exceeds the limits of the authority granted to it to serve the ends for which the state comes into existence, it arrogates to itself unauthorized power and commits the injustice of usurpation. The injury done by such usurpation lies in its infringement of the residual autonomy that belongs, by right, to the citizens, acting either as individuals or as organized in subordinate groups or associations.

The government of a republic cannot carry its usurpation of unauthorized power to the extreme of totalitarianism without destroying the republic itself. That extreme coincides with the extreme of despotism, for the totalitarian state (which is a state in name only) is one that permits no private corporations, that allows no measure of autonomy to individuals or to families for the administration of their own affairs, and that concentrates the control of everything in a single central government. Nevertheless, to whatever extent the constitutional government of a republic usurps unauthorized power and encroaches on the residual autonomy of its citizens or of subsidiary corporations or groups, it tends toward totalitarianism.

I would like to mention briefly two special forms of the injustice with which we are here concerned—the injustice of usurpation by a constitutional government.

One is the use of coercive force by government, especially in its exercise of police power, beyond the limited amount that is authorized in its constitution. The application of unauthorized force by government is, as we have observed, an act of violence that justifies violence in self-defense. Indeed, in extreme circumstances violent acts of reprisal might even be justified. In exceeding its authority to use force to sanction its laws and decisions and to maintain civil peace, government itself breaches that peace and warrants further violations of it. The principle here is clear; its application to particular cases is difficult.

The other special form of usurpation may appear to be so extreme that its likelihood may be questioned. The authority of government is limited to matters about which reasonable men can disagree. The right to life makes murder wrong beyond all reasonable doubt. It is, therefore, not within the authority of government to decide whether murder should or should not be prohibited by law or made a criminal offense. While it might appear unlikely that a *de jure* government would commit the injustice of sanctioning murder, it might sanction unprovoked and unmitigated killing by its police officers or by its soldiers in the field, on the ground that such action in the performance of their duties is not murder. The reason offered is spurious. The *de jure* government that took this course would be sanctioning murder and in doing so would exceed its authority by trespassing on a moral truth about which there can be no reasonable disagreement.

(6)

So much for the injustice of constitutional government that results from its exceeding its constituted authority. A second way in which *de jure* government can be unjust is through deficiency or defect in the discharge of its obligations. The extent to which this occurs is measured by reference to the whole panoply of natural rights that government must secure and safeguard if it is to avoid injustice.

As we observed earlier, despotic government that is not

tyrannical can involve a mixture of injustice with justice by violating certain rights while respecting and safeguarding other rights. The same holds true of constitutional government. Unless it recognizes and protects *all*—not just *some*—of the natural rights of its citizens, their economic and social rights as well as their political rights, its deficiency in this respect results in an admixture of justice and injustice. I will return to this matter in Chapters 12 and 13, when I will deal with the social and economic conditions that affect the justice of a constitutional government or of the republic that it serves. Here I would like to dwell for a moment more on one special defect that detracts from the justice of constitutional government.

The citizens of a republic have the right to resist injustice on the part of their government and to alter or reform it to rectify the wrongs it commits. They also have the right to seek redress for grievances or injuries that they have unjustly suffered at its hands. These rights cannot be effectively exercised unless constitutional government provides its citizens with juridical means of resistance and redress, as well as juridical means to rectify the injustice of the constitution itself or of the laws of the state by changes—amendments or reforms—achieved through due process of law.

In the absence of adequate juridical means, citizens acting in defense of their natural rights have no course open to them except resort to violence, with the consequent abrogation of the civil peace, one of the primary goods of communal life that a just government is obligated to achieve and preserve for its people.

Only when such juridical means are available can citizens resort to civil disobedience and peaceful dissent instead of being compelled to engage in the violence of revolution. When they are compelled to resort to revolution, their action goes beyond civil dissent and becomes a withdrawal of their consent to government. Dissent can occur within the boundaries of consent only if it is provided with effective juridical means. I will have more to say on this subject in the concluding chapters of this book. [6]

(7)

I come finally to a third way in which constitutional government can be unjust, that special form of injustice which political democracy is specifically designed to rectify. As constitutional government rectifies the injustice of despotism, so political democracy rectifies the injustice of an oligarchical constitution —one that grants citizenship to only a portion of its population and leaves the rest in subjection to despotic rule. In order to meet the objection that the disfranchised portion of a republic's population is not being despotically ruled, it is necessary to clarify the meaning of three basic terms—slavery, subjection, and citizenship.

There are three distinct relationships in which men can function as rulers. One is in relationship to things. In this relationship, the ruler serves his own good, not that of the thing governed. This is proper and just, not tyrannical. Things, as contrasted with persons, have no rights to infringe.

The second relationship is that between person and person, where the person ruling is a mature human being and the person being ruled is an immature human being—an infant. Here the ruler, the parent responsible for rearing the child, governs justly only if his government is benevolent and tutelary—for the good of the child, not for the parent's good. To the extent that he serves his own good rather than that of the child, the parent is tyrannical. But the avoidance of tyranny does not make his rule any the less absolute, for it is government without consent or participation of the governed. In addition, in order to be fully just, parental rule must be progressively self-liquidating; for the passage from immaturity to maturity, or from infancy to adulthood, is a gradual process that requires the parent to perform the difficult, almost impossible, task of gradually attenuating the absolutism of his rule. Failing in this, he does not fully discharge his obligation to govern the child for the child's good, which involves helping the child to grow up and become an adult.

The third relationship occurs in the government of adult

persons by adult persons, where none of the persons involved is in a condition of dependency or of incompetence for self-government that is characteristic of infants. In this third case, the government, to be just, must not only be for the good of the ruled, as it should be in the case of children; it must also be government with their consent and their participation, as it cannot be in the case of children. And unless it meets these requirements and is, therefore, self-government, it cannot possibly be government that adequately serves the good of the governed, since their good is adequately served only when they are ruled as free men and equals.

The consideration of these three relationships enables us to clarify the meanings of slavery, subjection, and citizenship.

When a person is governed as if he were a thing—managed, used, or exploited for the good of the ruler—the person thus governed suffers the injustice of tyranny and has the status of a slave, a thing without rights.

When a mature person or adult human being is governed as if he were an infant—ruled without his consent and participation—the person thus governed suffers the injustice of absolute rule or despotism and has the status of subjection. Like parental rule, despotic government may avoid tyranny by serving the good of the ruled; but since the ruled is not an infant in the process of growing up, the good of the ruled can never be adequately served by despotic government, no matter how benevolent it is or what natural rights it respects short of the right to be treated as a free man and equal.

Only when mature persons or adult human beings are governed with their consent and participation, do they have the status of citizenship. The creation of this status is inseparable from the creation of constitutional government. They are two faces of the same coin, on one side of which we have the citizen who rules only as a constitutional office-holder, and on the other side, the same citizen, whether in office or out of it, who is ruled by laws that he has had a voice in making and with the authority of a government of which he is a consenting constituent.

On the assumption that, except for pathological disabilities that call for hospitalization, no adult person is in the condition of dependency and incapacity for self-government that characterizes the infant, the justice of constitutional government is seriously blemished by the injustice of a constitution that grants citizenship to only a portion of the adult population and relegates the rest to subjection, suffering the injustice of despotic rule at the hands of a ruling class—the few or the many who enjoy the status of citizenship. Though they belong to the population of a republic, they are not constituents of it; they are not members of the people, in the political sense of that term; and even though some of their natural rights may be respected and safeguarded, so that they are not reduced to slavery, their good is not adequately served by the constitutional government that subjects them, for they are deprived of their right to self-government, their right to citizenship with suffrage, their right to be ruled as free men and equals.

The division of a population into a ruling class of enfranchised citizens and a subject class of disfranchised persons excluded from political life, and so, in Mill's phrase, treated as "political pariahs," places the latter in the same condition as that of men living under the despotism—although not necessarily the tryanny —of a *de facto* government. The injustice they suffer is all the more grievous because they belong to a population, some part of which enjoys the rights and privileges of citizenship. They live in a republic and under a constitutional government without being members of the body politic. They are deprived of goods enjoyed by their equals—men living beside them in the same community.

The injustice of the oligarchical constitution, with its restricted suffrage and its division of the population of a republic into a ruling class and a subject class, is the injustice of treating equals as unequals. Saying this brings us back to the assumption mentioned a little earlier; namely, that, except for hospitalized incompetents, all normal adult human beings are not only equal as persons, but are also equal in the sense that they all possess at least the minimum competence required for self-government —for citizenship and suffrage.

Until very recently, this assumption was flatly rejected as

false by political philosophers. Only in the last hundred years has its truth been affirmed by political theorists, and then tenuously or reluctantly. Only in the same period of time have some men of common sense, in the light of their experience with universal or almost universal suffrage, come to think of the whole population as "we, the people"—members of the body politic.

The history I have just recited reports but does not settle one of the most difficult and persistent issues in political philosophy— one that requires the defenders of political democracy to answer a wide variety of objections from many different quarters, some ancient and traditional and some contemporary. Because of the complexity of this issue, and the importance of the political principle that is challenged by oligarchs or anti-democrats of every variety, I am going to devote Chapter 11 to a defense of the democratic principle. But in Chapter 10, I am going to anticipate a resolution of the issue in favor of democracy, so that, in dealing with the question of how the state and government are not only compatible with but also indispensable to the maximization of liberty and equality for all, I can proceed in terms of a perfectly just society—an ideal that I regard as realizable in the socialist, democratic republic of the future.

CHAPTER 10

The Maximization, Through Justice, of Liberty and Equality for All

(1)

Iɴ Chapter 8, I engaged in a dialogue with the philosophical an-archist. The common ground which made that possible was our agreement on the ideal of maximizing liberty and equality for all, and we both recognized that the critical operative words in the statement of that ideal are the words "for all." Drop those words and there is no problem, or certainly none of great difficulty. But unrelenting insistence on universalizing as well as maximizing liberty and equality does create a difficult problem for which the philosophical anarchist and the political philosopher propose different solutions.

Let me remind you briefly of the opposite proposals before I proceed further in my attempt to support the political as against the anti-political solution. The philosophical anarchist maintains that the maximization of liberty and equality for all requires the abolition of the state and government. The political philosopher counters this with a double rejoinder, saying *on the one hand*, that the maximization of liberty and equality for all is impossible in the absence of a *de jure* state and government; and, *on the other hand*, that it is possible only if the *de jure* state and government become perfectly just.

When the issue is thus stated, we begin to see how it can be re-solved. The second part of the political philosopher's rejoinder concedes two points to the philosophical anarchist. *First*, that it is only within the framework of the *de jure* state and government that liberty and equality can be maximized for all. If the anarchist uses the words "state" and "government" for purely *de facto* institutions—manifestations of force or violence—then he is correct in thinking that their eradication is necessary for the maximization of liberty and equality for all. *Second*, that the *de jure* state and government must itself be rectified of all of the injustices that it has so far historically exhibited and must become perfectly or completely just in order to maximize liberty and equality for all. Here the philosophical anarchist is correct in thinking that the *de jure* state and government, *without such rectification*, does not solve the problem.

The ideal proposed by the philosophical anarchist and the ideal proposed by the political philosopher are thus seen to coincide, and justice is the indispensable solvent that brings them together. Leave justice out of the discussion and there is no way to achieve a resolution of the issue. A society, in which men live together in peaceful cooperation with one another, and in which liberty and equality are maximized for all (the philosophical anarchist's ideal), is identical with a *de jure* state and government that is perfectly just in its social and economic as well as its political institutions (the political philosopher's ideal).

I have denominated that ideal state as the socialist, democratic republic and, while admitting that it does not yet exist, I have asserted that the ideal is practically realizable, not utopian. The preceding chapter's analysis of the justice and injustice of *de jure* government is one step toward supporting that assertion; for none of the injustices that we have so far considered is incapable of rectification. I will outline further steps to be taken in the chapters to follow. Here I wish to complete my argument with the anarchist on one point only.

(2)

I propose to do this in the following way. If the philosophical anarchist were to concede that the ideal proposed by the political philosopher is practically realizable, then there would be no need for further argument. Let us, therefore, suppose the opposite rejoinder from the anarchist; namely, that the injustices mentioned cannot be rectified within the framework of any state or under any form of government. This amounts to denying that the political philosopher's ideal is realizable. Dismissing it as utopian, the philosophical anarchist then re-asserts the necessity of abolishing the state and government to achieve the maximization of liberty and equality for all. As we have already noted, the political philosopher maintains, on the contrary, that is is impossible to maximize liberty and equality for all in the absence of a *de jure* state and government.

Since these opposed assertions are contrary, not contradictory, both can be false; but since they exhaust the alternatives, their both being false would mean that *it is impossible to maximize liberty and equality for all.* I, for one, am not prepared to accept that conclusion. Whether, in subsequent chapters, I can show that the political philosopher's ideal is practically realizable remains to be seen; but I think I can show now, quickly and clearly, that it is impossible to maximize liberty and equality for all in the absence of a *de jure* state and government.

I will do this, first, by showing that liberty cannot be maximized for all unless the freedom of the individual is limited by the restraints of justice; and, second, by showing that conditions of equality cannot be established for all except through the creation and maintenance of just institutions. Please note that I am not begging the question whether the ideal of a perfectly just state and government can be realized. That, I repeat, remains to be seen. I am here only arguing that, *unless it can be,* the ideal of maximum liberty and equality for all cannot be realized, because the restraints of justice and just institutions are impossible in the absence of a *de jure* state and government. In short, it is false to assert that liberty and equality for all can be achieved by the abolition of the state and government.

(3)

I turn at once to the consideration of liberty for all. It is necessary to distinguish three forms of social freedom—the freedom of the individual in society. It is only the first of these that the philosophical anarchist has in mind.

The first is the unlimited freedom of complete autonomy, a freedom that is incompatible with civil law and government, for it consists in each man's obeying himself alone and being able to do exactly as he pleases. [1]

The second is the limited freedom of the residual autonomy that the individual retains when he acknowledges the limited authority of a *de jure* government, of which he is a consenting constituent. This is the freedom of being able to do as he pleases with respect to all matters not prescribed by the civil laws of a just government. Let us call such limited freedom "individual civil liberty." [2]

The third is the freedom of the individual as a consenting constituent and a participating citizen. In contrast to individual civil liberty, which consists in doing as one pleases where just laws prescribe no course of conduct, this freedom which I shall call "political liberty" consists in obeying laws that are made by an authority to which the individual has consented and made by a process in which, through his suffrage, he has participated. While they are not laws wholly of his own making, neither are they laws wholly imposed upon him by force. The citizen as a self-governing individual has the freedom of political liberty in his lawful conduct. [3]

Now, if the only liberty worthy of the name were the unlimited freedom of complete autonomy (which is the only freedom that the philosophical anarchist acknowledges), it would follow that such liberty cannot exist for men living in states and under government. However, it also follows that if such liberty were to be exercised *without the restraints of justice*, some individuals might enjoy unlimited freedom to the maximum, but in doing so they would encroach upon, limit, or reduce the freedom of others to do exactly as they pleased. In other words, unlimited freedom—freedom unrestrained by justice—*cannot be maximized for all*. [4]

Herein lies the distinction between liberty and license. Liberty is freedom exercised under the restraints of justice so that its exercise results in injury to no one. In contrast license is freedom exempt from the restraints of justice and, therefore, injurious to others in infringing their freedom as well as violating other rights. When no distinction is made between liberty and license, the freedom of the strong can destroy the freedom of the weak. For the freedom of any one individual to be compatible with an equal measure of freedom on the part of all others, the freedom of each must be limited and limited precisely for the purpose of preventing the freedom of one from encroaching upon or destroying the freedom of others. Hence maximization of freedom for all, with an equal measure of freedom for each, is impossible without the restraints of justice. which confines the freedom of doing as one pleases to conduct that in no way injures anyone else. [5]

It may be objected at this point, on behalf of the philosophical anarchist, that what has so far been shown is only that the maximization of liberty *for all* and with an *equal measure* for each, requires the restraints of justice. It has not been shown that it requires civil law and government. Let me meet that objection by proposing a hypothesis that I regard as contrafactual.

Let us suppose that individuals living together in a society without law and government not only could act in concert for their common good and cooperate peacefully, but also that each and everyone of them had perfect moral characters so that they would all act under the restraints of justice in everything that they did which affected others. On this supposition, they would have complete autonomy, for each would obey himself alone, but that complete autonomy would no longer be an unlimited freedom, for it would be limited by the *self-imposed* restraints of justice. This limited freedom exercised by completely autonomous individuals with complete moral integrity would not differ an iota from the limited freedom that can be enjoyed by individuals living in the state under just laws and government. I say "can be enjoyed" because, in civil society, those who are impelled to act unjustly may be coercively restrained by government, but even then they are not deprived of liberty when that is distinguished from license.

Hence if the philosophical anarchist admits that the restraints of justice are required for the maximization of liberty for all, with an equal measure for each, he must abandon his conception of liberty as an unlimited freedom for each individual to do exactly as he pleases whether he injures anybody else or not. Then the only question which remains is whether this liberty—freedom limited by justice—is compatible with the retention by everyone of complete autonomy. If so, then it can exist in a society without government; but if not, then it cannot exist in the absence of the state and government.

In proposing the hypothesis that we have been considering, I said that it was contrafactual. I need only recall points made earlier to show why that is the case. We have seen that it is impossible for individuals who retain their complete autonomy to live together in peace and act in concert for their common good. That would be true even if the individuals were men of perfect moral integrity, for even so they would still have the finite intelligence of human beings. They would be men, not angels or gods. In addition, men being as they are or even as they might be under the best of circumstances, they are rational animals, not purely rational beings; and it is therefore unlikely, to say the least, that all would achieve the perfect moral integrity that presupposes the power of reason completely to control the animal appetites and drives, or even the specifically human emotions or desires.

Hence, taking men as they are or as they might be under the best of circumstances, the limited freedom that is the only liberty that can be maximized for all in equal measure cannot be achieved solely by the self-imposed restraints of justice. For the whole assembly of men, including the criminal and the vicious along with the virtuous and including all degrees of moral character short of perfect integrity, the instructive prescriptions of just laws are required to supplement self-discipline where it is inadequate, and the coercive force of law is required to prevent the unrestrained exercise of freedom by those whose uncontrolled impulses are unjust.

Let me briefly sum this up. The unlimited freedom that some men would have access to in the absence of government and law would defeat the realization of the ideal of maximizing liberty for all. It is anarchy, not the state and government, that is incompatible with the realization of this ideal. When a man's limited freedom is seen as consisting in his individual civil liberty in all matters not regulated by just laws, together with his political liberty as a consenting constituent and a participating citizen of a *de jure* state and government, then, in principle at least, we can see no reason for denying that the fullest possible realization of freedom for all is not only compatible with, but is also dependent upon, the institutions of a just state with just government.

(4)

The consideration of equality for all parallels the reasoning just set forth with regard to liberty for all. Here as before certain distinctions must be made and observed.

The most important of these is the distinction between the personal equality or inequality of men and the equality or inequality of the conditions under which they live. Personal equality and inequality rest on the specific nature of man, upon the individual differences of men as members of the human species, and upon the differences in their personal attainments. All men have personal equality in one respect and one respect only; namely, in their common humanity and their common possession of the same species-specific powers or properties, even though as individuals they possess these powers and properties in unequal degrees. The many respects in which men are personally unequal consist, first, in all the differences of degree that attend their possession of the same specific human powers or properties; and, second, in all the differences of personal attainment that follow from the use they make of their native capacities and talents.

Equality and inequality of conditions include all the respects in which men have either the same degree or more and less of the benefits that external circumstances can confer on them, such things as economic goods or possessions, status, opportunity, privileges, respected rights, etc.

If the philosophical anarchist were correct in thinking that all men can enjoy an equality of conditions in all respects (which is maximization of equality for all) *only* when each retains the complete autonomy of an absolute sovereign, each the peer of everyone else, then, of course, it would follow that the state and government would have to be abolished in order to achieve the maximization of an equality of conditions for all. The same line of argument that showed him to be mistaken with regard to liberty shows him to be mistaken here. I need not repeat the steps of the argument in order to state the conclusions to which it leads. [6]

In the absence of a *de jure* state and government, the personal inequalities that exist among individual men—inequalities in intelligence, strength, rationality, and emotional drive—would, if unrestrained by just laws and government, result in inequality of status, inequality of opportunity, inequality of treatment, and inequality of economic goods or possessions.

If the state were to provide only equality before the law and not attempt to promote and maintain equality of conditions and treatment (which is what the leading conservatives have always advocated), the personal inequalities of men would result in the widest range of inequalities of condition. Anarchy would even more surely produce the same result.

Only the state and government can operate positively and constructively to establish and maintain the equality of conditions that justice demands as befitting the personal equality of men as human beings, regardless of all their personal inequalities at birth or in attainment.

It is anarchy, not the state and government, that is incompatible with the realization of the ideal of a universal equality of conditions. And there is, in principle at least, no reason for denying that the fullest possible realization of the ideal is not only compatible with, but also dependent upon, the institutions of a just state with just government.

(5)

Let me bring this chapter to a close with a comment on the controlling principle that has been operative throughout. The controlling principle is justice, not liberty and equality; for without justice, liberty cannot be restrained from becoming license, and the personal inequalities among men cannot be prevented from producing an inequitable inequality of conditions.

When it is said that the ideal is as little government as possible, the controlling principle is liberty rather than justice. This explains the falsity of Jefferson's maxim, that that government governs best which governs least, which is carried to absurdity in the statement by Thoreau, that that government governs best which governs not at all. The truth of the matter is that that government governs best that governs most justly, regardless of the amount of government that is required to achieve the fullest possible realization of the ideal of justice.

I hope, in Chapter 13, to be able to show that that government governs most justly which establishes the truly classless society— one that is devoid of economic and social as well as political class divisions and, therefore, one in which all men have, in equal measure, as much freedom as they can use justly and in which they are all treated in a manner that accords with their equality as persons and their equal possession of natural rights. [7]

It is only through the fullest possible realization of the ideal of justice—political, economic, and social justice—that the state and government can realize as fully as possible the ideals of liberty and of equality for all.

Political Liberty and Equality: The Answer to Oligarchs, Conservatives, and Reluctant Democrats

(1)

Iɴ Chapter 9, in the course of discussing the various injustices that can be committed by government, even by a *de jure* or constitutional government, I singled out one form of injustice as peculiar to constitutional government. It is the injustice that resides in the framework of the constitution itself. The name for such constitutional injustice is oligarchy, and it is the injustice of the oligarchical constitution that political democracy is specifically designed to rectify.

The oligarchical constitution is one that excludes some portion of the normal adult population from citizenship, and so divides the population into a ruling class of constituent citizens with suffrage and a disfranchised subject class, deprived of citizenship and suffrage. Hence oligarchical states are class-divided societies, and societies in which conditions of political equality do not prevail. Another way of saying this is in terms of the meaning of "the people" as comprising only those who are members of the body politic. In an oligarchical state, the people, whether they be relatively few in number or many, always includes less than the whole normal adult population. In that statement of the matter, the word "normal" covers the justified exclusion of the pathologically disabled who must be hospitalized for their own good.

And the word "adult" excludes those of an age that is legally defined as "infancy," however that age is specified by reference to years. Hence political democracy cannot be defined as government of, by, and for the people unless we add the qualification that the people is coextensive with the whole population, short of the two exceptions just mentioned.

When, as in the constitution of Athens under Pericles (regarded by the ancient Greeks as democracy carried to the extreme), the people comprised a quarter of the population; or when, as in nineteenth-century England or the United States, a comparable situation existed—their government of, by, and for the people exemplified oligarchical injustice, not democracy. Government was *of* the privileged minority who were its constituents. Government was *by* that privileged minority—the citizens with suffrage. And it was *for* them also, for it aimed at promoting the conditions of a good human life or the pursuit of happiness for them alone, not for the disfranchised majority who lived outside the pale of political life.

When Aristotle defines the state as a community of equals aiming at the best life possible, and when he says, "that form of government is best in which every man, whoever he is, can act best and live happily," he is far from declaring that all men are equal, or that all are capable of engaging in the pursuit of happiness. [1] The community of equals to which he refers is the community of the few who can engage in the pursuit of happiness. Only they should be constituents of the state, members of the body politic, citizens with suffrage. Aristotle describes the rest—the chattel slaves, the women, the manual workers (the artisans or mechanics)—as "necessary to the existence of the state," necessary in the sense that, as slaves, "they minister to the wants of individuals," or as "mechanics and laborers, they are the servants of the community." [2] Reiterating that "the state exists for the sake of the good life, and not for the sake of life only," he goes on to say that, like brute animals, slaves and laborers cannot be parts of the state or members of the body politic, for they have no capacity for human happiness, at which the state aims. [3]

The oligarchical position, thus explicitly stated by Aristotle, is, with some moderation, the position of those who call themselves political conservatives and of many others, even those calling themselves democrats and political liberals. Its central tenet is the denial that all men can or should be governed as free men and equals or that all men have the natural right to be consenting constituents and participating citizens of government.

In the view of political conservatives who espouse the oligarchical constitution on principle, it is the only just form of *de jure* government; and its justice is based on the division of mankind into natural superiors and inferiors—those with an inborn capacity for self-government and for the pursuit of happiness, and those bereft at birth of such capacities. Those who do not espouse the oligarchical constitution on principle—and this includes many who adopt the opposite, the democratic, principle, that all men are endowed at birth with the capacity for self-government and for happiness—nevertheless sometimes defend oligarchy as being justified by the unfortunate circumstances under which a portion of the population exists. While conceding that oligarchy is unjust, absolutely speaking, relative to the nature of man, they also maintain that it may be relatively just; that is, just in relation to conditions that prevent some men from engaging in self-government or the pursuit of happiness. They defend oligarchy as a temporary expedient, justifiable only by reference to conditions which are, in themselves, unjust and which, therefore, should be rectified. This group includes or shades off into those whom I shall describe as "reluctant democrats" because even when they move in the direction of universal suffrage, they do so with misgivings that they express in the form of various devices for preventing what they call "the tyranny of the majority."

I am going to devote this chapter to a defense of democracy against the oligarchical or conservative position, as well as against the position taken by the reluctant democrats. I will attempt to defend the democratic principle by reference to the natural equality of men; and I will also argue for the application of that principle under conditions that make it appear to be inexpedient.

Then, in Chapters 12 and 13, I will deal with the economic and the social equality that are indispensable to the effective operation of the political equality that is established by a democratic constitution. This will bring us back, finally, to a further examination of the ideal of the perfectly just state and government, proposed at the end of Chapter 10—the state and government that establishes a truly classless society.

(2)

Let me begin by clarifying the notion of political equality, ridding it of considerations that do not properly belong to it.

Political equality consists wholly and solely in the sameness of status, and of the rights and privileges appertaining thereto, that is enjoyed by men who are admitted to the basic constitutional office of citizenship. Men are politically equal as citizens when each has an equal voice in government through the exercise of suffrage. But while citizenship is always the primary constitutional office, since it is the *sine qua non* of eligibility for any other office in government, it is also the lowest in the hierarchy of offices that the constitution defines for the performance of the legislative, judicial, and executive functions of government. Being a citizen is, therefore, only a necessary, not the sufficient, condition for being eligible to be a legislator, a judge, or an executive. In addition to having the basic political capacity that fits men to exercise the consent and suffrage of citizens, some individuals have special talents or virtues, special training or skill, that fit them to exercise the authority that is constitutionally allocated to other offices in the hierarchy of governmental functions.

It is a profound misunderstanding of political equality to suppose that it involves an equal capacity to perform all the functions of government, those of the magistracies as well as those of citizenship. When, in ancient Athens, only a small portion of the population were admitted to citizenship and when the few who were citizens enjoyed the same external conditions of life, it may have been a sound policy to fill the various public offices by lot from among the citizenry. Even then, certain offices, such as that of the military commander, were filled by the election of individuals qualified by their possession of special competence, rather than by a lottery involving the whole body of citizens. Then, too, the problems of government were much simpler than they are now.

Under modern conditions, with universal suffrage, recourse to the lottery as a way of filling public offices would imprudently disregard the fact that all men are not equally competent, by native endowment or individual attainment, to perform all or most of the functions of government. That fact, however, does not provide an objection to political equality, properly understood. Political equality for all is affirmed by asserting that all men are capable of being citizens with suffrage; it is not contradicted by denying that they are equally capable of filling all or most of the other political offices.

Let me reinforce what I have just said by recalling that personal inequality in native talent or individual attainment always accompanies the personal equality that consists in being human. All men are personally equal only in their specific humanity; in all other personal respects, they tend to be unequal as they differ in the degree to which they natively possess their common human powers or the degree to which they cultivate them by their individual efforts. On the one hand, it is their personal equality as men, each possessing the same human powers to some degree, including the powers fitting them for self-government, that gives all men the natural right to participate in government, a right that is secured only when all men are granted the equal political status of citizenship with suffrage. On the other hand, it is their personal inequality in individual endowment and attainment that fits some men and not others to perform certain political functions and makes them eligible to hold this or that public office.

Though the citizen who does not have the competence to be a judge is, in this particular respect, individually inferior to the citizen who has such competence, he is in no sense the latter's political inferior. The man who holds a judgeship exercises the specific authority assigned to that public office, but all constitutional authority to perform this or that political function derives from the consent of the constituents who are citizens. In acknowledging the authority of the judge, the citizen respects the office, not the man. He obeys the judicial decision because it has authority over him by his consent; he does not obey the man who holds the judgeship because he is a political superior.

In short, personal inequality in individual endowment and attainment has political relevance only to the selection of men for the various public offices other than citizenship; and the hierarchy of these public offices does not establish grades of political inequality. The president of a republic and a private citizen are political equals. The only fact that has relevance to the admission of all to the basic office of citizenship, establishing all as political equals, is the fact of their all being human, with the same species-specific powers or properties, however much they vary in degree from individual to individual.

(3)

The aforementioned fact, affirmed by the democrat, is denied by the oligarch and the conservative.

The classic expression of this denial is, of course, Aristotle's statement that some men are intended by nature to be slaves and that it is, therefore, just for them to be treated as slaves. [4] He conceives the natural slave as a human being who does not have enough reason or intelligence to direct his own life or the affairs of others. According to this conception, the natural slave has the same human powers that are possessed by the man who is intended by nature to be free, but he has them to an inferior degree.

How, then, does a difference in degree result in a difference in kind? The Aristotelian answer is that the same human powers possessed to an inferior degree do not allow for the formation, through learning and development, of certain habits of mind and character. No amount of equality of nurture can overcome the deficiency of nature. In contrast, the man intended by nature to be free has, by native endowment a degree of reason or intelligence that proper nurture can cultivate into the habits of mind and character appropriate to political life.

Even if the facts were as Aristotle alleges, they would not, in by judgment, establish the justice of treating any man as a chattel slave, that is, as a thing rather than as a person, an instrument to be used wholly as a means. An inferior man, inferior in the degree of his human powers, is still a man, equal to every other man in his humanity and personal worth or dignity. Aristotle's admission that the natural slave is not a brute animal, but a man, with some degree of reason and human intelligence, as evidenced by speech, completely undermines his acceptance, as just, of the treatment of the natural slave as chattel—as a thing that can be owned and used. But if the facts were as Aristotle alleges them to be, which I shall now try to show is not the case, they would support the oligarchical and conservative thesis that only some men are fit by nature to be self-governing citizens and that some —the ones that Aristotle regards as natural slaves—are fit only to be subjects, governed as very young children are governed, without their consent or their participation. [5]

The critical threshold in the scale of degrees of human capacity, above which men have the power to form certain habits of mind and character and below which they do not, would then divide men into two groups: on the one hand, those whose native endowments and individual attainments fit them for citizenship; on the other hand, those whose native endowments are so deficient as to preclude their attaining the habits requisite for citizenship. Mankind would thus be divided into those intended by nature to be free, in the sense of self-governing citizens, and those intended by nature for political subjection. The first group would form a community of political equals, the citizens of a republic, members of the body politic. The second group would be their political inferiors, excluded from active participation in political life and treated, by analogy with children in the household, as wards of the state. Accordingly, the oligarchical constitution would establish the only just form of *de jure* government, and the democratic constitution would be, *ipso facto*, unjust, for it would treat alike those who do not deserve to be treated alike.

I think the following argument will suffice to show that the facts could not be as Aristotle alleged them to be and will also show the source of his error in construing them as he did. Aristotle himself declared that man is by nature a political animal. The statement is subject to two interpretations. One is that man in his highest development is political, which in effect asserts that *only some* men are fit for political life, for self-government, and for citizenship. The second interpretation is that *all* men are by nature political.

If the second interpretation is true, as I will try to show, it definitely contradicts the proposition that some men are by nature intended to be slaves or fit only for political subjection as wards of the state. The contradiction is as patent as the contradiction between saying that all men are intended by nature to be politically free and that some men are not intended by nature to be politically free. Or as patent as the contradiction between saying that all men deserve to be treated as politically equal and that some do not deserve to be so treated. [6]

What reasons can be adduced in support of the second interpretation as against the first?

That all men have the same species-specific powers, such as the power of propositional speech, the power of conceptual thought, and the power of free choice, powers that differentiate man from brute animals, leads to two conclusions about man that also differentiate him from brute animals.

One is that all men, through conceptual thought and free choice, have the power to plan their own lives for good or ill, and so are under the moral obligation to try to make good lives for themselves. The fact that some men have these same powers to a lower degree does not mean that they are precluded from making the best use they can of whatever capacities they have; and when they make the best use of their capacities, they are as fully engaged in the pursuit of happiness as are men of superior endowment, and more so than those among the latter who do not make the best use of their powers.

The second conclusion parallels the first. What makes men and men alone political animals are the specifically human powers of propositional speech, conceptual thought, and free choice, powers that all men have to some degree. [7] The fact that some men have these powers to a higher degree may fit them to discharge the functions of certain highly specialized political offices, but it does not entitle them and them alone to fill the basic political office of citizenship, for that belongs by right to anyone who can plan his own life and direct his own actions by free choice, which is every man. In short, the possession of human powers to any degree above that pathological deficiency that calls for hospitalization suffices for the self-direction of the individual life and for participation in self-government through citizenship with suffrage.

Hence men, being by nature equal as men (i.e., equal in their possession of the same human powers to whatever degree), deserve to be treated as politically equal and as politically free. This is just another way of saying that the natural rights of man, the same for all men, include the right to be a consenting constituent and a participating citizen. The oligarchical constitution is, therefore, in principle always unjust, for it relegates some men to political inequality and subjection. [8]

Before I turn to the defense of the oligarchical constitution on the ground that, though it is unjust in principle, it can sometimes be justified as befitting the circumstances under which a portion of the population lives, I would like to suggest an explanation of Aristotle's error, an error made not alone by him but by all later oligarchs who espouse the view that some men are unfit by nature to be citizens and so must be governed as subjects and treated as wards of the state. Rousseau, arguing against Aristotle's doctrine of natural slavery, points out that "nothing can be more certain than that every man born in slavery is born for slavery." Aristotle was right, Rousseau says, in thinking that some have slavish characters, but he mistook the effect for the cause. [9] The basic insight here is that defects of nurture can be mistaken for defects of nature. Regardless of the degree of his native endowments, the man who, because of the social and economic conditions of his birth, is nurtured as a slave or as a member of a subject class, will appear to have a nature that is unfit for citizenship and self-government.

(4)

The justification of the oligarchical exclusion from citizenship of certain portions of the population, by reference to the disabling circumstances of their life, also has its classic statement in Aristotle's *Politics*. In one form or another, it is repeated by later conservative writers and remained, even as late as the eighteenth and nineteenth centuries, the standard objection to universal suffrage.

Aristotle declared that the citizen should be a man of property, a man who has economic independence in the sense of not depending on the will of another man for his livelihood, and who also has enough wealth to be exempt from devoting all or most of his time to toiling for his subsistence. Only such a man can have the time for learning and for other pursuits of leisure, among them active engagement in politics. [10]

To understand the point being made, it must be separated from the disqualification for citizenship that rests on innate personal disability—the inferior degree of endowment that Aristotle attributes to the natural slave. The members of the laboring class who, according to Aristotle, should not be citizens—mechanics, artisans, husbandmen, and sailors—may be born with a degree of human intelligence sufficient to enable them, through proper nurture and development, to form the habits of mind and character appropriate for citizenship. They differ from the men of property only in the external circumstances of their birth, not in their inborn capacities.

Let us call the external conditions of life into which the children of the working classes are born "disabling circumstances"— deprivation of schooling, deprivation of free time, deprivation of economic independence, and so on. The oligarchical thesis can, then, be stated in the following manner. Those born into and living under disabling circumstances are thereby rendered unfit for active participation in political life. They should not be admitted to citizenship or granted suffrage. Though their disability is due to a deficiency of nurture rather than of nature, the effect is the same, and, therefore, they too should be treated as wards of the state.

Even if the exponents of the oligarchical or conservative position were to admit that those who are born into and live under disabling circumstances suffer social and economic injustices that should be rectified, they would still insist on the property qualification for citizenship, on the grounds of both expediency and justice. In their view, it is inexpedient to make citizens out of men whose defects of nurture and miserable conditions of life under disabling circumstances prevent them from making good use of their suffrage. It is also just, in their view, to treat as politically unequal men who are made unequal by the external circumstances of their lives.

Within the last few hundred years two major political thinkers, both of whom are reluctant democrats, agree that the unfortunate groups in the population who are circumstantially disabled may have to be excluded from active participation in political life until, under altered circumstances, they can be brought up to the level of their more fortunate fellows. One is Immanual Kant; the other, John Stuart Mill. [11]

In the very context of saying that *all* men have the right to be citizens, Kant introduces a distinction between active and passive citizenship, admitting at once that "the latter conception appears to stand in contradiction to the definition of a citizen as such." Nevertheless, Kant creates the anomalous role of passive citizenship to accommodate those members of the population who are circumstantially deprived of economic independence. He gives the following examples: "the apprentice of a merchant or tradesman, a household servant, a minor, all women, and generally everyone who is compelled to maintain himself not according to his own industry, but as it is arranged by others." Such individuals, he says, are "without civil personality, and their existence is only, as it were, incidentally included in the state."

Their "dependence on the will of others" disqualifies them "to exercise the right of suffrage under the constitution, and to be full citizens of the state"; they must be relegated to the inferior status of "mere passive subjects under its protection"—wards of the state.

How does Kant reconcile this disposition of the circumstantially disabled with their inborn rights under "the natural laws that demand the freedom of all human beings and the equality that is conformable thereto"? He provides the answer in his concluding statement that "it must be made possible for [the circumstantially disqualified] to raise themselves from this passive condition in the state to the condition of active citizenship." [12]

I interpret this to mean that society must do what it can to rectify the injustice done those who are born into and live under disabling circumstances. Disabling circumstances for some must be replaced by enabling circumstances for all; otherwise, it would not be possible for the circumstantially disabled to raise themselves, as Kant suggests. However, until social and economic reforms do effect the changes required, Kant appears willing to accept the political inequality of active and passive citizenship as both expedient and just.

In the first great book of political theory that argued the case for political democracy as the only just form of government, demanding suffrage not only for the working classes in mid-nineteenth-century England but also for its female population, John Stuart Mill introduced the qualification that political democracy may not be expedient under all circumstances. He had in mind men living under technologically primitive and barbaric, as contrasted with technologically advanced and civilized, conditions. [13]

For such populations, Mill thought that something akin to the tutelary and benevolent rule of a parent would be more appropriate. While recognizing that the parental rule of mature beings is despotic, he condoned such despotism in the rule of politically immature colonial populations as being the only form of government that is expedient under the circumstances. The injustice of despotism in this case must be ameliorated, Mill suggested, by an explicit effort on the part of the despotic government to liquidate itself by raising the subject population up to the level where it can become self-governing. If the despotic government of a subject population were to operate in this self-liquidating manner, it would be performing the tutelary function that is the essence of benevolent paternal rule. This, in Mill's view, would justify it as a temporary expedient under circumstances that make self-government inexpedient. While Mill himself did not propose such benevolent despotism as a justifiable temporary expedient for those members of a civilized society who are born into and live under disabling circumstances, his argument can be and has been applied to them by others, thus justifying the oligarchical division of a population into a ruling and a subject class.

This defense of political inequality maintains that an oligarchical constitution is a justifiable temporary expedient only if the despotism of the ruling class is self-liquidating, not only by performing the tutelary function appropriate to parental rule, but also by instituting the social and economic reforms necessary to remove the disabling circumstances that disqualify some portion of the population for citizenship. However, until such tutelary efforts and such reforms take effect, it remains not only just but also expedient, according to this view, for the disabled to be treated as wards of the state rather than as citizens with suffrage.

I will return later to the consideration of other proposals made by reluctant democrats, which attempt to hedge or undermine the principle of majority rule when the extension of suffrage to the working classes makes them the majority of the electorate. [14] At this point, my only concern is to argue against the defense of the oligarchical constitution as a justifiable temporary expedient. If it can be shown that oligarchy cannot be justified even as a temporary expedient, then, *a fortiori*, it cannot be justified as a permanent institution.

When we say that the just thing to do is usually expedient in the long run, we are conceding that it is often inexpedient in the short run. To grant citizenship and suffrage to those who suffer from disabling circumstances may, indeed, be inexpedient at the outset—inexpedient in the sense that men will be made citizens before they are in a position to function as good citizens, exercising an independent and critical judgment about public affairs. Nevertheless, unless they are made citizens before the reforms take place that remove the disabling circumstances which prevent them from being good citizens, it is unlikely that the necessary reforms will ever occur. In fact, it was only by extending suffrage to the working classes and thus making them a majority of the electorate that the necessary social and economic reforms were voted into effect. The extension of free public schooling to the whole population did not precede the extension of the franchise to all, but followed it. Similarly, reduction in hours of work, improvement in working conditions, raised standard of living—all reforms tending to remove or ameliorate disabling circumstances—came into effect after those who lived under disabling circumstances were made citizens with suffrage, not before. Hence I argue that the political justice of the democratic constitution will never be established if it is postponed until it is expedient to do so, by virtue of an antecedent rectification of the social and economic injustices that place some portion of the population—large or small—under disabling circumstances.

The unreluctant democrat is one who recognizes that, after the franchise has been extended, many citizens will still be prevented from being good citizens by the conditions under which they live, but he does not recommend taking their citizenship away from them as a temporary or permanent expedient. He recommends instead that the disabling circumstances be attenuated and, ultimately, eliminated. [15] For the same reason, the unreluctant democrat recommends that suffrage be extended to all before all are made ready for citizenship by the removal of the disabling circumstances under which many of them live. While conceding that some miscarriage of self-government may result from this course of action, I deny that the inexpediency of it is ever of such magnitude as to be disastrous. In any case, whatever be the extent of the temporary inexpediency, I maintain that it is never sufficient to justify, even for a short time, the injustice of treating some human beings as wards of the state, thus depriving them of their right to the political liberty and equality that is conferred by citizenship. [16]

Economic Equality and Welfare: Democracy and Socialism

(I)

IN the preceding chapter, I argued for the proposition that economic deprivations can prevent men from being good citizens but should not be made the reason for depriving them of citizenship. I turn now to the other face of that same proposition, which declares that economic equality is indispensable to the effective operation of political equality; or, in other words, that economic and political democracy must be conjoined in order to realize the ideal of the just state and just government.

While the democratic constitution creates a *de jure* government that, in terms of purely political institutions, is perfectly just, it does not by itself create a perfectly just state; nor is democratic government itself perfectly just unless it establishes economic as well as political equality. If democracy is conceived as doing political justice and only that, then that is not enough. With economic justice overlooked, it cannot do complete justice. Worse, in the absence of economic justice, political democracy is itself an illusory achievement.

Economic justice and equality are, in principle, akin to political justice and equality. To understand this is to understand how economic and political democracy involve parallel institutions. As the politically democratic state is the politically classless society, so the economically democratic state is the economically classless society. As the politically classless society is one in which there is no division between a ruling class and a subject class, i.e., those who are citizens with suffrage and those who are wards of the state, so the economically classless society is one in which there is no division between haves and have-nots, i.e., between those who have the economic pre-requisites for citizenship and for the pursuit of happiness and those who are deprived of them. [1]

We are thus led to the conclusion that political democracy cannot be effectively established unless government so controls and regulates the economy that economic inequalities do not make a travesty of the political equality that is instituted by universal suffrage.

Before going on to the question of what controls and regulations are needed to achieve economic equality, it is necessary, first, to be sure that we understand economic equality as a realizable, not utopian, ideal. It is utopian to the extreme of being manifestly absurd if it is conceived as consisting in an arithmetically determined quantitative equality of economic goods or possessions. While that is beyond any possibility of achievement and, in addition, may for many reasons be inherently undesirable, there is nothing impracticable about the ideal when it is conceived, in qualitative terms, as consisting in every man's having all the economic goods and conditions that he needs in order to make a really good life for himself. [2]

I have elsewhere enumerated the economic goods and conditions that are components of a really good life. While that enumeration may not be exhaustive, it suffices to delineate the range of goods required for an effective pursuit of happiness:

> a decent supply of the means of subsistence; living and working conditions conducive to health; medical care; opportunities for access to the pleasures of sense as well as to the pleasures of play and aesthetic pleasures; opportunities for access to the goods of the mind through educational facilities in youth and in adult life; and enough free time from subsistence-work, both in youth and in adult life, to take full advantage of these opportunities. [3]

Unless the individual has either income-producing property or purchasing power through other forms of income (wages, salaries), he will not have the economic goods he needs for the pursuit of happiness—things that are goods not only because they maintain his life and health, but because they facilitate his acquirement of other goods, especially the goods of leisure, the goods of mind and character that are related to the exercise of suffrage. Since every man is under a moral obligation to make a really good life for himself, and since this underlies his basic natural right to the pursuit of happiness, a just government and a just state are under the reciprocal obligation to promote every man's pursuit of happiness by doing what they can to facilitate or ensure the possession of the requisite economic goods by all. [4] They discharge this obligation by whatever measures or institutions promote the general economic welfare in such a way that every man has *at least the indispensable minimum* of economic goods that he needs for a good life. When this is the case, then all men are economically equal—equal in the sense of each *having* what he needs. They are all haves; none is a have-not, an economically deprived person, prevented by economic deprivation from leading a good life.

(2)

The foregoing exposition calls for three comments. First, the economic equality that consists in *all men having* and *none being deprived* of the requisite economic goods is established when every man has *at least the indispensable minimum* he needs, not when every man has the *identical amount* of economic goods or possessions. This is tantamount to saying that two men are economically equal if both have the *indispensable minimum*, though one has *considerably more* than the other. [5] In relation to the pursuit of happiness, the man whose possession of economic goods exceeds the indispensable minimum by a vast amount may suffer serious moral and other disadvantages, disadvantages almost as severe as those suffered by the economically deprived.

I have explained elsewhere how a life may be ruined by an

excess of good fortune as well as by an excess of bad fortune. [6] A superfluity or abundance of goods can militate against success in the effort to make a good life. It takes an almost heroic strength of character to resist the seductions of ease and affluence. Hence it might not be utterly far-fetched to think that a just government, in discharging its obligation to promote the pursuit of happiness by all, should take measures to limit the possession of economic goods to a *reasonable maximum*, even as it should take measures to ensure the possession of economic goods to an *indispensable minimum*. However, the protection of rights is one thing, and the enforcement of virtue is another. The latter is not the province of government.

In any case, the difference in the degree to which individuals possess economic goods when all have at least the indispensable minimum, may result in an inequality of power that jeopardizes their political and their economic equality. The possession of great wealth, vastly in excess of the indispensable minimum and greatly exceeding the amount possessed by most men, in addition to endangering the pursuit of happiness by the few who have such vast estates, confers inordinate power on them which they may be tempted to use in ways that militate against the common good. Hence justice may require the setting of a reasonable maximum to protect the common good against the eroding effects of self-serving interests, but not to protect individuals from the misfortune of excessive wealth.

Second, the foregoing enumeration of economic goods, even if not exhaustive, includes more than is needed for good citizenship, though not more than is needed for a good life. Of the goods enumerated, I would select and stress the following as being of critical importance for an intelligent and effective exercise of suffrage and for active participation in political life: first and foremost, a decent supply of the means of subsistence; that, supplemented by opportunities for access to the goods of the mind through educational facilities in youth and adult life, and sufficient free time from subsistence-work, not only to take advantage of these opportunities, but also to engage in political activity. These, taken together, would provide the economic conditions indispensable to political participation. Hence, in relation to citizenship, men who have these indispensable economic goods are, for political purposes, economically equal. To which the proviso must be added that no one should be permitted to accumulate wealth to an extent that confers an inordinate power to serve private interests in contravention of the common good.

Third and last, the foregoing enumeration of economic goods omits or glosses over one consideration that must be taken into account in relating economic to political equality. I said earlier that the individual may have the economic goods he needs for the pursuit of happiness *either* through his possession of income-producing property (his ownership of capital, the means of production) or through his having, through other means, equivalent purchasing power to obtain these economic goods. From the point of view of the good life, the difference between having income-producing property and having its equivalent purchasing power through other forms of income is negligible if both provide the indispensable minimum of economic goods needed for the pursuit of happiness. But from the point of view of economic equality in relation to political equality, the difference may be far from negligible.

The difference between owning income-producing property and receiving an income from any other source is the difference between being independent of and being dependent on the will of others for one's means of subsistence. This remains true in some measure even when the wage-earner's interests are secured or protected by welfare legislation and by the power of labor unions. It is relevant to recall at this point that Kant made economic independence—independence of the will of others in gaining one's livelihood—an essential condition for active citizenship. Those whom he regarded as, in one way or another, economic dependents, he relegated to passive citizenship or subjection. Hence a politically significant economic inequality may still exist in a society in which some of its members, usually a relatively small number, derive their income from their ownership of the means of production, while the rest derive their income solely from the wages of labor, even though both groups are equal in all other respects, i.e., have at least an indispensable minimum of other economic goods. [7]

(3)

With our understanding of the ideal of economic equality thus clarified, let us now proceed to the question of the means by which it can be realized.

I have identified socialism with the end to be achieved. Just as constitutional democracy can be defined by the goal at which it aims—political liberty and equality for all, so socialism can be defined by the goal at which it aims—economic welfare and equality for all. If, in the case of democracy, we turn from the end to the means, it suffices, at the level of principles, to specify universal suffrage, free elections, and a bill of civil rights as the indispensable means. Questions about the organization of government, the relation of its branches, the role of the legislature or of the judiciary, the operation of political parties, and so on, belong to the level of policy rather than to the level of principles, and so do not come within the sphere of political philosophy as a body of normative principles that have the universality and certainty appropriate to wisdom. [8] Similarly if, in the case of socialism, we ask about the means of achieving the economic welfare and equality at which it aims, we must restrict ourselves to the level of universal principles, and leave unanswered all questions of policy that are open to alternative solutions. [9]

To attempt to do what is required, let me begin by clarifying my use of two terms. One is capitalism; the other, property.

I will use the word "capitalism" to refer to any economic system in which human labor is neither the sole nor the primary means of production, as it is in primitive or early agricultural economies, in which labor is supplemented only by hand-tools and beasts of burden. Accordingly, any highly industrialized economy is a capitalistic, as opposed to a laboristic, economy, regardless of how its non-human means of production are owned and operated. [10] I will presently distinguish four varieties of capitalism according to four ways in which the means of production can be owned and operated.

I will use the word "property" to cover the ownership of the means of production, or capital goods, and the ownership of consumable goods, or commodities. In neither sense of the term is it possible to abolish property, as has sometimes been suggested. Consumable goods are usually owned by—are the property of— the person consuming them: the food he eats, the clothes he wears, the car he drives, and so on. If he rents a suit or a car, then they are owned by someone else, the lessor. Capital goods or the means of production must similarly be owned by whatever agency operates them to produce wealth and to distribute the wealth thus produced. It may be a single individual, a cooperative, or a group of associated individuals, a private corporation whose equities are owned by a number of individuals, a public corporation created by the state, or the state itself.

If capital goods are not owned and operated in one of these ways, they must be owned and operated in another. To abolish property in the means of production would be to abandon the use of capital goods for the production of wealth, i.e., to return to a purely laboristic economy. The demand for the abolition of property in capital goods cannot possibly mean that capital goods should be operated without being owned; rather it calls for transferring capital goods from one form of ownership to another, usually from individuals, cooperative groups, or private corporations to public corporations or the state itself. [11]

We are now prepared to distinguish four forms of capitalism, differentiated according to four ways in which the means of production can be owned and operated. Of these four, only the first is anti-socialistic in its aim; the other three all try to provide means for achieving the ends that define socialism. [12]

The first and oldest form of capitalism in an industrial economy is the form that Marx called "bourgeois capitalism" and that he regarded as the iniquitous system that the socialist revolution must overthrow and replace with communism. The defining traits of bourgeois capitalism are the private ownership of the means of production concentrated in the hands of relatively few, and the operation of the means of production for the private profit of its owners, without regard to the economic welfare of the rest of the population—the wage-earners. The resulting economic misery of the great mass of the population, and the great economic inequality that exists between owners and workers, is inimical to political democracy. When it is said that democracy and capitalism are absolutely incompatible, it is bourgeois capitalism that is meant.

The second form of capitalism is the form that replaces bourgeois capitalism when the private ownership of the means of production is abolished, and the ownership of all capital is transferred to the state or to its agencies. The resulting economic system, which is usually called communism, is just as properly described as state capitalism. Its defining traits are the concentration of capital ownership in the organs of the state, the operation of the means of production by agencies of the state, and the distribution by the state of the wealth produced, for the general economic welfare of its people.

The third form of capitalism is sometimes called socialized capitalism and sometimes the mixed economy. It can also be described as the economic system recommended by the revisionist socialist parties that part company with the communists on the nationalization of all industry and the complete transfer of capital ownership to the state. [13] I will use the name "mixed economy" for it, in order to stress the fact that the economy has both a private and a public sector. Some of the means of production are owned and operated by the state; some by private individuals or private corporations. So far as private ownership is concerned, it is still concentrated in the hands of the relatively few; but the distribution of the wealth produced is controlled by government to achieve a large measure of economic welfare and equality for many, if not for all.

The fourth form of capitalism, unlike the other three, has no existing embodiment. Unlike the mixed economy, it moves toward economic welfare and economic equality for all by going in the opposite direction from communism. Whereas communism or state capitalism replaces the concentrated private ownership of capital in the hands of the few by the concentrated public or state ownership of capital, this fourth form of capitalism proposes to replace the concentrated ownership of capital, whether public or private, by a diffused or universally distributed ownership of capital in private hands. Its ultimate aim is to make every citizen also a capitalist, one who derives all or at least part of his income from his ownership of income-producing property, replacing or supplementing his earnings from labor. I will, therefore, distinguish this form of capitalism from the other three by calling it "universal capitalism." Like communism and the mixed economy, universal capitalism aims at economic welfare and equality for all. [14]

(4)

The foregoing enumeration of the four forms of capitalism, three that actually exist and one that is only a possibility, sets forth, in principle, the alternative means for achieving the ends of socialism and of democracy. [15] We have already noted that bourgeosis capitalism opposes the ends of both. We must, therefore, move in the opposite direction, to one of the other forms of capitalism.

State capitalism, or communism, as two leading ex-communists —John Strachey and Milovan Djilas—have observed, substitutes a new class of concentrated "owners" and operators of capital for the concentrated private ownership that existed under bourgeois capitalism. The new class comprises the bureaucrats of the state, in whom economic power is not only concentrated but also united with political power. [16] In consequence, a communist society, so long as its government remains a dictatorship of the communist party in the name of the proletariat, is hardly a classless society, either economically or politically. Though it may be a welfare state, it also tends to be a totalitarian state, in which there is and can be little or no political liberty, even though it is nominally a republic with a constitution and with citizenship.

We are, therefore, left with only two economic systems as ways of achieving the economic welfare and equality for all that is indispensable to political equality and freedom for all. One is the mixed economy; the other, universal capitalism. Both are socialistic in their aims, and both are opposed to bourgeois capitalism and to state capitalism (i.e., communism) as means.

The mixed economy has the advantage of so far appearing to be a feasible economic system. In contrast, the feasibility of universal capitalism must remain an open question until it is tried and tested. [17] In principle, however, universal capitalism is designed to achieve a greater measure of economic equality, though perhaps not a greater measure of economic welfare, for all. In the mixed economy, the division between owners and workers still persists, with a small portion of the population having a degree of economic independence that the rest do not possess. In addition, the mixed economy can operate to achieve general economic welfare for all, and some measure of economic equality, only by making the central government the agency for redistributing wealth, so that those without income-producing property nevertheless have sufficient purchasing power. In consequence, it tends to concentrate economic and political power in the hands of the central government and verges toward the totalitarianism of state capitalism.

On these counts, the untested possibility which I have called universal capitalism is to be preferred. It is in no way inimical to political democracy, as state capitalism certainly is, and as the mixed economy might become. It would appear to be the economic system best able to achieve the combined ideals of economic and political democracy—the economically and politically classless society.

If universal capitalism should turn out not to be feasible, and if no fifth alternative can be devised, then the mixed economy, with all its inherent conflicts, would appear to be the only system that can achieve some measure of economic welfare and equality and achieve it in a manner that is compatible with the preservation of political liberty. [18] Should the mixed economy be our only available and feasible means, then the process of socialization must be carried further to eliminate poverty, to ensure the indispensable minimum of economic goods for all, and to set a reasonable maximum for the acquirement of wealth. In addition, a working balance of power must be maintained between the private and public sectors of the economy to prevent an excessive concentration of economic power in the hands of the central government, while at the same time giving the central government the authority it needs to regulate the private sector for the general economic welfare and the common good.

CHAPTER 13

The Classless Establishment
and the World Community

(1)

WE have seen why a just state must be both politically and economically classless; for the division of a population into a ruling and a subject class, or into haves and have-nots, is an unjust treatment of equals. With this understood, we pass to the question whether a just state must also be socially classless; and as soon as the question is asked, we are aware that it is both different from and more difficult than the problem of political classlessness and the problem of economic classlessness.

From the point of view of justice, the only political class division that is significant is that between a ruling class and a subject class; the only economic class division that is significant is that between men who have the prerequisites for citizenship and the pursuit of happiness and those who are deprived of them. But when we approach the question of social classes from the point of view of justice, we can think of no class division that has parallel significance. On the contrary, we are confronted with an innumerable variety of social class distinctions, none of which seems to be relevant to the basic problems of a normative political philosophy.

Our problem, therefore, must be restated as follows. Are there any other class distinctions, over and above the two just mentioned, of significance from the point of view of perfecting the justice of the state and of government?

The answer to that question, in principle, is contained in the notion of factions. When social classes are opposed in their interests and when this opposition converts them into political factions, then the existence of such classes as factions in conflict becomes significant from the point of view of justice. To explain their significance, I am going to use as my model the economically-based class distinction between the rich and the poor, the haves and have-nots.

From the begining of political history in the West, right down to the present, the basic class conflict in society has been between these two factions. Karl Marx did not discover class conflict in the nineteenth century. Plato, in the fifth century B.C., observed that there are always two cities, not one, the city of the rich and the city of the poor, and they are forever at war with one another. The discussion of revolution in Aristotle's *Politics* centers mainly on this class conflict. [1] When we come down to the eighteenth and nineteenth centuries, we find the same predominant concern with the conflict between these two factions in society. James Madison's discussion of this problem in the famous tenth *Federalist Paper* will help us to relate class conflict to a principle of justice other than the principle of equal treatment for equals.

(2)

Madison made two assumptions that had the look of truth in his day, but no longer need be granted. The first was that factional conflict cannot be eliminated from society, certainly not the conflict between the rich and the poor. The second was that the ever-present conflict between these two factions is a conflict between the few and the many, the rich being the minority and the poor the majority. [2]

Though Madison himself did not use the phrase "tyranny of the majority," he had that notion in mind when he sought to protect the minority faction against self-interested legislation on the part of the majority faction. That phrase was later introduced by Tocqueville and Mill; [3] and the same essential point is involved in one of the major objections raised by the philosophical anarchists against the state and government, namely, that it always involves the tyranny of a faction—in their view, always a minority faction. [4] From the point of view of justice, it makes no difference whether the tyrannical faction is a majority or a minority. What makes the faction tyrannical is the same in both cases.

As we observed earlier, tyranny, in the strict sense, is the government of persons as if they were things, thus reducing them to the status of slaves totally without rights. When we speak of factional tyranny, we are not using the term "tyranny" in this strict sense but are extending it to cover any exercise of power for the self-interest or good of the party in power, rather than for the common good of the community and all its members. Hence when the faction of the rich has predominant power in the state and exercises it for its own self-interest, rather than for the common good, we have the tyranny of a minority. Similarly, when the faction of the poor comes into power through being a majority of the electorate, and exercises its power in self-interested ways that do not serve the common good, we have the tyranny of a majority. Factional tyranny, thus defined, involves the injustice that consists in acting for a special interest as against the common good.

The factional tyranny that chiefly concerned the conservatives or the reluctant democrats of the late eighteenth and the nineteenth century (Madison, Tocqueville, Calhoun, and Mill) was the tyranny of a majority—the masses that were just then beginning to achieve political power through the extension of the suffrage. Assuming, as Madison did, that factional conflict could never be eliminated, they tried to devise ways of circumventing its injurious effects. Upon examination, their proposals turn out to be nothing but ways of circumventing the will of the majority, for good or ill.

The Federalist's advocacy of representative government as

against direct democracy, and the proposal of such things as the electoral college and the indirect selection of senators, were aimed at restoring the power of the minority to check that of the majority. Calhoun's proposal of a concurrent majority would, if adopted, have had a similar effect, for it would give a non-concurring minority the power to interpose a nullifying veto on the will of the majority. Mill's proposal of plural voting and of minority representation were aimed in the same direction. [5]

From the point of view of justice, the problem of factions cannot be solved by such proposals, which do no more than try to shift power from the majority to the minority, or at least to restore a balance of power in which each can check or stalemate the other. On the supposition, which must be allowed, that one faction is no less self-interested than the other, and, therefore, no less inclined to tyrannize over the other, justice is not served by any of these proposals. I submit, therefore, that the only way to solve the problem of factional self-interest and the tyranny in which it is likely to result is to eliminate factional conflict itself by abrogating the class divisions from which it arises.

To say this is to challenge Madison's assumption that factional conflicts cannot be eliminated from society. The conflict between the rich and the poor certainly can be. As I pointed out earlier, that assumption may have had the look of truth in Madison's day, but the socialist revolutions and movements since his time support the contrary view, for there is now at least a reasonable hope that the ideal of economic equality can be realized. With that, the factional conflict between the haves and the have-nots can be eliminated from the socialist, democratic republic just as the conflict between a ruling minority class and a subject majority class has been eliminated by the democratization of the constitution.

(3)

The principle we have learned is that the tyranny, or injustice, that is the almost inevitable result of factional conflict cannot be remedied by shifts in power from one faction to the other, but only by eliminating conflicting factions from society, as they are eliminated in two important respects by the establishment of political and economic equality for all.

In addition to the two factional conflicts just considered, are there others? Are there social—not political, not economic—class distinctions that create factional conflicts that must also be eliminated to rectify the ever-threatening tyranny of one faction over another?

Racial and ethnic class distinctions suggest themselves at once. There may be others, but the consideration of these two will suffice to exemplify what is meant by saying that the socially classless state is one in which there are no factions of this type. As long as racial and ethnic class distinctions persist, factional conflict between the racial or ethnic majority and one or another racial and ethnic minority is likely to occur; and if it does, the tyranny of the majority is a likely result.

The socially classless state will come into existence only when all social class distinctions that might generate factional conflicts and factional injustice have been eliminated. Since the ideal at which we are aiming is the perfectly just state, or the best possible society, the elimination of the factional injustice that is the ever-threatening result of factional conflict must supplement the elimination of the injustices that are rectified by democracy and socialism.

At one time it was thought impossible to eliminate the injustices just mentioned by achieving a politically classless and economically classless society. Revolutionary historical changes have altered our view of what is possible. Even if the ideal of the politically and the economically classless society is not yet fully realized, its realization can be projected from steps in that direction which have already been taken.

The possibility of eliminating the factional conflicts that arise from racial and ethnic and, perhaps, other social class distinctions is not, of course, as clear. What is clear, however, is that their elimination is necessary for the sake of justice; and if we are given to believe, as I for one am, that the necessary must be possible, such faith is at least the first step in the direction of making every effort to create the socially classless state by eliminating all social class distinctions that generate factional conflicts. [6]

(4)

I would like to add two comments. The first concerns the notion of social equality. We have seen that political and economic equality can be defined with precision. Can we define social equality with a comparable degree of precision? I think it is possible to do so. Individuals are treated as socially equal when they are treated as having the worth or dignity that is inherent in being a person, not a thing. Their social equality is violated only when they are subject to discrimination on the basis of one or another social class to which they happen to belong. Discrimination among persons is justified only by their individual inequality in native endowment and personal attainment. [7]

The elimination of all social class distinctions—not just those that generate factional conflicts—is probably impossible and clearly undesirable. Social equality can be established simply by not allowing such nonfactional class distinctions to become the basic for a discriminating treatment in favor of one human being as against another.

The second comment I would like to make concerns the notion of "the establishment" that has such currency today, at least in speech. The term is, for the most part, used invidiously or dyslogistically, to refer to a dominant faction exercising its power tyranically in a self-interested fashion and, therefore, in contravention of the common good. Thus used, the term "establishment" connotes a source of injustice. In the eighteenth and nineteenth centuries, the establishment that revolutionary movements sought to overthrow was a minority faction of the ruling and propertied few. Today, the establishment that the new left seeks to overthrow is a majority faction which, in their view, oppresses racial minorities and ignores the injustice being done to those still impoverished. The achievement of a truly classless society, with all factional conflicts eliminated, is the only way in which the injustices done by factional establishments, whether they are minority or majority establishments, can be rectified.

The ideal of a truly classless society takes two forms: the one proposed by the anarchist or anti-political philosopher, the other by the political philosopher. For Bakunin or for Marx, as for the extremists of the new left in our own day, the truly classless society can come into existence only with the destruction of the state and of government. The new left often has this in mind when it speaks of destroying the establishment. For the political philosopher, the ideal of the truly classless society cannot be achieved except through perfecting the justice of the state and of government—the establishment that the anarchists wish to destroy. [8]

I, therefore, purpose to use the word "establishment" in a non-invidious way to refer to all the institutions of the state and of government, through which justice must be done to realize the ideal of a truly classless society, with liberty and equality for all. These are the institutions that must be established to create the truly classless society; and, therefore, I think it proper to refer to the ideal at which political philosophy now aims as the ideal of the classless establishment. [9]

(5)

We have come to an understanding of the ideal that now seems possible of attainment—the best society that the perfection of our institutions can achieve. At this point in history, as at any other, our vision of the possible cannot avoid being limited by the experience on which it is based; but it is, nevertheless, a larger vision than was vouchsafed our ancestors.

Reviewing the careers of historic civilizations, Toynbee has observed that they have all been beset by the twin evils of class and war. While that is still true of all existing civilizations, we are living in the first century in which the eradication of these evils appears to be a practicable possibility, not a utopian dream.

This is the first century in which world government has been envisaged as a practicable remedy for the international anarchy that is identical with a permanent state of war between sovereign states. It is not their nationalism or the fact that they are national states, but rather their sovereign independence that puts them at war with one another—the cold war of diplomacy, espionage, and terrorism, or the hot war of bombs and bloodshed. [10] It is also the first century in which the injustices of slavery, serfdom, subjection, poverty, and racism can be and have been considered eliminable, not merely for some favored segments of humanity but for all mankind.   ,

I have used the term "classless" to describe the ideal of a society from which all factional conflicts have been eliminated; and I have shown that, in order to provide the maximization of liberty and equality for all, the classless society must be achieved not through the destruction of the state and government, but rather by perfecting the justice of our social, economic, and political institutions. The classless society thus conceived—or, as I have called it, the "classless establishment"—is an ideal that is new in the history of normative political theory. Its newness is certified by the recency of the judgments that democracy and socialism are not only possible but desirable.

To be sure that this is not misunderstood, let me recall that by democracy I mean the democratic constitution of a republic in which there is no division of the population into a ruling and a subject class; and that by socialism, I mean the economic counterpart of political democracy, achieved by the participation of all in the general economic welfare so that there is no division of the population into haves and have-nots. The socialist, democratic republic is only a first approximation of the new ideal of a classless society. A fuller realization of that ideal calls for the elimination of other class divisions, based on racial, ethnic, or other discriminations that create factional conflicts and result in injustice to one or another segment of society.

Though the ideal now envisaged as possible is new, it is subject to one qualification that is not new in principle. Yet our understanding of the principle *is* new. The just state and just government are not ultimate ends to be achieved for their own sake. The best society that is capable of institutional achievement is only a means to the good life for human beings. Our moral obligation to do whatever can be done to bring it into existence derives from a more fundamental moral obligation—the obligation that every man has to make a good life for himself.

The truth of this basic normative insight was imperfectly understood when, in earlier periods of history, it was thought to be impossible to universalize it—that is, to extend its application to all men, all without exception, not just the privileged few or even the privileged many. This gives us the measure of the imperfection of the ideal that earlier centuries aimed at, for the best society that they could conceive, even when they conceived it properly as a means to the good life and not as an end in itself, provided the external conditions of a good life for only a portion of the population, usually considerably less than all.

"All"—when what is meant is *all without exception*—is the most radical and, perhaps, also the most revolutionary term in the lexicon of political thought. It may have been used in the past, but it was never seriously meant to include every individual member of the human race, not just the members of one's own class, or even one's fellow countrymen, but every human being everywhere on earth. That we are now for the first time in history begining to mean all without exception when we say "all" is another indication of the newness of the emerging ideal of the best society, the institutions of which will benefit all men everywhere, by providing them with the conditions they need to lead good human lives.

Local or parochial justice and local or parochial peace are, therefore, not enough. World-wide justice and world-wide peace are not embellishments of the ideal; they are of its essence. If we think of the socialist, democratic republic as something to be achieved in this country or that, we are not thinking of the ideal to which we should now be committed; we should think instead of a world-wide union of socialist, democratic republics that would be a world state and a world government, establishing justice and preserving peace on a global basis. This and this alone is the proper and adequate representation of the ideal to which we should now be committed because we can no longer justify aiming at less, on the ground that only parochial goals are practically achievable. On the contrary, as I hope to show, the goal of a good society is no longer achievable within parochial limits but only on a world-wide basis.

Understanding the best possible institutions as means rather than as ends, and the best possible society as a means to the good life for all, still further enlarges our conception of the ideal at which we should aim. More is required than the maximization of liberty and equality for all; even world-wide justice and world-wide peace are not enough; for all these things could conceivably be accompanied by conditions that would militate against or prevent the achievement of the ultimate end—the pursuit of happiness by all. Wealth must be produced in a sufficient quantity to provide every man with more than the bare necessities of life, and it must be produced in such a manner that every man, in addition to having the requisite physical comforts and conveniences, also has ample free time in which to improve the quality of his life by engaging in the pursuits of leisure and enjoying the pleasure of play. Even this is not enough, as we have now come to realize with justified anxiety, if we allow the over-population of the earth and the deterioration or destruction of the life-sustaining and life-enhancing biosphere to occur.

Hence our conception of the best society must include considerations, both economic and ecological, that have never heretofore been regarded as essential to the ideal that men have projected for realization.

Part Four

The Goal of Progress and the End of the Revolution

CHAPTER 14

Three Needed Developments:
Prescriptions, Not Predictions

(1)

THE framework of normative principles that I have expounded in this book so far and that, in the immediately preceding pages, I have just summarized leads us to the conclusion that all existing states are defective means to the end that they ought to serve; that no government is yet completely just, for none has yet achieved, in the fullest possible measure, liberty and equality for all. What is more important, no parochial government, even if it were perfected within its local limits, would be able to provide the external conditions prerequisite to a good life even for its own citizens, much less for every man on earth.

This, however, should not lead us to think that what does not yet exist cannot be achieved. There is nothing about the principles enunciated that should lead us to the conclusion that the good society is only a utopian dream. There is nothing in the nature of man or of human institutions that makes it impossible—however difficult it may be—to rectify all injustices, to remove all deprivations, and to prevent all the hazards that threaten the continuation of life on earth or threaten to reduce it to almost unimaginable misery.

The problem with which we shall be concerned in the concluding chapters of this book is, therefore, the question of what must be done to realize the ideal that is now seen to be capable of achievement. Let me say at once that I am not predicting that it will be achieved. Prophecy is not the business of political philosophy. Being a normative discipline, it is concerned with prescriptions, not predictions.

I can imagine a monkish philosopher living in the year 970, when prophecies of imminent doom abounded as the millennium approached. Overcome by the anxieties of his time, he probably would have dimissed as folly any attempt to think normatively about the future of life on earth. I am aware that, in the year 1970, there are many secular scholars and thinkers who are in the same state of mind. The predicted imminence of doom preoccupies their attention and causes them to reject concern with remote ideals as almost insanely irrelevant.

The end of the world did not occur in the year 1000, and it may not occur in the year 2000. If it does, it will have been a vain undertaking to think seriously about what ought to be done to realize an ideal that may take much more than the next thirty years to achieve. But if the cataclysm is averted, we will have addressed ourselves to a problem that will be of genuine concern for many generations.

In any case, it should be recognized that the prescriptions which it is the business of a normative political philosophy to formulate have a truth that is independent of what will happen, just as their truth is independent of what has happened. Ought, however, does presuppose can; we are obliged to do only what is possible. It is in this connection that a knowledge of the past, of what has happened, has a bearing on the projected ideal as a realizable possibility. The technological, political, economic, and social progress that mankind has made in the last 6000 years gives us reason to think that still further progress can be made by further changes in our institutions. As we observed earlier, great steps forward have been accomplished by revolutions that were progressive in their effect, especially the three great revolutions that were formative of the best societies that now exist. To say, as we must, that these societies are far from good enough is to say that more progress must be made and that more revolution may be needed to effect the changes that are requisite. [1]

(2)

My optimism does not consist in thinking that the human race *will necessarily* survive the dangers that now threaten it, but only in thinking that it *may* survive by overcoming those dangers. It does not consist in thinking that further progress in human institutions will *necessarily* occur, but in thinking that it *can* be achieved, whether by revolutionary or other means. And if it can be achieved, then knowing what ought to be done to achieve it is the normative wisdom that political philosophy should be able to provide.

I am aware that my optimism about institutional progress is based on a reading of the past that differs radically from the interpretation of it now current among revolutionists who aim not at perfecting our existing institutions but rather at destroying them and making a fresh start by non-institutional means. All that they see is the continuing existence today of certain injustices or evils that have always existed in the past, and so they conclude that our institutions are incorrigible. What they fail to see is that certain injustices or evils that existed in the past no longer exist today precisely because our institutions have been improved; and their manifest corrigibility is ground for attempting to improve them further rather than doing away with them entirely. Only if the past were what a noted anthropologist has recently reported the disaffected young as thinking, namely, "a colossal, unintelligible failure," would total pessimism about the future be justified; believing that would undermine those who hope to improve human affairs by making a fresh start as much as those who look for progress through the improvement of our institutions. [2]

These preliminary observations should serve to clarify the problems with which I will deal in these concluding chapters and to indicate the self-imposed restraints that will govern the manner in which I shall address myself to them. I propose to proceed as follows.

In the next three chapters, I will discuss developments that are prerequisite to the realization of the best society that now seems possible: in Chapter 15, technological advances for the sake of eliminating poverty and pollution; in Chapter 16, world government; and in Chapter 17, universal liberal schooling. Then in Chapter 18 I will consider the role that revolution plays in the accomplishment of progress; and in this connection I will deal with the question whether revolution is a permanent feature of society or a transient one. If, as I will try to show, it is the latter, then there will be an end to revolution, even as there may also be an end to progress in human institutions. We shall be left, therefore, with a concluding question about the future of man after the limit of improvement has been reached in all the external conditions of human life.

CHAPTER 15

The Control of Technology

(1)

THE first of the three developments that are needed is economic. The production of wealth in sufficient quantity as well as a just distribution of the wealth produced is needed for the elimination of poverty; and the mode of its production must be such that the employment of human labor is minimized, so that everyone has ample free time for the tasks of citizenship and for other pursuits of leisure. These objectives can be attained only by further advances in technology, though not by them alone.

Technological advances during recent centuries have contributed substantially—perhaps indispensably—to the promotion of democracy and socialism. Industrialization, which is a manifestation of advanced technology in the production of wealth, replaced the feudalism of an agrarian economy with its serfdom and peonage. The organization of labor that is coincidental with the industrial system of production led to the further emancipation of the working classes. The extension of the franchise came first in the technologically advanced, industrialized countries and was accompanied by the introduction and expansion of free public schooling. The harbingers of socialism also appeared first in the industrialized economies; and when revolutionary socialism won a victory in an industrially backward country, such as Russia, its initial effort to solidify its gains involved plans for augmenting industrialization.

I mention these facts to indicate the contribution of technology

to the democratic and socialistic revolutions that began and pro-
liferated in the nineteenth and twentieth centuries. The reforms
they initiated and established—the democratic constitution and the
programs of the welfare state—underlie our projection of still
further reforms to be made, among which the elimination of
poverty and the emancipation of all men, not just some, from
grinding toil have high priority. No one, I think, would question
that these objectives have become realistic and practicable for us,
as they were not for our ancestors, because of the estimates we can
now make of technological advances still to come.

These estimates have led some contemporary prophets to fore-
cast the coming of what they have called "post-industrial society."
That, I submit, is a misnomer for the society that will be conditioned by the predicted advances in technology. When we speak
of a post-agrarian society, we refer to the replacement of the
agrarian by the industrial economy, including the industrialization
of agriculture. If we were to use the phrase "post-industrial" in a
parallel fashion, its connotation would be the replacement of the
industrial production of wealth by some other mode of production.
But that is not what the prophecies envision. They envision instead
a future in which the increased production of wealth by industrial
means will involve less and less need for manpower. Far from being
post-industrial, the society projected will be super-industrial.

As the productive power of machinery increases and the automa-
tion of production advances, the input of human toil will be
steadily diminished. Industrialization at its onset and in its early
stages changed the relative contribution of men and machines to
the production of wealth. With technological improvements, industrial development has steadily altered that ratio in favor of
machines. The super-industrial society of the future will merely
carry that change forward, while at the same time resulting in an
increased supply of economic goods.

I would like to propose what I think is a more accurate name
for the society of the future that should be the goal of our efforts
to realize the ideal that we are now able to project. I am not predicting that it will necessarily come into being as the result of
forces now inexorably at work. I am rather prescribing the direc-

tion in which we ought to move in order to create a society better than any which now exists. Speaking in that vein, I would say that the most apt description of our objective is the post-parochial civilization of a world political community under world government. At their best, all the societies of the past and all that now exist in the world have been and are parochial civilizations. Until very recently, until the democratic and socialistic revolutions of the recent past, they have all been parochial civilizations of privilege, with a dominant minority enjoying the political and economic privileges that are the indispensable conditions of a good human life, and with a submerged and oppressed majority deprived of these conditions.

With the technological advances of the last few hundred years, which made the democratic and socialistic revolutions possible, we have seen the proportions reversed. We have not yet achieved the classless society that is the goal of democracy and socialism, but it is now a minority rather than a majority of the population that is submerged and oppressed. The best societies in the world today are still parochial civilizations of privilege, but with the striking difference just noted, which portends the ultimate elimination of privilege. [1]

Further technological advances and augmented industrialization are needed to produce that result, but with them we shall also be in a position to eliminate the parochialism as well as the privileged classes that have characterized all societies up to this time. World government did not emerge as a practicable ideal until world wars, more and more global in their extent as well as more and more destructive in their effects, became technologically feasible.

The proposition that world government is necessary for world peace does not depend for its truth on the technology of the twentieth century. Dante reached that conclusion by cogent and valid arguments at the beginning of the fourteenth century. Kant reached the same conclusion at the end of the eighteenth century. But neither Dante nor Kant could have seen, as we can see today, that the formation of a world political community is a practicable possibility, an achievable goal. In addition, with our understanding not only of the power conferred on us by technology but also of the problems created by the misuse of that power, we recognize that world government is necessary for the control of technology itself, as well as for the establishment of world peace. The biosphere is global not local; its protection from pollution and deterioration cannot be effectuated by the best efforts of local governments.

(2)

In the foregoing discussion, I have referred to technological advances—to improvements in technology—rather than to technological progress. I have done so in order not to beg the question whether the benefits conferred by advanced technology outweigh its detrimental effects. When we face that question, we must also face the current criticisms of technological advances as productive of more evil than good.

All forms of power are instrumentalities to be used. In themselves they are neither good nor bad; their moral quality depends entirely on the use which men make of them. The fact that some instrumentalities are more powerful than others does not alter this, but the misuse of more powerful means is productive of greater evil. Technology confers power on man; and advances in technology, increments of power. The moral problem remains essentially the same whether the technology is primitive or advanced, but with advances in technology, the magnitude of the problem requires the action of the organized community. The use of available instrumentalities ceases to be an individual problem and becomes a social problem. [2]

In saying that technological advances made the democratic and socialistic revolutions possible, we are saying, by implication, that in certain respects a good social use has been made of the instrumentalities afforded us by improved technology. If only these advantages accrued and were accompanied by no disadvantages, we would find it reasonable to conclude that the technological advances had been put to the service of progress. But we must also take into account the many and varied abuses or misuses of advanced technology, with far-reaching consequences pre-eminent among which is the deterioration or destruction of the ecological balance in the biosphere. If the destructive use of technology is not averted, or even if its deteriorating effect on the quality of human life is not overcome, then clearly the use that has been made of advanced technology is not on the side of progress, when that is understood, as it should be, to consist in an increase in good over evil, not just an increase in the power of the means at our disposal or in the efficiency of their use.

(3)

As I said before, it is not the business of normative political philosophy to predict the future, but rather to prescribe what should be done to make the society of the future better than any society of the past or present. Unless the political philosopher can assume not only that technology is subject to effective political control, but also that advances in technology will be able to provide ways of overcoming pollution and reversing present ecological trends, he has nothing to say. Making the requisite assumption provides him with the basis on which he can make the only two prescriptions that fall within his competence.

One rests on the insight that man's natural rights, subservient to his basic right to the pursuit of happiness, include the right to an environment that is conductive to a healthy and pleasant life. This is merely an expanded understanding of the right to life itself. When this right is seriously infringed by the misuse of technology, and even threatened with total violation, then the control of technology becomes a paramount objective of government, taking precedence over almost every other consideration. To do the work of justice, which involves securing all natural rights, government must give an over-riding priority to the conservation and enhancement of a healthful environment, without which the possession of of other rights becomes ineffectual. The governments of parochial societies may not be able to discharge this obligation to even a minimal extent unless they act in concert; doing so may be a step toward the post-parochial world community of the future.

The other prescription concerns the role of scientists and technologists in government. One of the current concerns, occasioned by advanced technology, is the rise of a new elite—a new ruling class consisting of the men whose special knowledge or expertness might put them in positions of power in what has come to be called "the technological society." Were this to occur, it would be as inimical to political democracy as the substitution of the edicts of a philosopher king for the voice of the people in the determination of public policy. [3]

The basic thesis of democracy is that the people should govern themselves, for good or ill, and not be governed, even if it appears to be for their good, by philosophers, scientists, or technologists, no matter how useful their wisdom, knowledge, or expertness may be to the body politic. To whatever extent it is useful, it should, of course, be used, but how it should be used is a question to be decided by the citizens as a whole. They are the rulers, and the experts are at best their good servants. [4]

CHAPTER 16

World Government

(1)

THE discussion so far has indicated the need for world government to overcome the defects intrinsic to parochial communities, defects that are not remediable by local governments. I would now like to treat this subject more extensively, for the formation of a world political community is the second major development required for the realization of the ideal that we can now project as possible.

At the conclusion of Chapter 7, I pointed out that nothing short of the world state can adequately serve the end that the state, teleologically defined, should aim at, since peace in the fullest sense of that term is an essential condition of the good human life. Nothing less than the world state, therefore, perfectly realizes the idea of the state. [1]

Peace must be understood in positive, not negative, terms. If it were merely the absence of overt violence, then we would have to admit that peace exists between sovereign states during such periods as they are not engaged in actual fighting. But we also know that peace in this purely negative sense is often replaced by actual warfare, especially if the sovereign states have conflicting interests that put them in the posture of hostility toward one another. [2]

Positively conceived, peace exists only when institutions are operative to resolve conflicting interests and settle all serious differences without recourse to violence. It is in this positive sense of peace that civil peace—the peace that obtains within the boundaries of a state—is one of the boons conferred upon the members of a society by its institutions of government. They have ways of settling their differences without recourse to violence. [3]

In sharp contradistinction to peace in this positive sense, the negative use of the word "peace" to signify nothing but *the absence of overt violence* conceals the fact that what is being described is a state of war—what we have come to call the "cold war," in which military establishments, active espionage, and propaganda are manifest threats of violence that has not yet become overt. While it is true that the cold war is an active enterprise only between hostile rather than between friendly nations, it is always present in some degree between sovereign states. Between sovereign states, whether friendly or hostile, peace in the positive sense of that term has never existed and cannot exist; the alternatives for them are not peace and war, but only cold war and hot war—threatening violence that cannot be prevented from turning into overt violence, because the relation of sovereign states precludes the one factor that is required for the preservation of civil peace—government.

In the history of mankind up to this moment, peace—or what I shall call *civil peace* to signify the positive sense of that term—has existed only within states, not between states. Even there, as we shall presently observe when we come to consider the violence of revolutions, it may be illusory to the extent that the institutions of the society are unjust and breed revolution. Nevertheless, such civil peace as has obtained on earth, to whatever degree, has been the product of civil government. [4]

If civil government is necessary for civil peace within the boundaries of a parochial society, then, for exactly the same reason, world civil government is necessary for world civil peace; and to achieve this we must replace the plurality of parochial societies, each a sovereign state, with the unity of a world state. The elimination of war between states—hot war or cold war—is identical with the elimination of a plurality of independent states, each of which is sovereign or subject to no superior in its external relations with other states. The elimination of war between states is not identical with the elimination of all forms of violence, for injustice may still breed revolution in a world community, as it has and does in parochial societies. Nevertheless, if we regard revolutionary violence as civil war, whether within the confines of a parochial society or in a world community, the replacement of international war by civil war through the formation of a world state is an advance, because civil war can lead to the restoration and improvement of civil peace, as international war cannot. [5]

(2)

The foregoing constitutes an answer to the question, why world government is necessary for world civil peace, and, in part at least, it also answers the question of its desirability; for if world-wide civil peace is an indispensable means to the happiness of mankind, and if world government is an indispensable means to world-wide civil peace, then its necessity as a means makes it as desirable as the end it is needed to serve. But this leaves quite open the question whether world government is possible, as well as fails to touch on other considerations with regard to its desirability. [6]

However appealing or persuasive it may be to say that if something is necessary as a means to an end that we are morally obligated to seek, it must be possible, that proposition by itself need not be our only answer to the question about the possibility of world government. The feasibility of world government depends on our being able to overcome two formidable obstacles. One of these is technological, the other political. Let me deal with each of these briefly.

The technological obstacle to world government appeared to be insurmountable in earlier centuries when the geographical barriers to communication and interaction among the peoples of the earth were of such an order that they could not function as fellow-citizens in a single community under one government. Technological advances have now shrunk the world, not in geodesic space, but in social space, to a size small enough to make its political as well as its economic unification feasible. If we are persuaded that the economic interdependence of the peoples of the world has now reached the point that makes their political unification desirable, we should also be able to see that the same technological factors that have produced global economic interdependence now make political unification feasible. Another sign pointing in the same direction is the advent of world wars, new in the twentieth century. The same technological advances that ushered in the era of world war—conflicts that have been and threaten to become more and more global in their extent—also provide the underpinnings for world peace by reducing the distances in social space and in communication and transportation time that were, in the past, obstacles to world political unification, as in the past they were also obstacles to global war.

The technological obstacles to world government being overcome, the only question of its feasibility concerns the political obstacles that remain. The difficulty of the problem that these present is such that one cannot be assured of its solution in the immediate future. All we can be sure of is that, in principle, it is solvable, which is tantamount to saying that world government is, in principle, politically feasible, as well as being, in fact, technologically feasible.

If world government is to be, as it should be, the *de jure* government of a republic, the best hope for its coming to be lies in the adoption of a federal constitution for the world state, creating a federal union of participating states that have surrendered every vestige of external sovereignty in dealing with one another. The chief political obstacles to the adoption of a constitution for a world federal republic lies in the requirement that all the participating states must themselves be republics. I would go further and say that if the world state is to embody the political ideal to which we are committed, the participating states must not only be republics, but also socialist, democratic republics. This requisite degree of political homogeneity among all the participating members of a world federation—a union of socialist, democratic republics— may be extremely difficult to achieve in a relatively short time, though there is no reason whatsoever to suppose that it cannot be achieved if sufficient time is allowed for revolutions and reforms to occur in the parochial societies that now exist. [7]

One positive indication of its feasibility is afforded us by the adoption in 1948 by the United Nations of the *Universal Declaration of Human Rights*. Agreement on this basic charter of rights betokens the possibility of agreement on the constitutional provisions needed to secure these rights for the citizens of a world political community—constitutional provisions that would have to be democratic and socialistic in their institutional enactment. [8] I would like to mention one other indication of the possibility, in principle, of overcoming the social, economic, and political heterogeneity that would prevent world federation, while preserving cultural pluralism and a diversity of institutions in the federating states. It is afforded by the Preliminary Draft of a World Constitution prepared at the University of Chicago in the years 1945–1948. This document deserves the most careful study. I regret that I must refrain from quoting it in its entirety, contenting myself with the following passages— from its Preamble and from its Declaration of Duties and Rights. The Preamble declares:

> The people of the earth having agreed that the advancement of man in spiritual excellence and physical welfare is the common goal of mankind;
>
> that universal peace is the prerequisite for the pursuit of that goal;
>
> that justice in turn is the prerequisite of peace, and peace and justice stand or fall together;
>
> that iniquity and war inseparably spring from the competitive anarchy of the national states;
>
> that therefore the age of nations must end, and the era of humanity begin;
>
> the government of the nations have decided to order their separate sovereignties in one government of justice, to which they surrender their arms;
>
> and to establish, as they do establish, this Constitution as the covenant and fundamental law of the Federal Republic of the World.

The Declaration of Duties and Rights begins by saying that "the universal government of justice as covenanted and pledged in this Constitution, is founded on the Rights of Man," among which are the rights of everyone everywhere to claim

> release from the bondage of poverty and from the servitude and exploitation of labor, with rewards and security according to merit and needs;
>
> freedom of peaceful assembly and of association, in any creed, or party, or craft, within the pluralistic unity and purpose of the World Republic;
>
> protection of individuals and groups against subjugation and tyrannical rule, racial or national, doctrinal or cultural, with safeguards for the self-determination of minorities and dissenters;
>
> and any such other freedoms and franchises as are inherent in man's inalienable claims to life, liberty, and the dignity of the human person. . . .

to which is added the following clause:

> The four elements of lffe—earth, water, air, energy—are the common property of the human race. The management and use of such portions thereof as are vested in or assigned to particular ownership, private or corporate or national or regional, of definite or indefinite tenure, of individualist or collectivist economy, shall be subordinate in each and all cases to the interest of the common good.

The sections of the World Constitution that follow these opening declarations of principle then prescribe governmental institutions and procedures designed to achieve the ends in view. It is not my purpose here to defend the proposed constitutional provisions. They are details in what was admittedly a preliminary draft submitted for emendation and improvement. I cite this draft of a world constitution only as evidence of the juridical feasibility—or feasibility in principle—of a world federal republic against those who would claim that the political obstacles to its formation are intrinsically insurmountable. [9]

(3)

But can the political obstacles, which represent real difficulties of a high order, be surmounted in the immediate future, or will it take several centuries or more of revolutionary changes and institutional reforms to remove the social, economic, and political heterogeneities that stand in the way of world government? That is a factual question and one that calls for a prediction which lies beyond the scope and competence of political philosophy as a normative discipline. However, one consideration can be mentioned as having a bearing on the question of time.

Twenty-five years ago, when the preliminary draft of a world constitution was published, the urgency to create a world government rested solely on the need to prevent a third world war—more nearly global in its extent and, with the advent of atomic weapons, irremediably destructive of life on earth. [10] Today there is the additional urgency that stems from the even more desperate need to prevent the destruction of the biosphere which, according to leading technologists, cannot be effectively accomplished by the action of parochial governments. A third world war has been postponed for twenty-five years and may be postponed indefinitely by the widespread fear of its cataclysmic consequences; but the destruction of the biosphere in the next twenty-five or fifty years can be prevented only by strenuous positive measures undertaken rapidly and carried out globally. The urgency of mounting and effectuating this program does more than reinforce the urgency of preventing global war: it sets a relatively short time as the period allowed us for doing what must be done. Men and nations everywhere may not be able much longer to close their eyes to the inexorable alternatives of one world or none.

I said earlier that the necessity of world government as an

indispensable means to world-wide civil peace is only one point in answer to the question about its desirability as a political objective. Its indispensability as a means to preserving a life-sustaining and life-enhancing environment for mankind is another positive consideration. But there are still other considerations that should be mentioned before we face the objectionable features of a world state that might make it undesirable. Let me mention three briefly.

(1) The formation of a world community under world government is needed to eliminate the inequitable distribution of resources and wealth that has allowed the rich nations to dominate and exploit the poor nations. The same reforms that have been operative to overcome poverty within the technologically advanced welfare states must become operative on a world-wide basis to rectify the injustices suffered by the have-not nations. We must, in the words of Gunnar Myrdal, go beyond the parochial confines of the welfare state to extend participation in general economic welfare to all the peoples of the world; and this can be done only by the regulation of a world economy by a world government that aims at the economic welfare of men everywhere. [11] It should be added here that so long as the cold war exists and the hot war threatens, the wasteful employment of our productive powers to maintain military establishments can prevent us from producing enough wealth to remove poverty, no matter how far our productive technology may advance.

(2) What is true of poverty on a world-wide basis is similarly true of racism on a world-wide basis. This, like poverty, is not an evil confined within the borders of this or that parochial society. It is an evil that pervades a world in which nationalism generates ethnic and racial hatreds and hostilities. The elimination of racism requires a world community in which all men, of whatever stock or complexion, are fellow-citizens, and no one is a foreigner, a barbarian, an enemy, or a sub-human alien. [12]

(3) The formation of a world community under world gov-

ernment is needed to safeguard constitutional government and democratic processes from the political schizophrenia that besets parochial states whose foreign policies undermine or conflict with their domestic programs. The machinations of international politics usually evade or violate the principles of justice that the best parochial societies attempt to apply within their own borders. In addition, with the advent of war on a global scale, the so-called military-industrial complex has grown to such power that it has become a serious threat to the institutions of political democracy; but so long as parochial states remain in the posture of war toward one another, there may be no cure for this evil, which afflicts all the great powers—China and Russia as much as the United States.

(4)

With all these things in its favor, what disadvantages attach to world government that might raise a serious question for us about its desirability?

Certainly not that world government would require the abolition of the external sovereignty and independence of the parochial national states in existence today. That, as we have seen, counts as one of the great benefits world government would confer, not only serving the cause of peace but also helping to eliminate poverty and racism. Only myopic provincialism or, what is worse, an over-riding commitment to short-term gains for a favored few against the interests of all the rest would lead anyone to regard the loss of national sovereignty as an unmitigated evil that over-balances all other considerations.

The only respectable objection with which I am acquainted derives from the fear that a monolithic world state would embody a centralization of authority and a concentration of power so massive that if it were converted into an instrument of despotism and tyranny, it would be one against which no countervailing force could ever prevail.

In reply to this objection, let me say, first, that the same constitutional safeguards that prevent a republic from becoming a despotism can be built into a world constitution in a manner that is appropriate to the organization of the government it sets up. Once again I would refer to the *Preliminary Draft of a World Constitution* for a vision of how constitutional limitations on public officials and departments of government can safeguard the citizens of a world republic from abuses of authority or power, as these have been safeguarded by comparable devices in parochial societies.

In the second place, everything that has already been said about the preservation of residual autonomy for individuals and subordinate associations applies to world government, and with even greater force because of the number, variety, and size of the subordinate communities, corporations, and associations that would not only be included but would also be granted some measure of local autonomy in the organization of a world federal republic. In other words, the centralization of ultimate authority in the organs of a world government should be counter-balanced by a decentralization of the functions to be performed by its subordinate components, each exercising the measure of residual autonomy that is requisite for an effective performance of its special function. [13]

Finally, with all military power abolished, and with the only implements of authorized force available to government those which can be justified as means of preserving peace and protecting individuals against criminal violence, the power at the disposal of the world government might be considerably less than that provided by the armaments under control of the national governments of parochial societies. One of the great advances that will come about with the formation of a world republic will be the substitution of a legally constituted and civilly controlled police power for all the other forms of force that have been available to government. The only authorized force will be that of police operating solely to protect rights and to render the acts of government efficacious.

If injustice of one sort or another still persists in the world community after world government is instituted, or creeps back into it, and if the legal means for the redress of grievances are not adequate to rectify serious wrongs, revolutionary violence would still remain the only option, and having recourse to it would not be precluded; for world government, if properly constituted, would not have overwhelming force at its disposal, as it might if it were empowered with a vast military establishment proportionate to its global scope, rather than confined to the use of a civil police force designed primarily to preserve civil peace. [14]

CHAPTER 17

The Education of Mankind

(1)

THE third major development needed for the realization of
the ideal society that we are now able to envisage as
practically possible demands a greater act of faith on our
part than either of the other two.

We can be reasonably sure that further technological advances
in the production of wealth and in the manner of its production
will enable us to provide the economic conditions of a good life
for everyone on earth, especially if we are, in addition, able to
eliminate war and replace parochial societies with a world
state. We may even be persuaded by reflection and experience
that world government is not only necessary and desirable, but
that it is also feasible in principle, whether or not it can be
consummated in time to forestall the disasters that appear to
threaten us.

But can the human race—by which I mean *all men without
exception*—be educated to the degree required for citizenship
in the union of socialist, democratic republics and beyond that
for the pursuits of leisure that are the essential ingredients in
the good life that every man is obligated to make for himself?
To answer this question affirmatively calls for an act of faith
beyond all the evidence that experience affords.

The development that is projected here is the development
of an effectively administered, purely liberal schooling for all
children who do not require hospitalization for feeble-minded-

ness; and, after such schooling is completed, the continuation of liberal learning by everyone throughout adult life. The only aim of liberal schooling should be to make the young *learners*, not learned. Becoming *learned* is the work of a life time. Neither the liberal schooling of the young nor the liberal education of adults has ever been accomplished for the whole population of even the most advanced parochial societies, wealthy enough to support fairly elaborate systems of public education, both in schools and apart from them. The only positive evidence that historical or present experience affords us reveals some measure of success in the education of a relatively small number of persons belonging to the privileged classes. The attempt to provide liberal education for the whole population of a society, in school and after, was not made in the parochial societies of privilege that existed in the past and still exist in many parts of the world today; nor is the attempt yet being made in those among existing societies that represent first approximations to the ideal of classlessness.

If the educational development that I am saying is needed has not yet been begun in the U.S.A., in the U.S.S.R., in Sweden, or Japan—to take as examples the countries where it might be expected to show itself first—then what grounds do we have for believing that it is possible? Let me counter this question by observing that the proposition has never been put to the test. If an attempt had been made and had failed, that might put the matter in a negative light, though not decisively. Since we have no experience to go on, either positive or negative, we can only appeal to faith in the potentialities of the normal human mind of any degree of endowment above the minimum which requires hospitalization. If man is by nature a political animal, as I maintain he is; and if man is morally obligated to make a good life for himself by devoting a major portion of his time and energy to the pursuits of leisure, as again I maintain he is; then man must be by nature—by his intellectual endowment—educable for the duties of citizenship and for the pursuits of leisure.

What I have just said is meant to apply to all men, with the exception only of the pathologically defective, not just to the fraction of mankind who, in the normal distribution of innate intelligence, are men of superior endowments. In support of this faith in the educability of mankind, it seems reasonable to surmise that all the educational efforts so far made have not yet adequately explored or assessed the potentialities of the human mind. It may hold learning power to be released as far in excess of the power that we now employ by any educational means known to us, as thermonuclear power exceeds all other available forms of physical energy.

(2)

We must proceed on this faith to invent the ways and means of providing effective liberal schooling for every child and for sustaining liberal learning throughout the lifetime of every adult My reason for saying this is that the educational development projected in these terms is as necessary as world government and a world-wide economy of plenty for the coming to be of a society that will serve and promote the pursuit of happiness by every member of the human race.

There is nothing novel or strange about stipulating an educational effort or outlining an educational program commensurate with the aims that the political institutions of a society are designated to serve. In the oligarchical republics of the past, the effort to provide liberal education for the ruling class was commensurate with the aim of such societies to promote the pursuit of happiness by the privileged few, as well as to prepare that few for the duties of political life. With the emergence of what are at best only first approximations to the classless society in the socialist democracies that exist today, the same quality of education that once was provided for the few should be provided for all, in order for the educational effort to be commensurate with the aims of the classless society. But all that we have managed to accomplish so far is the gradual extension of free public schooling so that no children are left out; but neither the number of children in school nor the quantity of schooling provided them answers the need if the quality of the schooling that all of them receive does not correspond to what is needed for citizenship and the pursuits of leisure. [1]

The educational maxim to which a socialist, democratic republic is committed demands equal educational opportunity for all— equal in quality as well as equal in quantity. What this means is that every human being should be educated up to his capacity, with the proviso added that every human being should be recognized as having a capacity to be educated for citizenship and for the pursuits of leisure, not just a capacity to be vocationally trained for the performance of some task involved in earning a living. As we contemplate a future in which a world political community in the form of a union of socialist, democratic republics will replace the parochial societies that exist today, the educational maxim just stated imposes a burden that may be difficult to discharge, for it dedicates the ideal society of the future to an effective liberal education for all members of the human race. [2]

Whether or not this burden *can* be discharged or *will* be discharged is a matter of prediction about which there can be reasonable disagreement; but that it *should* be discharged is a prescription that is inseparable from the other prescriptions which derive from our vision of the best society that it is now possible to achieve. If the educational development that is called for is not forthcoming, then the other developments with which we have been concerned as necessary steps toward the realization of the ideal will either be frustrated or rendered futile. Even if that were not the case, even if the best society that is now possible were to come into existence and become operative in the absence of any effective educational effort commensurate with that society's aims, its ultimate end would not be served; for without liberal schooling, the pursuit of happiness is crippled at the outset.

Before I leave this matter, I would like to add one concluding observation. The fact that all human beings would probably not make a good use of the best educational opportunities, were they provided, does not alter the rightness of the prescription that they should be provided for all. The same holds true for all the other institutions of a good society. The fact that everyone would not utilize the beneficent conditions that such institutions afford for leading a good life does not in any way detract from the rightness of the commitment to develop the best society that is possible on earth. To think otherwise would be to question the rightness of emancipating all men from slavery and subjection on the ground that all are not likely to use their freedom well.

CHAPTER 18

Change, Revolution, and Progress

(1)

THE three developments that we have been considering can, in a loose sense of the term, be called revolutionary changes. They can also be described as changes that constitute progress toward the realization of the political ideal. But if, when it is asked how these changes are to be brought about, the answer is "By revolutions," another meaning of that troublesome term is introduced, and we must make a few distinctions if we are to keep our discourse clear.

The three terms that require clarification, especially in relation to one another, are change, progress, and revolution. Two of these three terms are value free; that is, they do not involve a moral judgment. Change may be for better or for worse, but change itself is neither good nor bad. To desire change for its own sake, without regard to the moral quality of the end result, is moral idiocy. Words that are sometimes misused as synonyms for change—such as "growth" or "development"—may have, but do not necessarily have, the moral connotation of change for the better. Other words in the same family of terms, such as "increase" and "decrease," are, like "change," morally neutral. Change of quantity, whether in the direction of more or of less, may be a change either for better or worse.

What is true of "change" does not, at first glance, appear to be true of "revolution," for we do not use that word to signify *any* change, but only changes that we think are important or great, not insignificant or slight. It is in this sense of the term that we speak of an industrial revolution or a technological revolution, or of an educational revolution, a cultural revolution, a revolution in the arts, and so on. On closer examination, however, we find that the question of values is not definitely answered, though it is frequently begged. The change that we call a revolution because we deem it to be a large change of some importance may be a change for better or for worse.

As we have already observed, the technological advances that we sometimes refer to as the technological revolution, involve extraordinary increases in the power available for use; but while this is an important change and a large one, it remains an open question whether it is a change for better or for worse. How that question is to be answered depends on the quality of the use to which the power is put. In the sphere of our political institutions, it should be obvious that what we call a revolution may result in either a better or a worse state of affairs. Republics have been overthrown and replaced by despotisms, as in ancient Rome and modern Germany or Greece; and, as we know, changes in the opposite direction have also taken place. When we regard these changes as revolutions, regardless of the direction in which they move, we are making the judgment that the changes are important, but not that they involve improvements.

In the political sphere, there is another variable that enters into our use of the term "revolution." An important institutional change that may be a change either for better or worse may also be a change brought about by violence or by peaceful means. The overthrow of the Tarquins in Rome and the establishment of the republic exemplify an important change for the better accomplished by violence; the democratization of the American republic by the amendment of its constitution and by gradual extensions of the franchise represents an important change for the better by legal or civil means—without the violence of insurrection. It must be added that history affords us few if any instances of important changes in the opposite direction— the replacement of republics by despotisms or of democracies by oligarchies—that were not accomplished by fraud or violence.

What we have learned so far is that the notion of revolution involves only one note that distinguishes it from change; namely, that of importance or magnitude. The other variables remain inteterminate—whether it is change for better or worse, and whether it is brought about by violence or by peaceful means. Revolution, thus understood, is, like change, morally neutral. In itself, apart from the moral quality of the result or the manner in which the result is achieved, it is neither good nor bad. Hence to desire revolution for its own sake is, like desiring change for its own sake, a manifestation of moral idiocy.

(2)

In contradistinction to change and revolution, progress is not a value-free or morally neutral term. It is sometimes misused to signify any important change that involves augmentation or increase—a change in the direction of more rather than less. But just as no one would regard an increase in the size of a cancer as an improvement in health, so no one would call an increase in the size of the military establishment an improvement in the body politic. Neither constitutes progress when that is conceived as a change for the better. I shall use the term in that sense and that sense only.

Since some revolutions are changes for the better, some are instances of progress. Revolutions in the opposite direction are instances of regress. As we have seen, changes for the better in the sphere of politics—improvements in the institutions of society—can be accomplished either by violent or by peaceful means. It would be useful to employ terms in such a way that we can distinguish the manner in which the institutional improvement is accomplished.

The reason is that violence can be justified only as a last resort. If there is no way of rectifying injustice other than by resort to violence, then and only then is violence to be condoned as a means to the good result that is desired. To recommend violence for its own sake or even as preferable to non-violent means is to prefer war to peace, or anarchy to government.

Since political justice and civil peace are both indispensable conditions of a good human life, our aim should be to achieve the one without sacrificing the other, so far as that is possible. Only if the rectification of injustice requires breaching the peace because no peaceful means are readily available, is violence justifiable as a last resort—a drastic remedy *in extremis*. [1]

To keep this basic normative principle clearly before our minds, I propose to use terms in the following manner. I will describe all changes for the better as progress. I will use the term "civil progress" for institutional improvements accomplished by peaceful means. Those that involve a justifiable resort to violence, I will call "revolutionary progress."

The distinction that should be made between civil dissent and revolutionary action is related to the distinction that I have just proposed. Civil dissent is protest by peaceful means and, therefore, presupposes consent to the general framework of government. It is a way of opposing a particular act or policy of government without withdrawing consent from the government as constituted. Revolutionary action is dissent carried to an extreme that involves a temporary or permanent withdrawal of consent. It is opposition to the government as constituted, and so it inevitably becomes dissent by violent means. Like civil dissent and unlike revolutionary action, civil disobedience is non-violent and occurs within the boundaries of consent. But civil disobedience should not be confused with civil dissent for, unlike civil dissent, it is always and only refusal by an individual to obey a particular law that he regards as repugnant to his conscience because it commands him to perform an act that he regards as unjust; and his disobedience, while law-breaking, remains lawful by virtue of his willingness to accept the legal penalty for breaking the law. In contrast, civil dissent, as a form of peaceful protest by individuals or groups against governmental acts or policies that do not require them to perform acts that they regard as unjust, need not and should not involve unlawful action on their part even when it is directed against laws—or policies or acts of government—deemed by them to be unwise or unjust. [2]

A well-constituted government should provide juridical means for the redress of all grievances, including juridical allowances for all forms of civil dissent and civil disobedience. The ideal just stated is difficult to achieve perfectly, especially if considerations of time become important—the time required to rectify injustice by juridical means. [3] Nevertheless, the ideal is approximated to some degree by all *de jure* governments, as it is not approximated in the least by *de facto* governments.

In other words, in societies under *de facto* government, only revolutionary action is possible, and it is justified when it is employed for the sake of revolutionary progress—improvement in the institutions of society by violent means. In societies under *de jure* government, revolutionary action may be justified if juridical means are either not available or not temporally adequate for the rectification of injustices that should be quickly remedied; [4] but in such societies, it will also be possible to achieve civil progress through the improvement of institutions by peaceful means. To whatever extent that is possible, revolutionary action cannot be justified as a way of bringing about those improvements.

With this clarification of terms, we are now in a position to ask two concluding questions, both looking to the future.

One concerns the limits of political progress and, in that context, asks whether we can look forward to a future in which no further institutional progress will be made, either by peaceful or by revolutionary means. The other question involves clairvoyance, for it calls upon us to imagine the future of man if the human race continues in existence after the limits of institutional progress have been reached. I will attempt to answer these two questions briefly in the concluding chapter of this book.

CHAPTER 19

Our Limited Vision of the Possible

(1)

THIS book, in attempting to state the principles of a normative political philosophy, has been devoted to projecting
a realizable political ideal, not a utopian fancy—the best
society that is now seen to be possible, one that is perfectly just
in its institutions and one that provides all men with the conditions which they need in order to lead good human lives.
Until that ideal is realized, there is room for progress—either
civil progress or revolutionary progress.

We can look forward to a future in which there will be
progressive revolutions, as there have been in the past, so long
as violence must be resorted to as the only means available for
rectifying the injustices that still prevail in all existing societies.

The three major developments that I have described as necessary for the realization of the ideal—developments needed for
the conservation of the biosphere, for the elimination of poverty,
racism, and war, and for the intelligent participation of all men
as citizens of a world republic—are of such magnitude and such
urgency that it may not be possible in the time allowed to con-
summate them by peaceful means. In that case, revolutionary
action will have to be taken and will be justified. But if the
revolutions do occur and are successful or if the ends in view
are achieved wholly or partly by peaceful means, then the
state of affairs that will result from the civil or revolutionary
progress that is made may represent the limit of institutional
progress.

The need for institutional progress is always the same: injustice or deprivation of one sort or another. In all the class-divided societies of the past, and in the still imperfect approximations to the ideal of the classless society that are to be found in the best of existing socialist, democratic republics, revolution is always brewing, and there is room for progress to be made. There is no reason to suppose that this will not continue into the future as long as the same causes are operative. And as long as institutional progress is possible, revolutionary action may be justifiable, but there can be no justification for revolution when further progress cannot be made. [1] On the other hand, there is no reason to suppose that institutional progress by whatever means must necessarily continue forever or beyond the point at which the causes cease to be operative, because no injustices will remain to be rectified and no deprivations will remain to be remedied.

In other words, institutional progress, whether civil or revolutionary, can and should continue until the rights of all men everywhere are secured by the justice of the state and its government and until the conditions of a good human life are provided all men everywhere by the effort of the organized community to supply its people with goods that they need but which they, as individuals, cannot obtain for themselves. There is thus a limit to institutional progress and one that is conceivably not beyond attainment within a finite time.

(2)

If that conclusion seems unduly optimistic, let me hasten to qualify it by one comment on politics as the art of the possible. I have proceeded throughout this book in terms of the vision of the possible that is now available to us in the light of past and present experience. Our enlarged conception of the possible, I have said, has enabled us to project a political ideal far beyond anything that our ancestors would have thought attainable. But I have also said that political philosophy is always conditioned by the historic limitations of the time in which it is being formulated. This is as true of any twentieth-century effort as it was true of the political formulations made in earlier centuries. The same mote that clouded the vision of earlier political philosophers still clouds our own, even if we are not so aware of it.

In the uprising that took place at the Sorbonne a few years ago, a student chalked up on the wall the following graffito: *Be realistic; attempt the impossible!* On the face of it, considered soberly and strictly, the statement is, of course, false. The impossible is that which cannot be done; and, therefore, it should not be attempted by anyone in his right mind. Nevertheless, the statement is a witty way of expressing the truth that the determination of what is possible or impossible is an extremely difficult matter, involving more knowledge of facts than is generally available at any time; and so, as this student was really saying, the spirit of progress should always challenge those who seek to preserve the *status quo* by claiming that the changes called for by justice lie beyond the bounds of the possible.

The same insight applies to our vision of a future state of affairs that precludes the possibility of further progress because all the institutional improvements that are needed for the happiness of mankind have been achieved. That vision may be defective, because we cannot foresee the effect on human life of factors that have not yet become operative. The further development of space exploration, for one thing, and, for another, the development of our power to manipulate the genetic code may bring with them social problems and social opportunities so novel and so consequential that the possibility of progress may be enlarged beyond anything that we can now conceive. This, however, suggests the conclusion, not that institutional progress is without limits, but only that our present view of what its limits are may be inaccurate.

(3)

On the assumption, which it seems reasonable to make, that institutional progress has a definite limit even if we cannot correctly define it at this point in history, we are left with the question: Would reaching that limit mean the end of progress in human affairs? The answer is clearly no.

Before elucidating that answer, let me say a word in defense of the assumption on the basis of which the question is asked. There is nothing in the nature of man or of society and its institutions that makes it impossible to rectify all injustices and to remove all deprivations. If the limit of institutional progress is defined formally as the best possible society, in which all men will have the opportunity to make good lives for themselves, then that limit will be reached, or at least very closely approached, when revolutionary or civil progress has brought into existence a classless society that embraces all men in a world state under a world government that is constitutional, democratic, and socialistic. Nothing less than this will completely abolish war, racism, and poverty from the face of the earth; or maximize, through justice, freedom and equality for all.

Let us further suppose that the fullest realization of this political ideal is accompanied by satisfactory solutions of the population problem, the problem of preserving a healthful ecological balance in the environment, and the problem of providing effective liberal schooling for all. What then? What does the future hold for man beyond the point at which his institutions are perfected so that no injustices remain to be rectified and no deprivations remain to be remedied? What is the ultimate goal toward which the human race can and should collectively strive after all the external conditions of human life are optimal and stable?

Only one answer seems to be possible. Progress in human affairs will shift from the realm of externals—the realm of social, economic, and political institutions—to the interior life of man, the life of the mind and the spirit. Progress in institutions will be replaced by progress in individuals. The ultimate goal of human striving ought to be the fullest development of the potentialities of the human mind and spirit, a development that will not begin in earnest until the realization of the political ideal provides all men with the external conditions under which they can devote themselves to the highest pursuits of which the human race is capable—teaching and learning. [2]

When no obstacles or barriers stand in the way of the effective and sustained communication of the members of the human race with one another, and when the human mind is no longer distracted from concentration on what is important by the urgency of practical problems that press for solution, then the cooperative engagement of men in teaching and learning as lifelong pursuits should be the chief source of progress toward fulfilling the capacities for understanding and wisdom, for friendship and love, that are the distinctive powers of the human mind and spirit. [3]

Notes

NOTES TO CHAPTER 1

1. Proudhon's *What is Property; an Inquiry into the Principle of Right and Government* appeared in 1840–41; his *General Idea of the Revolution in the Nineteenth Century*, in 1851; Bakunin's *God and the State*, in 1871–72; Kropotkin's *The State, Its Historic Role*, in 1903; his *Anarchism: Its Philosophy and Ideal*, in 1904; Sorel's *Reflections on Violence*, in 1908.

2. Robert M. Hutchins, "Doing What Comes Scientifically," in *The Center Magazine*, January, 1969, p. 60.

3. See Paul Goodman, *The New Reformation: Notes of A Neolithic Conservative*, pp. 54–56; and J. H. Plumb, *The Death of the Past*.

4. See *The Conditions of Philosophy*, Ch. 8.

5. See *The Time of Our Lives*.

6. Published in 1936.

7. Cf. Leo Strauss, *What is Political Philosophy?* pp. 10–14, 17, 22; Isaiah Berlin, "Does Political Theory Still Exist?" in *Philosophy, Politics, and Society*, ed. by P. Laslett and W. G. Runciman, pp. 1–33; John Plamenatz, "The Use of Political Theory," in *Political Philosophy*, ed. by Anthony Quinton.

8. See my discussion of the three levels of normative or practical thought in *The Time of Our Lives*, pp. 193–196.

9. Cf. Leo Strauss, *op. cit.*, pp. 63–64.

10. *Ibid.*, p. 322; see also pp. 18–21, 194.

NOTES TO CHAPTER 2

1. See *The Time of Our Lives*, Ch. 19, esp. pp. 94–95.

2. See *ibid.*, pp. 5–6, 258–261, Note 2 on p. 333; and Note 17 on pp. 301–302. Since the end with which politics is concerned is the

good society, and since the good society is not an ultimate end but only an indispensable means to the good human life, which is the ultimate end of human action and the end with which ethics is concerned, politics is subordinate to ethics in the order of means and ends. But since the end with which ethics is concerned is the good life for the individual, whereas politics, in aiming at the good society, is concerned with the good life of a number of individuals, politics has a greater good in view, though it aims at this greater good indirectly through the ordination of the good society, which is its direct and immediate objective, to the good life for man, which is its remote and ultimate objective.

3. See *ibid.*, pp. 140–143.

4. See *ibid.*, pp. 122–123, 203–205, and Notes 17 and 18 on p. 293.

5. See *ibid.*, pp. 183–184.

6. See *The Time of Our Lives*, esp. Ch. 9–11, 13–16, for argument in support of the ethical principles presupposed by the political philosopher.

7. See *ibid.*, pp. 104–109.

8. See *ibid.*, pp. 207–209.

9. See *ibid.*, pp. 140–147.

10. See *ibid.*, pp. 182–184.

11. See *ibid.*, pp. 180–182, and Note 7 on pp. 315–316.

NOTES TO CHAPTER 3

1. See *The Time of Our Lives*, Ch. 17; and also an earlier book of mine, *The Difference of Man and the Difference It Makes*, esp. Ch. 8–11.

2. See *The Difference of Man and the Difference It Makes*, pp. 268–273, 288–290; and also my two volume work, *The Idea of Freedom*, Vol. I, Ch. 20–24; Vol. II, Ch. 8–12, 19.

3. See *The Time of Our Lives*, Ch. 12, esp. 122–123, and Notes 17 and 18 on p. 293.

4. See *ibid.*, Note 2 on pp. 307–308; and cf. *The Difference of Man and the Difference It Makes*, pp. 115–118, 271–279.

5. See *Man and Aggression,* ed. by M. F. Ashley Montague, esp. the essays by S. A. Barnett, Geoffrey Gorer, T. C. Scheirla, Sir Solly Zuckerman, and John Beatty.

6. See *The Time of Our Lives,* p. 120, Note 16 on p. 293, and Note 5 on p. 295. The fact that species come into existence and that extant species become extinct does not affect the point here being made; namely, that while a species remains extant, in the interval between its origin and its extinction, its genetic determination remains relatively constant. Correlative to that genetic constancy is the constancy of the species-specific properties that characterize all the members of a species so long as the species endures. The evidence is overwhelmingly clear that the distinctive functional characteristics of the genus *Homo,* and of its several species, are the related powers of propositional speech and conceptual thought. See my summary and appraisal of the evidence in *The Difference of Man and the Difference It Makes.* The successive speciation within the genus *Homo,* which first produced *Homo erectus* and then *Homo sapiens,* represents a transition from a lower to a higher degree of the same generic powers and of the species-specific properties to which they give rise. Further successive speciation would result in changes of the same sort. Since *Homo sapiens* is the only extant species in the genus *Homo,* no confusion should result from speaking of man's species-specific properties as those which are grounded in the genetically determined and genetically constant characteristics of the genus *Homo*—the power of conceptual thought and the derivative power of propositional speech. For a fuller discussion of species and of man as a species, see J. N. Deely, "The Emergence of Man," in *The New Scholasticism,* Vol. XL, No. 2, April, 1966, pp. 141-176; and "The Philosophical Dimensions of the Origin of Species," in *The Thomist,* Vol. XXX, Nos. 1 and 2, January and April, 1969, pp. 75-149, 251-342.

7. Cf. *The Difference of Man and the Difference It Makes,* pp. 263-268.

8. See *The Time of Our Lives,* pp. 149-150, and Note 11 on p. 301.

9. The single fact that man and man alone is a political animal, when that is fully understood in both its negative and its positive significance, completely repudiates books like Robert Ardrey's *The Social Contract,* which treat human society as essentially similar to other forms of instinctive animal association. The impertinence of Ardrey's title and of the dedication of his book to Jean-Jacques Rousseau, whom Ardrey does not begin to understand, is exceeded only by the pretentiousness of the argument and the irrelevance of the animal stories that abound in its pages.

NOTES TO CHAPTER 4

1. See *op. cit.*, Postscript, pp. 235–265.

2. See also Chapter 3, Note 6, *supra.*

3. In my Postscript to *The Time of Our Lives*, I pointed out that Aristotle's *Politics* "suffers much more from the limitations of the historic circumstances under which it was written than does the *Nichomachean Ethics*. It is relatively easy to universalize the truths found in the *Ethics* concerning the good life for man. . . . But to state the truths about the good society in an equally universal manner, one would have to repudiate much that is said in the *Politics*, transform in radical ways the sound conceptions it offers, and deal with many subjects it does not treat at all." The chief contribution of the *Politics* "lies in its one controlling insight that the standard by which a society, in all its aspects, is to be judged good or bad, better or worse, is the good life for the individual man"; in addition, it makes important contributions "to the theory of the state and of government (such as its account of the origin and nature of the state, its conceptions of constitutional government, of citizenship, and of political liberty)." See *op. cit.*, p. 261.

   Professor Leo Strauss criticizes the historicism, so prevalent in modern times, which denies that the classic works of ancient and mediaeval political philosophy contain any principles that are true for all times. See *What is Political Philosophy?* pp. 26, 40, 57, 59–60, 64–65. But he himself goes to the opposite extreme of denying that changing historical circumstances can lead to the discovery of new political truths and even to a better understanding or elucidation of truths already known. See *op. cit.*, pp. 67-72.

   The position that I am taking in this book occupies a middle ground between these two extremes. Against the extreme of historicism, I maintain that some of the principles discovered by earlier political philosophers are still true today in spite of the many technological and institutional changes that have occurred since their day. And against the opposite extreme represented by Professor Strauss, I maintain that altered historical conditions enabled modern political philosophers to discover truths not known to their ancient and mediaeval predecessors, that the radical changes of the last hundred years have occasioned radically new departures in political philosophy, and that our present vision of what is possible in the foreseeable future allows us to project as realizable ideals that would have been dismissed as utopian a hundred years ago.

4. See *The Conditions of Philosophy*, Ch. 7.

5. If one takes into consideration the ethical presuppositions of political philosophy, the latter cannot avoid some secondary reliance on common experience in the positive sense. Nevertheless, its primary reliance—so far as its own, purely political principles are concerned—is upon common experience in the negative sense.

6. Cf. Jacques Maritain, *The Rights of Man and Natural Law*, pp. 29–38, 49, 58–64; *Man and The State*, pp. 89–94; *On The Philosophy of History*, Ch. II–III. See also Yves Simon, *Community of the Free*, Ch. 3; and also Charles Van Doren, *The Idea of Progress*, Ch. 22–23.

7. See Note 3 *supra*.

NOTES TO CHAPTER 5

1. The revolutionary idea may be formulated and accepted only after institutional changes embodying that idea have been brought about by revolutionary action; but it is more often the case that the revolutionary idea first occurs as a protest against conditions that revolutionary action is needed to change. Even in these cases, the general acceptance of the idea follows upon the institutional changes that such revolutionary action succeeds in bringing about.

2. See Charles Howard McIlwain, *Constitutionalism Ancient and Modern*, Ch. II–IV.

3. See "An Agreement of the People," in *The People Shall Judge*, Vol. I, pp. 40–48.

4. See *The Annals of America*, ed, by M. J. Adler and C. Van Doren, Vol. 5, pp. 4–25.

5. Cf. Hans Morgenthau, *The Purpose of American Politics*, esp. pp. 11–37, 307–323.

6. While the United States had the good fortune to be born free of the heritage of European feudalism, its acquiescence in the African slave trade and its acceptance of the institution of chattel slavery have had social, economic, and political consequences that constitute a major blot on the American record, so far as the realization of the democratic ideal is concerned.

7. See Plato, *Republic*, Bk. 5; J. S. Mill, *Representative Government*, Ch. 8 (concluding pages). See also J. S. Mill, *The Subjection of*

Women, published in 1869; and V. I. Lenin, *The Emancipation of Women*. In the controversy between oligarchs and democrats over the extension of the suffrage, most of the early proponents of the democratic position—in fact, all except Mill—meant "all males" when they said "all men"; and their oligarchical opponents, when they argued for the exclusion from citizenship of some portion of the male population, either assumed or explicitly proclaimed the exclusion of all women. Cf. Chapter 11.

When in this book I discuss and defend the democratic ideal of political equality for all men, I hope that my readers will understand that I mean all human beings regardless of gender, not just all males. At this point in the twentieth century, I would like to think that that should not have to be said, but it certainly should not have to be said more than once.

8. See Yves Simon, *Community of the Free*, Ch. 4 on "Socialism and the Democracy of the Common Man"; *The Philosophy of Democratic Government* pp. 231–259.

9. See Chapter 12, *infra*.

10. See George Lichtheim, *The Origins of Socialism; A Short History of Socialism*.

NOTES TO CHAPTER 6

1. The argument here rests on three sets of exhaustive alternatives. (a) There are only two ways in which a group of individuals united for a common purpose can achieve concerted action under agreed upon decisions for their common good: one is for them to reach these decisions unanimously; the other is for them to institute an agency for making decisions the authority of which they unanimously acknowledge. (b) The authority that they institute must be either personal (one man or some number less than the number of the group as a whole) or collective (a determined upon preponderate fraction of the group as a whole, e.g., a majority). (c) The only alternative to the institution of authority by consent is the imposition by force of an agency for decision making. See Yves Simon, *The Philosophy of Democratic Government*, pp. 7–9, 18–20, 25–33, 190–194; cf. *A General Theory of Authority*, pp. 39–41, 47–49, 57–60; *Nature and Functions of Authority*, pp. 12–18, 16–18, 40–41. See also Jacques Maritain, *Scholasticism and Politics*, pp. 92–93, 97–98; R. S. Peters and P.

Winch, "Authority," in *Political Philosophy*, ed. by Anthony Quinton.

2. See Hobbes, *Leviathan*, Part II, Ch. XVII, XX; Locke, *Concerning Civil Government*, Second Essay, Ch. VIII, Sect. 95–98, 106, 112, 122; Rousseau, *The Social Contract*, Bk. I, Ch. 4–5; Kant, *The Science of Right*, Sect. 44, 46.

   Earlier expressions of the same fundamental insight do not employ the term "consent"; nor do they explicitly stress unanimity, as do Hobbes, Locke, Rousseau, and Kant. Nevertheless, both notions are implicitly present in Aristotle's conception of constitutional government as the government of free men and equals, in which the citizens rule and are ruled in turn; and also in Aquinas's view that governing and law-making belong either to the whole people or to someone who functions as vicegerent for the people as a whole. See Aristotle, *Politics*, Bk. I, Ch. 1, 1252^a 13–16; Bk. III, Ch. 4, 1277^b 7–9; Aquinas, *Summa Theologica*, Part I–II, Q. 90, A. 3.

   Unanimous consent on the part of the people as a whole defines the meaning of that often misused phrase "popular sovereignty"; it also helps us to distinguish "government of" the people from "government by" and "government for" the people. Government of the people does not mean that the people are the subjects of government; on the contrary, it means that they are its consenting constituents—the ultimate source of its authority. Cf. John Plamanetz, *Consent, Freedom and Political Obligation*, Ch. 1.

3. When the principle of authority is established by unanimity, a particular decision has authority for the individual who would himself have decided the matter differently. The individual, who may be a minority of one, may be practically right about the decision that ought to have been reached; but, nevertheless, the practically wrong decision of the leader or of the majority has authority for him if he has voluntarily acknowledged the decision-making authority that is essential to government.

4. See Locke, *Concerning Civil Government*, Second Essay, Sect. 19–20, 89–90; Kant, *The Science of Right*, Sect. 44.

5. See Yves Simon, *Nature and Functions of Authority*, pp. 7–9; 45; *Freedom and Community*, pp. 117–130; Jacques Maritain, *Scholasticism and Politics*, pp. 101–102.

6. An unjust law is a law in name only; lacking the authority of law, it represents an imposition of unauthorized force. See Yves Simon, *A General Theory of Authority*, pp. 163–166.

7. A civil police force is the coercive arm of a *de jure* government. It operates with constitutional authority and under constitutional limitations. This being the case, it is an astounding fact that the institution of a civil police force is a relatively late development in the history of constitutional government. See, for example, James F. Richardson, *The New York Police.* The republics of antiquity and, until fairly recently, modern republics employed civil police power only in the most rudimentary form, if at all. The military power at the command of a *de facto* government and one or another form of "secret police" are agencies of unauthorized force; their utilization for coercive purposes is violence. Cf. Charles Reith, *A New Study of Police History*; Raymond Fosdick, *European Police Systems.*

8. In the field of medicine, a drastic remedy which is necessary for the cure of an illness but which has injurious side effects that cannot be eliminated is a necessary evil. If the injustices to which even a *de jure* government is prone could not be eliminated, then government might be considered a necessary evil in an analogous sense. I will attempt to show in Chapters 9–13, *infra*, that there is no injustice that cannot be eliminated.

9. It may be objected that the need of even a perfectly just government to employ coercive force is analogous to an injurious side effect which cannot be eliminated; and so, like a form of therapy that cannot effectively serve the cause of health without also introducing an injurious side effect, a perfectly just government is a necessary evil because it cannot serve the purposes which make it good without also introducing the evil of coercive force. The answer to this objection consists in pointing out that in a society under a perfectly just government only unjust men are subject to coercion—only those who are inclined to disobey the rules or decisions of a duly constituted authority. Since the coercion of the unjust is not itself unjust, the objection fails.

10. See Yves Simon, *Nature and Functions of Authority*, pp. 28–30; *Philosophy of Democratic Government*, pp. 68–71.

NOTES TO CHAPTER 7

1. Those who identify the state with the institutions of civil government must, in consequence, distinguish between the state and civil society. In their view, civil society or the political community

includes the state as a component part of itself and is not coextensive with it. Even though the opposite view departs from what has come to be established usage, I think it is to be preferred. In this book, I will always use the word "state" to designate the political community or civil society as a whole, distinguished from other forms of society or community, such as the family or the tribe. Just as the family or the tribe is not coextensive with domestic or tribal government but involves many aspects that are not governmental, so the state—the political community or civil society—is not coextensive with civil government; it involves social, economic, and cultural activities, institutions, and relationships that lie outside the sphere of government. They may or may not be affected by the acts of government. Whether they should be or not is a point of critical importance in drawing the line between those aspects of the state or civil society that transcend the authority of government or fall outside its proper scope and those that are properly subject to its operations. See Yves Simon, *Freedom and Community*, p. 114; and cf. Maritain, *Man and the State*, pp. 9–19.

2. An independent community in relation to other independent communities is usually said to have "sovereignty" or to be a "sovereign state"; it is *not* under the jurisdiction of or government by any other state, in contrast to a colony or a dependency. Since this in effect means that an independent community is one which is not subject to rules or decisions except those of its own making, "autonomous" should be used to replace that troublesome word "sovereign."

3. In a federation of states, such as Switzerland or the United States, it is only the federal state itself that has autonomy or independence *vis-à-vis* other states. None of the Swiss cantons and none of the fifty states in the American federal union is an independent or autonomous state. Strictly speaking, therefore, none exists as a state, but only as an inferior corporation or community that is part of a state.

4. See Aristotle, *Politics*, Bk. I, Ch. 1–2. Cf. Yves Simon, *Freedom and Community*, pp. 130–140.

5. Three things distinguish parental from civil government: (a) the infant subject to parental government is governed without his consent; (b) parental government is absolute, not limited; and (c) when just rather than tyrannical, it aims directly at the good of the child, not directly at the good of the whole community, thus serving the good of its members indirectly. In consequence, the

authority of parental government differs from that of civil government; its justification lies in the infant's need to be governed for his own good and in the infant's incapacity to govern himself. See Locke, *Concerning Civil Government*, Second Essay, Ch. XV; and cf. Yves Simon, *Nature and Functions of Authority*, pp. 12–15.

6. What Locke says of absolute monarchy applies to any form of *de facto* government: "absolute monarchy is indeed inconsistent with civil society, and so can be no form of civil government at all" (*Concerning Civil Government*, Second Essay, Sect. 90). Cf. *ibid.*, Sect. 13, 91, 226.

7. Aristotle's declaration that "a state is not a community of living beings only, but a community of equals, aiming at the best life possible" (*Politics*, VII, 8, 1328ᵃ 37–38), combined with his definition of constitutional government as the government of free men and equals, entails the conclusion that the state that does not have a *de jure* government is a state in name only. The same conclusion is implied in the passages of Locke's second essay that are cited in Note 6, *supra*. The identification of a state with a republic is explicitly affirmed by Rousseau: see *The Social Contract*, Bk. I, Ch. 6. Kant uses the term "state" less restrictively, though he does assert that "the only rightful constitution . . . is that of a *pure* republic" (*The Science of Right*, Sect. 52). Cf. Yves Simon, *Freedom and Community*, pp. 130–140.

8. In the least perfect of states—the oligarchical republic—there is usually a multitude of human beings who are not members of the civil society or body politic, for they are not citizens with suffrage. Aristotle speaks of them as necessary to the existence of the state, though not participants in it. See Politics, III, 5, 1278ᵃ 1–6. Cf. *ibid.*, III, 9; VII, 8.

9. Chapter 16, *infra*, offers a fuller discussion of this subject. Cf. Jacques Maritain, *Man and the State*, pp. 188–211; Yves Simon, *Philosophy of Democratic Government*, pp. 67–68; and Robert M. Hutchins, *Aquinas and the World State*.

10. I have elsewhere dealt extensively with the question whether the state is ever justified in requiring the sacrifice of happiness (*totum bonum commune hominis*) for the good of the organized community (*bonum commune communitatis*). See *The Time of Our Lives*, pp 172–174, 177–182; Note 6 on pp. 311–315; and Note 7 on pp. 315–316.

11. The two passages in Aristotle that must be put together in order to see that he asserts that the state is conventional in the order of

efficient causality while at the same time natural in the order of final causality, occur within the campass of the same short chapter —Chapter 2 of Book I of the *Politics*. The chapter begins by emphasizing that the naturalness of the state consists in its being an indispensable means to the end that men ought to seek, namely, a good human life (1252^b 27–30). After several repetitions of the point that the state is needed because men cannot live well without it and that it is natural because man is by nature a political animal, Aristotle conjoins the remark that men are by nature gregarious or social (impelled to associate in communities, whether families, tribes, or states), with the observation that "he who first founded the state was the greatest of benefactors" (1253^a 30–31). That benefactor was the inventor of constitutional government—a man like Solon or Lycurgus.

Although Rousseau explicitly asserts that, "of all societies, the only one that is natural is the family" (*The Social Contract*, Bk. I, Ch. 2), the reason he gives for the naturalness of the family is one that he himself makes applicable to the state. The family, he says, is natural because it is needed for the preservation of its offspring during their infancy or immaturity. Its naturalness, in short, is in the order of final causality—as a means indispensable to an end desired. "If they [children and parents] remain united" after this need is satisfied, then, according to Rousseau, "they continue to do so no longer naturally, but voluntarily; and the family itself is then maintained only by convention" (*ibid.*). At the very point at which he introduces the social compact as the convention which is the originating efficient cause of the state's coming into existence, Rousseau explains that the human race would perish unless it departed from the "state of nature" and entered into "civil society" (*ibid.*, Ch. 6). Since civil society or the state is needed by man for his survival, it is natural or necessary as an indispensable means to an end desired, just as the union of children and parents in the family is natural or necessary. The difference between Aristotle and Rousseau lies not in the fact that one asserts the state to be purely natural and the other asserts it to be purely conventional, but rather in the fact that, for Rousseau, the naturalness of the state (in the order of final causality) consists in its being needed for survival, whereas for Aristotle it consists in its being needed for the perfection of human life—for human happiness. With regard to the conventionality of the state (in the order of efficient causality), they differ in language rather than in principle: for Aristotle, the efficient cause of the state's origin is the invention of a constitution; for Rousseau, it is the social contract, but since the social contract results in the formation of a republic (a state under *de jure* or constitutional government), the difference disappears.

The foregoing interpretation of Rousseau applies to Hobbes, Locke, and Kant. The "natural laws" that impel men to enter into the contract that forms the state or body politic are all remedies for the infelicity and misery of human life in a "state of nature" (i.e., a state of anarchy). Nothing could be plainer than that, in Hobbes's view, the state of nature is totally repugnant to the nature of man. See *Leviathan*, Part I, Ch. XIII–XIV, and Part II, Ch. XVII. Similarly for Locke, men are impelled to quit the "state of nature" and to enter into civil society by compact, in order to overcome all the "inconveniences" that result from the absence of civil government—inconveniences that include the deprivation of freedom, equality, and peace, all of them goods that are indispensable to the pursuit of happiness. Hence for Locke as for Aristotle, the state or civil society is necessary as a means to the good life, not just as a means of survival. See *Concerning Civil Government*, Second Essay, Sect. 13, 123, 127. Though for Kant the replacement of the "state of nature" by civil society springs from a moral obligation rather than from a natural need, the underlying point remains the same: men cannot live as men—humanly or morally—in the absence of civil society. See *The Science of Right*, Sect. 41–42, 44.

The misinterpretation of the modern social-contract theorists would probably not have occurred had the misleading phrase "state of nature" been totally avoided and the absence of civil society under civil government always been described as a condition of "anarchy." With this pair of opposites or contraries—anarchy, on the one hand, and civil society, on the other—it would have been immediately obvious that if anarchy is the most unnatural condition for man as a social and political animal, then civil society is the most natural. And when the naturalness of civil society or the state is thus understood, there is no difficulty in understanding that though it is natural in the order of final causality (as the necessary means to ends naturally desired by man), the state is also conventional in the order of efficient causality (as something invented by men and instituted voluntarily by agreement and consent).

12. If men could live well—achieve happiness or make good lives for themselves—without living in states, the state would not be practically or morally necessary; and it is solely by virtue of its being practically or morally necessary that the state is natural. The state is not naturally necessary as the beehive and the ant-mound

are. The beehive and the ant-mound are instinctive, not voluntary, associations, arising, by way of efficient not final causality, from the nature of the species of organisms that populate them. Precisely because it is a voluntary association that is necessary only as a means, the fact that the state is a whole of which its human members are parts does not lead to the false conclusion that the parts exist for the sake of the whole. Herein lies the truth of the proposition that man is not made for the state, but the state for man. The opposite and false view is held by those who regard the state as an organic whole, either by analogy with the living body, the members of which are its organic parts; or by analogy with the beehive or ant-mound, the members of which are instinctively driven to act for the preservation of the hive or mound and so for the perpetuation of the species. The beehive and the ant-mound do not exist for the good of its individual members, but for the good of the instinctively formed animal society and, ultimately, for the preservation of the species. For the preservation of the body, it is sometimes necessary to sacrifice one or another of its organic parts —the loss of an arm or a leg; but it is never necessary to sacrifice the human common good for the good of the organized community. (See Note 10, *supra*.) If the state were either like a living body or like a beehive and ant-mound, then the good of the state would be paramount, and men would serve it as mere means. Instead, the good of man is paramount, and the good of the organized community is always subordinated to that supreme good.

There are passages in Aristotle and Aquinas that appear to speak in an opposite tenor. They are inconsistent with what I regard as the controlling texts in these two authors. For an interpretation and criticism of these passages, see "The Theory of Democracy, Part III," by Mortimer Adler and Walter Farrell, in *The Thomist*, Vol. IV, 1942: p. 137, Note 130; pp. 336–337, Note 263. For an exposition of the controlling texts with which they are inconsistent, see *ibid.*, pp. 132–133; 135, Note 129; 318–319, 341–343, and esp. Note 299 on p. 343.

13. The ant-mound or beehive is natural in a sense that precludes voluntariness and convention. On the other hand, a business corporation or a baseball club is conventional and adventitious in a sense that precludes its being natural in any sense. Only the basic human communities—the family, the tribe, and the state— are both natural and conventional: the way in which they are natural not only allows but calls for their conventional formation; the manner in which they are conventional is grounded in their naturally desired ends.

14. See Note 11, *supra*. That the "state of nature," which is more properly to be called a "condition of anarchy," is unnatural or contrary to nature confirms the truth of the proposition that man is by nature not only a social but a political animal—social in that he needs the goods of communal life, especially civil peace, in order not only to live but to live well, humanly and morally; political, in that he is able by intelligently contrived arrangements and by voluntary agreements, to institute civil society and civil government as means to achieve these ends.

NOTES TO CHAPTER 8

1. See the passages cited in Notes 1, 2, and 4 to Chapter 6; and in notes 6, 7, 11, and 12 to Chapter 7, *supra*. Cf. Charles Howard McIlwain, *The Growth of Political Thought in the West;* Leo Strauss, "Plato," Harry V. Jaffa, "Aristotle," Laurence Berns, "Thomas Hobbes," Robert A. Goldwin, "John Locke," Allan Bloom, "Jean-Jacques Rousseau," in *History of Political Philosophy*, ed. by Leo Strauss and Joseph Cropsey; Sheldon S. Wolin, *Politics and Vision*, Ch. Two, Eight, Ten; E. F. Carritt, *Morals and Politics*, Ch. I, II, VI–VIII; John Plamenatz, *Man and Society*, Vol. I, Ch. 4, 6, 10; John Dunn, *The Political Thought of John Locke;* Ernst Cassirer, *The Question of Jean-Jacques Rousseau.*

2. See Chapter 1, Note 1, *supra*. The one always mentioned exception to the recency of philosophical anarchism is Zeno the Greek Stoic. See D. Novak, "The Sources and Varieties of Anarchism," in *Patterns of Anarchy*, ed. by Leonard I. Krimerman and Lewis Perry, pp. 6–9; J. Joll, *The Anarchists;* G. Woodcock, *Anarchism.*

3. See *Patterns of Anarchy*, pp. 38–39, 44–46, 83–93, 104–115, 185–206, 223–237, 281–330, 336–345. Cf. P. J. Proudhon, *General Idea of the Revolution in the Nineteenth Century;* G. P. Maximoff, ed., *The Political Philosophy of Bakunin: Scientific Anarchism,* Peter A. Kropotkin, *Anarchism: Its Philosophy and Ideal; The State, Its Historic Role;* Georges Sorel, *Reflections on Violence.*

4. See V. I. Lenin, *State and Revolution*, esp. Ch. 1 and 5; and also G. Plekhanov's critique of Bakunin and Kropotkin, in his *Anarchism and Socialism*, pp. 96–100, 128–141. The Marxist doctrine, as expounded by Lenin, of the gradual withering away of the state differs from the direct action anarchism of Bakunin as the gradualism of the Fabian Socialists differs from the direct action socialism of the Marxists.

5. See Herbert Spencer, *The Man versus The State*, with an intro-
   duction by Albert Jay Nock; Henry David Thoreau, *Civil Dis-
   obedience*; Bertrand Russell, *Roads to Freedom*, esp. Ch. II–III, V,
   VIII; Paul Goodman, *The New Reformation: Notes of a Neolithic
   Conservative*, Part III; *People or Personnel*. Cf. Milton Mayer,
   Man v. the State; Noam Chomsky, "Notes on Anarchism," in the
   New York Review of Books, Vol. XIV, No. 10, May 21, 1970, pp.
   31–35.

6. See *Patterns of Anarchy*, p. 44; and cf. Max Stirner, *The Ego and
   His Own*.

7. See Georges Sorel, *Reflections on Violence*, Ch. 4–5; and cf.
   Mortimer J. Adler, *The Idea of Freedom*, Vol. I, pp. 373–375.

8. See V. I. Lenin, *State and Revolution;* and Mortimer J. Adler,
   The Idea of Freedom, Vol. I, pp. 375–379. Cf. Note 4, *supra*.

9. See *Patterns of Anarchy*, pp. 68–69; and cf. Henri De Lubac,
   The Un-Marxian Socialist: A Study of Proudhon; James H. Jack-
   son, *Marx Proudon, and European Socialism;* George Lichtheim,
   A Short History of Socialism, pp. 131, 203, 213–223, 230–231, 311.

10. See *Patterns of Anarchy*, pp. 185–206, 223–237, 281–330, 543–553.

11. See *ibid.*, pp. 559–561.

12. See *ibid.*, p. 38, 188–191, 195–203, 252–253, 511–514, 559–560; and
    cf. Franz Oppenheimer, *The State*, pp. 3, 5, 14–15, 27.
    If, on the other hand, the distinction between *de jure* and *de
    facto* government is valid and tenable, there can be an authorized
    use of coercive force which is as distinct from violence as auth-
    orized or *de jure* government itself is distinct from unauthorized
    or *de facto* government. Furthermore, when in the operation of *de
    jure* government, a minority obeys a law with which it disagrees
    and against which it voted, it does so voluntarily and not under
    coercion. See Chapter 6, Note 3, *supra;* and also Chapter 13, *infra*.
    See also V. I. Lenin, *State and Revolution*, p. 68; and Bertrand
    Russell, *Roads to Freedom*, pp. 50, 68, 197–201.
    The error made by the anarchists is the identification of author-
    ity with coercion. This leads them to wish to supplant the authority
    of government with the complete autonomy of individuals, and to
    hope for the maintenance of society and civil peace entirely by
    means of decisions unanimously agreed to, and persuasively, not
    coercively, enforced. One can reject these errors while agreeing
    with the anarchists' repudiation of all forms of illegitimate or
    usurped authority, the injustices of tyranny and despotism, the
    use of coercive force in excess of what is authorized or needed, the

monolithic centralization of the totalitarian state, with no residual autonomy for subordinate corporations, associations, or individuals, and so on.

The extremism to which the anarchist goes is, perhaps, best exemplified by Godwin's vision of a society in which civil peace is maintained without the existence or enforcement of criminal law. See *Patterns of Anarchy*, pp. 195–204. It is such extremism that caused Bertrand Russell to reject the anarchist position as unsound: see *Roads to Freedom*, pp. 121–123, 125–136, 144–145, 197–199.

13. See *Patterns of Anarchy*, pp. 386–396.

14. See *ibid.*, pp. 107, 110–111, 113. Cf. Mortimer J. Adler, *The Idea of Freedom*, Vol. II, Ch. 7, esp. pp. 215–217. See also Note 17, *infra*.

15. See Chapter 3, Note 6, *supra*.

16. The critical point here being made is one that Godwin is compelled to ignore or deny, for to acknowledge its truth would require him to depart from his view that society and civil peace are compatible with the retention of complete autonomy by individuals associated in a common life. See *Patterns of Anarchy*, pp. 186–188, 191.

17. Alexander Hamilton said: "If men were angels, no government would be necessary." See *The Federalist*, No. 51. But even if men were somewhat like angels, in being able to act like purely rational beings even though, unlike angels, they had bodily passions, government would still be necessary because purely rational beings having finite or limited intellectual power could still find themselves in reasonable disagreement about what should be done in particular cases.

The consideration by the Christian theologian of the purely hypothetical society that might have existed in Eden if Adam and Eve and their progeny had not been expelled from their earthly Paradise, provides us with another confirmation of the necessity of government even under the contrafactual supposition that men are not only perfectly rational but also completely virtuous. The human beings the theologian is imagining are in every way as idyllic as the "new men" posited by the anarchist for the realization of his dream of a society without government or law.

Thomas Aquinas, answering the question "Whether in the State of Innocence [i.e., in Eden] Man Would Have Been Master over Man?" points out that "mastership has a twofold meaning. First, as opposed to slavery, in which sense a master is one to whom another is subject as a slave. In another sense . . . even he who has the office of governing and directing free men can be called a master. In the state of innocence man could have been master of men, not in the former but in the latter sense. . . . A man is the master of a free subject by directing him towards his proper welfare or to the common good" (*Summa Theologica*, Part I, Q. 96, A. 4). Hence in Eden, with man in a state of innocence, government would have been necessary for the promotion of the common good, though there would not have been any need to resort to coercive force for the maintenance of civil peace. See Yves Simon's commentary on this statement by Aquinas, in his *Philosophy of Democratic Government*, pp. 59–62.

18. The proposition that man is pacific by nature and the proposition that man is aggressive by nature are contraries, not contradictories, and so while both cannot be true, both can be false. All the evidence indicates that they are both false; i.e., that man is by specific nature (by species-specific genetic determination) neither pacific nor aggressive. The truth of the matter is that some men are more or less pacific and some are more or less aggressive. This being so, the varying degrees of pacific and aggressive characters are manifestations of individual differences, not of species-specific human nature. As such, they may be in part the result of inherited individual differences in bodily make-up and emotional temperament, but they are probably also, in larger part, the result of nurtural influences and cultural conditioning. See Chapter 3, pp. 33–36, *supra*.

19. It is interesting to observe that the philosophical anarchist sees eye to eye with the extreme political conservative in rejecting the doctrines of the social contract and the consent of the governed. See *Patterns of Anarchy*, pp. 246–250; and cf. Jonathan Boucher, *A View of the Causes and Consequences of the American Revolution*, in *The Annals of America*, ed. by M. J. Adler and C. Van Doren, Vol. 2, pp. 346–347; George Fitzhugh, *Sociology for the South*, in *ibid.*, Vol. 8, pp. 249–250.

20. What states and governments have been from their historic beginnings up to the present moment does not support the conclusion that the injustices to which they have always been prone cannot be eliminated in the future. Those who sympathize with the anarchist position see only one face of history; they are exclusively preoccupied with the fact that certain evils or injustices which still exist have existed throughout the past, and from this they infer that injustice is inherent in the very nature of the state and government. But history has another face to show for those who will

look at it: therein can be seen the progress that has been achieved through the improvement of institutions, resulting in the elimination or reduction of injustices. The fact that certain injustices have been rectified and others have been minimized is ground for the reasonable hope that all can be removed, in the future as in the past, by institutional reforms or improvements.

NOTES TO CHAPTER 9

1. See *The Time of Our Lives,* pp. 143–144; see also *ibid.,* pp. 144–146, 183–184, 205–209.

2. Justice as applied to states and governments is multidimensional or multifaceted. Clearly, if a government can be unjust in a number of different ways, it can also be just in diverse ways. When we speak of one state or government being more or less just than another, this attribution of a higher or lower degree of justice must be interpreted as meaning that the state or government which is said to be more just is just in more of the various respects in which justice can be done by states or governments. A perfectly just state or government would be one that is just in all the respects in which it is under an obligation to do justice.

   Three aspects of political justice can be distinguished: political institutions or acts are (a) just insofar as they respect or secure natural rights, and unjust insofar as they transgress or violate them; (b) just insofar as they treat equals equally and unequals unequally in proportion to their inequality; and unjust insofar as they do the reverse; and (c) just insofar as they promote the goods of communal life, and unjust insofar as they act against the accomplishments of these ends. The summary statement that justice consists in rendering to each man what is his due covers all three aspects, if it is broadly enough interpreted; the same might be said of the summary statement that justice consists in acting for the common good *(bonum commune hominis,* not merely *bonum commune communitatis).* See Otto Bird, *The Idea of Justice,* Ch. 5–7, esp. pp. 163–168.

   With regard to the diverse respects in which a law can be just or unjust, see Thomas Aquinas, *Summa Theologica,* Part I–II, Q. 96, A. 4. There is no difficulty in discerning the justice of laws that prohibit acts that injure other individuals. But regulations such as those that proscribe the possession or use of certain harmful drugs would appear to prohibit harming one's self rather than others. Such laws or the laws prescribing compulsory education derive their justice from their being directed toward the good of the organized community *(bonum commune communitatis)*, not from the fact that they direct the individual to act for his own ultimate good *(bonum commune hominis)*. Cf. John Stuart Mill, *On Liberty*, Ch. 4.

3. The anarchist would say that everyone has a right to govern himself, meaning by that being completely autonomous and obeying one's self alone. Self-government, when it is properly understood as a political institution, does not consist in complete autonomy (which excludes all political institutions); it consists rather in being subject to *de jure* government, the authority of which the individual has acknowledged by freely given consent, and in the processes of which he is juridically entitled to participate as a citizen with suffrage. An association of self-governing individuals, in this sense of the term, is a community of persons who are governed as free men and equals.

   With regard to *de jure* or constitutional government as the government of free men and equals and, therefore, as the only form of government that secures man's natural right to political liberty and equality, see Mortimer J. Adler and Walter Farrell, "The Theory of Democracy," Part V, in *The Thomist*, Vol. VIII, No. 1, January, 1944, pp. 85, 87–88, 91–94.

4. In other words, a government can be despotic without being tyrannical; that is, it can deprive men of the right to self-government while at the same time not depriving them of other rights. We need not turn back to the benevolent despotisms of the past to illustrate the point. Many of the welfare states in the world today operate under governments that are in practice, if not in principle, despotic; but in being dedicated, through the adoption of one or another socialist program, to promoting the general economic equality and welfare of their people, they do justice in respect of the natural rights they serve, while also doing injustice in respect of the natural rights they violate, especially the rights to political liberty and equality.

5. Cf. Yves Simon, *Philosophy of Democratic Government*, pp. 129–137; *Nature and Functions of Authority*, pp. 45–46; *A General Theory of Authority*, pp. 137–139.

6. See esp. Chapter 18, *infra*. The right to dissent through juridical means is inseparable from the right to self-government, which is in turn an aspect of the natural right to political liberty and equality. But the right of rebellion, understood as the right to resort to force

or violence in order to overthrow an unjust government, is not a natural right in and of itself, though revolutionary action may be justified by an appeal to natural rights that have been violated. When we speak of the "right of revolution," we are saying no more than that, under certain circumstances, revolutionary action can be rightful or justifiable action. There are no natural needs or real goods to which the so-called "right of revolution" corresponds, as there are in the case of the right to earn a decent subsistence, the right to an education, the right to political liberty and freedom of action, etc.

It is sometimes said that governments have the right to suppress or put down revolutionary action attempting to accomplish their overthrow. As in the case of the so-called "right of revolution," the question being raised here is not a matter of natural right, but rather an issue concerning the justifiability of the action in question. Under certain circumstances, governments are justified in suppressing revolutionary action, even as, under certain circumstances, rebels are justified in having recourse to such action as a last resort. Cf. the opposed views of John Lewis and Jacques Maritain in the UNESCO Symposium on Human Rights, pp. 54–77.

NOTES TO CHAPTER 10

1. If the freedom of complete autonomy is possessed by individuals attempting to live socially or lead a common life, it will, of course, be accompanied by the total absence of governmental coercion, but it will also probably be attended by the coercion or intimidation of one individual by another or of one group by another.

2. See Locke, *Concerning Civil Government,* Second Essay, Sect. 21.

3. Whereas John Stuart Mill makes freedom from law or government the individual's only freedom, Locke regards such liberty, to do as one pleases where the law prescribes not, as but a part of the individual's freedom in society. He is also free in obeying laws or complying with decisions that have the authority of a government to which he freely consented and in the making of which he has participated through suffrage. See Locke, *op. cit.,* Sect. 57, 59, 61, 87, 95, 106, 112, 171. See also Rousseau, *The Social Contract,* Bk. I, Ch. 8; Kant, *The Science of Right,* Sect. 42. Cf. Mortimer J. Adler, *The Idea of Freedom,* Vol. I. Ch. 14, Ch. 17, esp. pp. 323–327, Ch. 18, esp. pp. 358–367; Vol. II, Ch. 6.

4. When individuals living together in a society begin by having the unlimited freedom they would have with complete autonomy in the absence of government, they can exercise their liberty to use whatever force or guile is at their disposal to coerce or intimidate others. The ultimate result cannot avoid being an inequality in the possession of freedom rather than an equal measure of it for each, each having the maximum that is compatible with every one's possessing an equal measure.

5. See *The Idea of Freedom*, Vol. I, Ch. 14 and 17, esp. pp. 318–327.

6. Only on the false view that political equality consists in each individual's being an absolute sovereign, the peer of every other sovereign individual, with no one giving orders or directions to anyone else, and with no cooperative activities that involve a hierarchy of functions or tasks that involve some relation of men as superiors and inferiors in their conjoined efforts—only on this view, cherished by the anarchist, is government incompatible with political equality.

7. To ask for more freedom than this is to ask for freedom to invade the rights of others and to injure them or the community. When the epithet "libertarian" is employed invidiously, it connotes one who wants liberty at any price, without regard to equality and justice. Similarly, the "egalitarian" is one who seeks equality without regard to liberty and justice. These errors can be avoided only by making justice the primary consideration, for then and only then is it possible to maximize both liberty and equality for all.

NOTES TO CHAPTER 11

1. See *Politics*, VII, 2, 1324^a 24–25; and cf. III, 9, 1280^b 39–1281^a 2; VII, 8, 1328^a 37–38.

2. See *ibid.*, III, 5, esp. 1278^a 10–12.

3. See *ibid.*, III, 9, 1280^a 31–34.

4. See *ibid.*, I, 5–7.

5. If the natural slave is thus conceived as a person with limited intellectual powers, comparable to those of a child in arrested development, he would be unable to form the habits of thought and action required for participation in political life. On this view, the differ-

ence between the man who is by nature fit and the man who is
by nature unfit for citizenship is a superficial difference in kind
(having or lacking certain habits), based on an underlying difference in degree (the difference between the degree of intellectual
power that permits the formation of the habits in question and the
degree that does not). The difference is, therefore, both a difference in nature (with respect to the degree of innate intellectual
power) and a difference in nurture (with respect to the requisite
habit formation).

If the difference were a radical difference in kind, that is, if the
natural slave totally lacked the intellectual powers possessed by one
who is born to be a free man, then the natural slave would not
be a human being or a person and would not have the natural
rights that make the treatment of a person as chattel unjust. See
The Difference of Man and the Difference It Makes, pp. 8–10,
30–31, 262–273.

To deny, as I would deny, that there are any natural slaves, on
either of the foregoing conceptions of what is involved in the
difference between being by nature a slave and being by nature a
free man, is to assert that all men have the same species-specific
intellectual powers, and that, with the exception of the pathologically arrested, all have them to a degree that suffices for the
nurtural development of the habits of thought and action requisite
for political life.

6. The proposition "man is by nature political" (that is, all men are
both capable of and inclined toward self-government) is contradicted by the proposition "some men are by nature slaves"
(that is, some men are incapable of self-government and so are
in need of despotic rule). One of this pair of propositions must
be true, and the other false. The proposition "some men are by
nature slaves" is also contradicted by the proposition "all men are
by nature fit to be governed as free men and equals." Hence the
denial of the proposition that some men are by nature slaves entails the affirmation of two propositions that are equipollent: on
the one hand, that all men are by nature political; on the other
hand, that all men are by nature fit to be governed as free men
and equals.

7. These species-specific powers give all men both the *capacity* and
the *inclination* to participate in political life. To say that all men
have the capacity but only some the inclination is like saying that
some men have the capacity for happiness but only some the inclination to pursue it. In addition, a capacity or power that is
inherent in human nature engenders a natural need for the good
that can be achieved by its exercise or employment; and that in

turn grounds the moral obligation to seek the real good that satisfies the natural need. Because we have the capacity for it, we have
a moral obligation to engage in political life, as well as a natural
inclination to do so.

8. Cf. Mortimer J. Adler, "The Future of Democracy," in *Humanistic
   Education and Western Civilization*, ed. by Arthur A. Cohen, pp.
   35, 38, 43.

9. See *The Social Contract*, Bk. I, Ch. 2.

10. See *Politics*, VII, 9; also *ibid.*, I, 7, 1255^b 35–37. Cf. Robert M.
    Hutchins, "The Theory of Oligarchy: Edmund Burke," in *The
    Thomist*, Vol. V, January, 1943, pp. 61–78.

11. It is not quite fair to associate Mill with Kant on this point without
    observing that what Kant says explicitly, Mill says only by im-
    plication. Kant argues for withholding suffrage or active citizen-
    ship from the working classes on the grounds that they suffer
    from disabling circumstances. Mill argues for admitting the work-
    ing classes to citizenship but tries to offset the effect of the numer-
    ical majority they would possess by a variety of devices that, if
    instituted, would have the same result as withholding the suffrage
    from them. In addition, the very same argument that Kant employs
    to justify a temporary disfranchisement of the working classes,
    Mill employs to justify despotic government for peoples who,
    suffering from disabling circumstances, are for the time being
    incapable of self-government. See Note 13, *infra*.

12. *The Science of Right*, Sect. 46.

13. See *Representative Government*, Ch. 4. Cf. Mortimer Adler and
    Walter Farrell, "The Theory of Democracy, IV" in *The Thomist*,
    Vol. IV, No. 3, July, 1942, pp. 503–504, 510–514, 518–520.

14. See Chapter 13, pp. 157–159, *infra*.

15. "No man can be a good citizen," declared Theodore Roosevelt in
    1910, "unless he has a wage more than sufficient to cover the bare
    cost of living and hours of labor short enough so that after his day's
    work he will have the time and energy to bear his share in the
    management of the community, to help in carrying the general
    load. We keep countless men from being good citizens by the
    conditions of life with which we surround them" ("The New
    Nationalism," in *The Annals of America*, ed. by M. J. Adler and
    C. Van Doren, Vol. 13, p. 253). Cf. the Progressive Party Plat-
    form of 1912, in *ibid.*, pp. 347–355, esp. pp. 348–349, 353–354.

16. Cf. my earlier treatment of the question about postponing en-

franchisement in "The Future of Democracy," *loc. cit.*, pp. 36–39; and in "Footnote to the Theory of Democracy," in *From an Abundant Spring*, pp. 137–151. I now fully agree with the objector to the Aristotelian position, against whom I argued in 1952, though I must add that I still have some sympathy for a reluctant democrat such as J. S. Mill. It is much easier for us, a hundred years later, to see that his fears were unfounded than it was for him to overcome them in the face of what appeared to be very real dangers at the time.

NOTES TO CHAPTER 1 2

1. Economic justice in general parallels political justice; the one aims at securing the right of every man to have the economic conditions prerequisite to effective pursuit of happiness; the other aims at securing the right of every man to the political liberty and equality that are conditions of leading a good human life. Quite distinct from this broad meaning of economic justice, there is a narrower conception of it applicable to the economic transactions involved in the production and distribution of wealth. See the exposition of the three principles of economic justice in this narrower sense in *The Capitalist Manifesto*, Ch. 5, by Louis Kelso and Mortimer J. Adler.

2. Anyone who attempts to define economic equality must consider four possibilities: economic equality can be thought of as consisting in (a) all having no possessions at all; (b) all possessing the same arithmetically definite amount of economic goods; (c) each having economic goods in the variety and amount to satisfy all his individual wants; (d) each having the variety and amount of economic goods to satisfy the natural needs common to all men. These four possibilities being exhaustive, the elimination of the first three of them as impracticable or untenable, leaves us with the fourth as the only practical conception of economic equality. The fact that economic equality so conceived permits some men to have more than others is quite consistent with the fact that every one has enough for a good human life. Those who have more than enough are in moral danger of being seduced by the superfluities of their excessive affluence. Still, it is possible for them by virtue to overcome the seduction, as it is not possible for those who, through poverty or destitution, are deprived of the requisite economic goods to overcome such deprivation. The pursuit of happiness may

be threatened by undue affluence; it is frustrated by poverty. The basic natural right to the pursuit of happiness engenders the subsidiary natural right to a sufficient quantity of the economic goods requisite for its effective pursuit. This right is secured by the justice of a society that establishes economic equality, conceived as everyone's having a sufficient quantity of goods to satisfy man's natural economic needs.

If, in such a society, some men have more wealth than they have a natural right to or more than they naturally need, the resultant inequality of possessions is quantitative rather than qualitative. Quantitative economic inequality does not remove qualitative economic equality, but it creates the political problem of protecting society from the inequality of power that results from quantitative inequality of wealth. See p. 148–149, *infra.*

3. *The Time of Our Lives,* p. 206; see also *ibid.,* pp. 207–209. For a discussion of economic freedom as distinct from economic equality, see *The Capitalist Manifesto,* Ch. 2.

4. Providing equality of economic opportunity does not discharge society's obligation to establish an equality of economic conditions, including an equal measure of economic freedom for all.

5. See Note 2, *supra.* R. H. Tawney endorses the conception of economic equality in qualitative rather than quantitative terms: economic equality, he writes, is not "an identical level of pecuniary incomes, but [an] equality of environment, of access to education and the means of civilization, of security and independence, and of the social consideration which equality in these matters usually carries with it" (*Equality,* p. 43).

6. See *The Time of Our Lives,* pp. 24–25.

7. Even if economic equality obtained in all other respects, a society divided into owners of capital and wage-earners is one in which there remains a basic distinction between *haves* and *have-nots,* i.e., those who have the economic freedom, security, and power conferred by the ownership of income-producing property and those who lack these economic goods. On this point, cf. George Lichtheim, *A Short History of Socialism,* esp. Ch. 9–10. The only alternatives would appear to be for *all* individuals in society to be owners of capital, or for *none* to be. Since property in capital instruments cannot be abolished (i.e., capital cannot become like land that is a tract in common—not property in any sense), the second of the foregoing alternatives consists either in the state's ownership of all, as in Soviet or Chinese communism, or in the

ownership of capital instruments by syndics, i.e., functional co-operatives, formed by those associated in a productive enterprise. The syndicalist system of ownership has never been tried in any advanced industrial economy. See Lichtheim, *op. cit.*, pp. 312–329, esp. 318–319.

8. For example, as a matter of practical politics below the level of philosophical principles, one might propose a middle ground between representative and participatory democracy. To cure the defects of representative democracy without going the whole way to the extreme of direct or participatory democracy, the legislature might be empowered to institute referendums on critical public issues, with the result of a referendum being decisive of the issue only if a particular solution of the problem has a two-thirds majority, but having no more than an advisory influence if it is approved by a simple majority. Such a device, if put into operation, would substitute formalized institutional procedures for the informal ways in which the electorate now exercises some influence upon the government, such as public opinion polls, letters and telegrams to legislators, signed notices in newspapers, protest demonstrations in the streets, etc.

9. Normative political economy, in the sense indicated, is an integral part of normative political philosophy. In contrast, economics and politics as descriptive behavioral sciences are quite distinct.

10. See *The Capitalist Manifesto*, Ch. 6. The term "capitalism" is used pejoratively by socialists to designate an economy in which the means of production are privately owned by the relatively few who comprise a distinct class in the population, opposed in their interests to another class—the proletariat, or propertyless workers. If all members of society were owners of capital, or if capital instruments were owned by workers' cooperatives, the economy would be capitalistic in my descriptive sense of the term, though such capitalism would also serve to realize the socialist's ideal of the economically classless society. The mixed economy, sometimes called "socialized capitalism," and the communist economy, sometimes called "state capitalism" or "state socialism," are also forms of capitalism, in the descriptive sense of the term which applies only to the technologically advanced, industrialized societies; but there is a difference of opinion among democratic socialists about their acceptability as ways of achieving both economic and political democracy—the ideal of a classless society in which there is political liberty and equality as well as economic equality and freedom.

11. An industrialized economy without property in capital is as im-

possible as a civil society without civil government. Both are anarchistic illusions. The end at which socialism aims is the abolition of economic inequality and of poverty, not the abolition of property in capital or even the transfer of capital ownership to the state. See Lichtheim, *op. cit.*, pp. 284–285.

12. See *The Capitalist Manifesto*, Ch. 6–7.

13. See John Strachey, *The Challenge of Democracy*, esp. pp. 10–18, 33–34, 40–41; see also C. A. R. Crosland, "The Future of the Left," in *Encounter*, Vol. XIV, No. 3, March, 1960, pp. 3–12; and his *The Future of Socialism*; also R. H. Tawney, *Equality*, Ch. VI.

14. In *The Capitalist Manifesto*, Mr. Kelso and I failed to come up with a satisfactory name for this fourth form of capitalism: see *op. cit.*, p. 107. Since then, in a more recent book, Mr. Kelso has proposed the name "universal capitalism," which I am adopting here: see *The Economics of Reality*, by Louis O. Kelso and Patricia Hetter, Ch. 1, 2, 6. The appropriateness of this name will be apparent to anyone who sees in universal capitalism the economic counterpart of political democracy: as the latter, through universal suffrage, makes all men citizens, so the former, through universally distributed ownership of the means of production, makes all men capitalists.

15. Each of the four forms of capitalism is a political economy in the sense that a certain framework of political institutions is required for its existence, and certain legislative measures or regulations are required for its effective operation. Cf. Joseph Schumpeter, *Capitalism, Socialism, and Democracy*; see also *The Capitalist Manifesto*, pp. 151–158.

16. See John Strachey, *op. cit.*, pp. 19–23, 26–27, 31–34; Milovan Djilas, *The New Class, The Unperfect Society: Beyond The New Class*.

17. The long-term viability of the mixed economy is highly doubtful. It does not and cannot have a remedy for the built-in inflationary spiral that is engendered by its mode of redistributing wealth; nor can it succeed in maintaining the policy of full employment, to which it is dedicated. See *The Capitalist Manifesto*, pp. 129–137, 149–151; *The Economics of Reality*, Ch. 24.

18. See Note 17, *supra*. The one possibility that I have not fully explored may be the fifth alternative mentioned in the text; namely, the syndicalist capitalism that places the ownership of capital instruments in the hands of workers' cooperatives. See Notes 7 and 10, *supra*. This, like the fourth possibility, has never been put into practice; its feasibility therefore remains questionable.

NOTES TO CHAPTER 13

1. See Plato, *Republic*, IV, 423; Aristotle, *Politics*, V, and also VI, 3.

2. See *The Federalist*, Number 10, in *Great Books of the Western World*, ed. by R. M. Hutchins and M. J. Adler, pp. 50–51. Cf. James Madison, "A Plurality of Interests and a Balance of Powers," in *The Annals of America*, ed. by M. J. Adler and C. Van Doren, Vol. 3, pp. 145–149.

3. See Alexis de Tocqueville, *Democracy in America*, Vol. I, Ch. XV; John Stuart Mill, *Representative Government*, Ch. 6–7.

4. See Bertrand Russell, *Roads To Freedom*, p. 50, 197–201; *Patterns of Anarchy*, ed. by Leonard Krimerman and Lewis Perry, pp. 511–514; V. I. Lenin, *State and Revolution*, p. 68.

5. See *The Federalist*, Number 10, *loc. cit.*, pp. 51–53, and Number 39, pp. 125–128; *A Disquisition on Government*, in *The Annals of America*, ed. by M. J. Adler and C. Van Doren, Vol. 7, pp. 552–562; John Stuart Mill, *Representative Government*, Ch. 7, 10, 12.

   In "The Future of Democracy," I wrote: "The remedies—proportional representation and plural voting—which Mill proposed as ways of safeguarding democracy from its own deficiencies would as effectively have nullified democracy in practice if they had been carried out, as the devices proposed by James Madison and John Calhoun to prevent the will of the majority from prevailing. To be in favor of universal suffrage (which makes the ruling class coextensive with the population) while at the same time wishing to undercut the rule of the majority, is as self-contradictory as being for and against democracy at the same time" (*loc. cit.*, p. 38).

   The anti-Federalist papers plainly reveal the suspicion on the part of the opponents of Hamilton, Madison, and Jay that the framework of government that they favored tended to give the balance of power to a ruling class of property owners. As John Jay expressed it in the slogan of the Federalist Party, "Those who own the country ought to govern it."

6. The classlessness that would eliminate all factional conflicts may be an ideal limit that can be approximated but never fully realized. As Jonathan Swift pointed out in *Gulliver's Travels*, it was human

folly, not political injustice, that precipitated the conflict between the Big-Endians and the Little-Endians (see Part I, Ch. IV). To eliminate the factional conflicts that arise from unjust institutions or arrangements may be the most that one can hope for. One cannot expect institutional improvements of any sort to eliminate those that stem from the mo.al perversity or folly of men. Cf. Yves Simon, *Philosophy of Democratic Government*, pp. 253–259.

7. See R. H. Tawney, *Equality*, Ch. II, esp. pp. 71–72, 78–80, 90; and John Strachey, *The Challenge of Democracy*, pp. 33–35.

8. It is necessary to call attention to the difference between a realistic and a utopian conception of the classless society. The anarchist's conception of the classless society as one that will come into being when the state has withered away and government no longer exists is utopian or impracticable on all counts. See Djilas, *The Unperfect Society: Beyond The New Class*, esp. pp. 62–64. However difficult it may be to achieve to the fullest extent, the political philosopher's conception of the classless society is eminently practicable, for it looks toward the elimination of factional conflicts by just institutions and arrangements. Aristotle anticipated this conception of classlessness in his vision of the polity or constitutional government in which the middle class became, for all practical purposes, the only class. See *Politics*, V, 1, 1302^a 13–16; V, 7, 1307^a 5–27. Cf. Mortimer Adler and Walter Farrell, "The Theory of Democracy, Part IV," in *The Thomist*, Vol. VI, No. 1, April, 1943, pp. 81–93, esp. pp. 83, 89–90, 92–93.

9. Those who think that all governments are *de facto*, unjust, and oppressive use the word "establishment" in a dyslogistic sense when they apply it to the network of institutions that have their center or support in government. Those who think that governments can be *de jure*, just, and non-oppressive use the word "establishment" in a eulogistic sense when they apply it to the institutions of society that derive their power from the authority of government.

10. See John Strachey, *The Challenge of Democracy*, pp. 41–45.

NOTES TO CHAPTER 14

1. The advances made in the twentieth century hav crossed a critical threshold in the line of progress. In all earlier centuries, the populations of the best societies that existed were divided into

an oppressed majority and a privileged minority. In this century for the first time that situation has been reversed. In the technologically advanced, socialized democracies, it is a minority that is oppressed, and a small minority at that—considerably less than a third. The vast majority enjoy the privileges—the beneficent conditions of life—that are in justice due to every man. Injustice still remains, and it is no less grievous or onerous because it oppresses the few rather than the many; but the reversal that has taken place in this century give us reasonable ground for optimism about the removal of the injustice that remains to be rectified. To reverse the relation of the majority and minority is comparable to a change in kind as contrasted with the change in degree which further progress may achieve—the step forward from beneficent conditions of life for the majority to beneficent conditions of life for all.

2. See Margaret Mead, *Culture and Commitment: A Study of the Generation Gap.* To call the past a "colossal failure" because the best societies that now exist are not yet perfect is wilfully to overlook all the respects in which they are better than any societies that ever existed before; and especially to overlook the critical reversal described in Note 1, *supra*. It is unreasonable not to acknowledge that the small but persistent steps of progress made in the past are responsible for the remarkable jump forward in this century.

NOTES TO CHAPTER 15

1. See Chapter 14, Notes 1 and 2, *supra*.

2. All forms of power available to men, all instrumentalities for use by men, are morally neutral: they can be employed for good or for evil. Any utility or instrumentality is good only insofar as it is put to a good use; and it is always equally susceptible to a detrimental employment. This applies to the most powerful technology as well as to the simplest hand tools or weapons. Cf. Yves Simon, *Philosophy of Democratic Government*, Ch. V, esp. pp. 283–288, 318; and see also Paul Goodman, *New Reformation: Notes of a Neolithis Conservative*, Ch. 1, esp. pp. 7–12, 17–20.

3. See John McDermott, "Technology: The Opiate of the Intellectuals," in *The New York Review of Books*, Vol. XIII, No. 2, July 1, 1969, pp. 25–35. Cf. Harvey Wheeler, *The Political Order:*

Democracy in a Revolutionary Era (Praeger, New York, 1968), Ch. 5.; John G. Burke, "Technology and Values," in *The Great Ideas Today, 1969,* ed. by R. M. Hutchins and M. J. Adler (Encyclopaedia Britannica, Chicago, 1969), pp. 191–235, esp. pp. 227–233.

4. See William Letwin, "Social Science and Practical Problems," in *The Great Ideas Today, 1970,* ed. by R. M. Hutchins and M. J. Adler (Encyclopaedia Britannica, Chicago, 1970), pp. 92–137, esp. Sect. IV. "An expert," Professor Letwin writes, "is someone who knows a good deal about something, and to use his knowledge properly his client must understand what it is that the expert knows. The answer, to put it a shade too bluntly, is that the expert knows only about means. . . . The expert's advice is always properly a *conditional* imperative, in the form 'If you desire to achieve this end, you must do this and this.' . . . Whenever an expert goes far beyond this formulation, he is exceeding his brief, putting himself in the place of a ruler over a subject instead of his right place of servant to a master" (pp. 134–135). Professor Letwin, unfortunately, fails to recognize the existence of moral philosophy as objective and valid knowledge of ends. He maintains that "there are no experts about ends, nobody who is knowledgeable about what goals anybody else should pursue." I maintain, on the contrary, that there are no experts about ends because everybody through common sense is knowledgeable about what goals all men should pursue. The basic moral principles concerning the good life and the good society—the categorical oughts that are universally binding on all men in their individual and social lives—are matters of common-sense knowledge. With such knowledge and with sound practical judgment or prudence in the assessment of means, which, like basic moral knowledge, is not the exclusive possession of experts, the ordinary man as citizen has the capacity to make decisions on the basis of the special knowledge afforded him by every variety of expert.

Cf. Yves Simon, *Philosophy of Democratic Government:* "In an entirely normal state of affairs, leadership belongs to prudence, not to expertness. . . . Perfect order would want experts to be kept in subordinate positions under leaders who should be good men rather than good experts" (p. 279). "Violence is done to the nature of public life whenever government is in the hands of an expert rather than in those of a prudent man. In public life government by experts is government by outsiders. But in technological societies the expert often becomes so important that is is hard to keep him in purely instrumental functions" (p. 307). The difficulty of subordinating experts may increase with technological complexity, but the basic normative principle remains unaltered: moral knowledge and prudence being within the capacity of every man, the citizens as rulers should make the ultimate decisions on all critical political, economic, and social issues affecting the pursuit of the good life and the good society. The subordination of the military to civilian control is merely a special case of the general maxim that the people as a whole should be in control, not technical experts of any variety.

NOTES TO CHAPTER 16

1. See pp. 90–91, *supra*.

2. "War consisteth not in battle only, or in the act of fighting, but in a tract of time, wherein the will to contend by battle is sufficiently known; and therefore the notion of time is to be considered in the nature of war, as it is in the nature of weather. For as the nature of foul weather lieth not in a shower or two of rain, but in an inclination thereto of many days together, so the nature of war consisteth not in actual fighting, but in the known disposition thereto during all the time there is no assurance to the contrary" (Hobbes, *Leviathan*, Part I, Ch. 13). Sovereign states are always in the posture of war toward one another, whether they appear to be hostile or friendly in their interchanges. As Hobbes observes, they have "their weapons pointing, and their eyes fixed on one another; that is, their forts, garrisons, and guns upon the frontiers of their kingdoms, and continual spies upon their neighbors, which is a posture of war" *(ibid.)*.

3. In slightly differing language, Cicero, Machiavelli, and Locke all point out that men have only two ways of settling their differences —by fighting or violence, or by law, persuasion, and the use of authorized force. When the second set of means is not available through the institutions and instrumentalities of government, men are in a state of war with one another. This is just another way of saying that civil government is indispensable to civil peace, positively conceived as the condition in which men can settle their differences without recourse to violence.

4. When the force exerted by a *de facto* government maintains what appears to be civil peace, the peace is illusory rather than real: first, because the force employed, being unauthorized, is violence; and, second, because those unjustly treated are justified in having recourse to violence in order to remedy the abuses they suffer. As

Locke observes in his comment on the meaning of *rebellare, de facto* or despotic government, being incompatible with the peace of a civil society, is a return to the state of war. Aquinas goes further. In his view, any injustice imposed by force renders civil peace defective: "for if one man enters into concord with another not by a spontaneous will but through being forced by the fear of some evil that threatens him, such concord is not really peace" *(Summa Theologica*, Part II–III, Q. 29, A. 1, Reply 1). "There is no peace where a man agrees with another man counter to what he would prefer. Consequently, men seek by means of war to break this concord, because it is a defective peace, in order that they may obtain a peace in which nothing is contrary to their will" *(ibid.,* Q. 29, A. 2, Reply 2). Hence "peace is the work of justice . . . insofar as justice removes the obstacles to peace" *(ibid.,* Q. 29, A. 3, Reply 3).

5. The American civil war, sometimes incorrectly referred to as "the war between the states," and properly described as a war between the federal government and the states attempting to secede from the federal union, is a case in point. That war was concluded with a declaration of amnesty, restoring the civil peace of the federal union, not by a "peace treaty" of the kind that concludes an international war. Since sovereign or autonomous entities —whether individuals or states—do not co-exist in a condition of civil peace, the "peace treaty" that the victors impose upon the vanquished never restores civil peace; it only establishes an armed truce between the recent combatants.

6. See my discussion of the necessity, possibility, and probability of world government as the indispensable condition of world peace, in *How to Think About War and Peace,* esp. Ch. 5–10, 13, 14, 16, 19–20.

7. Toynbee, confident that world government is inevitable in the relatively near future, remains in doubt whether it will come into being by legal means, such as a world constitutional convention, or by violent means, such as the domination of the world by the conqueror in a world war. (See *Civilization on Trial,* Ch. 7; cf. Ch. 2, 5.) Should it be accomplished by violence, the resultant *de facto* world government would not establish world civil peace, but only an illusory counterfeit of it. See Note 4, *Supra.* A world war would probably then be necessary to overthrow the despotic or *de facto* world rule and replace it by a *de jure* or constitutional world government. Cf. Harvey Wheeler, *The Political Order: Democracy in a Revolutionary Era,* Ch. 7–8.

8. See Jacques Maritain's address at the Second International Con-

ference of UNESCO in Mexico City, November 6, 1947; reprinted in *The Range of Reason*, Ch. 13: "The Possibilities for Co-Operation in a Divided World." If the basic moral principles that underlie the formation of a just world order were derived from theological dogmas or were matters of religious faith, the difficulties in the way of cooperation or agreement among men of different religious persuasions would be as formidable as Maritain supposes, and one might have to fall back on his minimalist, pragmatic approach to the problem. I maintain, on the contrary, that common sense supplies the basic moral principles that can bring men into agreement about the constitutional provisions that should be enacted to establish a just world order. See *The Time of Our Lives*, pp. 264–265.

9. See *Preliminary Draft of a World Constitution*, as Proposed and Signed by Robert M. Hutchins, G. A. Borgese, Mortimer J. Adler, Stringfellow Barr, Albert Guerard, Harold A. Innis, Erich Kahler, Wilbur G. Katz, Charles H. McIlwain, Robert Redfield, Rexford G. Tugwell. Cf. G. A. Borgese, *Foundations of the World Republic*; and Elizabeth Mann Borgese, *A Constitution for the World*.

10. Cf. my prediction, made in 1944, that it might take as much as five hundred years to establish world peace through world constitutional government; in *How To Think About War and Peace*, Ch. 22, 24. With the advent of atomic weapons a year or so later, I shortened the time considerably; and I came to share with my associates in the drafting of a world constitution the hope that a world republic might become more and more imminent.

11. See Gunnar Myrdal, *Beyond the Welfare State*; and cf. Harvey Wheeler, "The Politics of Revolution," in *The Center Magazine*, Vol. I, No. 3, March, 1968, pp. 49–65, esp. pp. 62–64.

12. See Yves Simon, *Community of the Free*, Ch. Two.

13. By applying the principle of subsidiarity, calling for the retention of autonomy on the part of subordinate corporations for the performance of subordinate functions, it should be possible to limit the authority of world government to those matters that affect the common good of the world community, reserving to local governments autonomy in the disposition of local affairs. As Wheeler conceives it, "the world will be larger on the outside and smaller on the inside. It will be the entire world but made up of man-sized autonomous communities possessing their own individual integrity" ("The Politics of Revolution," *loc. cit.*, p. 65). In other words, a world federal government would be constitutionally authorized to deal only with matters that cannot be effectively handled by subordinate communities, corporations, or groups.

14. The top cabinet posts in a world federal government might be a secretary or minister of the future (who would be concerned with technological change and economic development), a ministry of peace (that would also be the department of justice and of law enforcement), a ministry of the environment (that would be the department concerned with political ecology), and a ministry of education. There would be no ministry of foreign affairs, no department of war or of defense. Their place would be taken by a ministry of internal affairs, concerned with the relations of the subordinate communities or corporations which had a certain measure of autonomy in local affairs or subordinate functions; and by the ministry of peace, which would develop and control a world-wide civil police force, adequately trained, in accordance with the highest professional standards, for the performance of what might prove to be the most difficult function of world government.

I recommend the study of a proposed new constitution for the United Republics of America as a model that suggests certain types of provisions that should be considered for inclusion in any constitution drafted for a worldwide Union of Socialist, Democratic Republics. It was formulated in discussions that have taken place over the last eight years at the Center for the Study of Democratic Institutions in Santa Barbara; the major part of the work and the actual drafting of the document was done there by Rexword Guy Tugwell. The thirty-seventh draft version has just been published, accompanied by a discussion of the project by Robert Hutchins, Rexford Tugwell, and others. See *The Center Magazine*, Vol. III, No. 5, September/October, 1970. The Tugwell project at the Center in Santa Barbara represents the institutional reforms and inventions within the creative power of those who retain their faith in politics—in institutional change—as the best, if not the only, way to solve the serious and difficult problems that have caused those who lack such faith to turn toward destructive violence or anarchistic illusions. The improvement of America will come from this kind of mature thinking about its problems, not from the juvenile vagaries of Charles Reich.

NOTES TO CHAPTER 17

1. Such evidence as we now have tends to suggest that prolonged compulsory schooling for all children has anti-educational effects as well as being productive of that pathological condition of the human personality known as adolescence. It is only in the last fifty

years or less that any society has undertaken the experiment of universal compulsory schooling carried on for twelve years and followed by four years more of classroom instruction made socially, if not legally, mandatory for equality of opportunity. Even if these sixteen successive years spent in classrooms had been properly directed toward the ends of purely liberal training for the young —toward disciplining their minds in the arts of learning and toward fostering their natural appetite to know—the confinement of the young in classrooms for so extended a period of time would have had the unhealthy results that are now becoming widely apparent. When, as in fact is the case, the schooling is anything but liberal in a manner that would be suited to the development of learning in every growing mind, the result cannot help being a striking and dismal failure.

But that should not lead us to abandon the ideal of genuinely liberal schooling for all, as Ivan Illich appears to recommend in his uncompromising attacks on the whole system of formal education as it is now constituted. The fundamental thrust of his attack is thoroughly justified, as is also the case with the anarchist's attack on all the historic embodiments of the state and government so far. But just as the anarchist calls for the total abolition of the state and government instead of calling for the reform of institutions that are not intrinsically evil or irremediable, so Illich makes the mistake of recommending the abandonment of schooling instead of recommending a thorough over-hauling and re-constitution of the school system. Cf. Paul Goodman, *Compulsory Mis-Education & The Community of Scholars*, and *New Reformation: Notes of a Neolithic Conservative*, Part Two. Goodman's criticisms of the miscarriage of universal compulsory schooling in the United States are as sound and trenchant as those leveled by Illich against the school systems of Latin America, but Goodman has more constructive proposals for the reform of schooling, with respect to its organization, its methods, and its aims.

The whole effort of schooling should be to habituate and capacitate the young person, every young person, for learning, thus enabling him to become one who wants to learn and is able to learn for the rest of his life. That is the only purpose that a system of liberal and liberating schooling should serve, not the utterly preposterous aim of trying to make the young learned, knowledgeable, or wise, much less the enslaving effort to train them for the roles they are to play in a technologically complex industrial society or the equally abusive attempts to stunt their growth by premature specialization or to shackle it with imposed patterns of conformity. If liberal schooling were exclusively directed to its one proper end, it not only could be made effective by individualized means of instruction for every child, with due regard for their individual differences in intellectual endowment and temperamental propensity; but it could also be accomplished in twelve years, beginning at the age of four and ending at the age of sixteen. The Bachelor of Arts degree, properly understood as signifying nothing more than proficiency in the arts of learning and an habitual inclination to engage in learning, would mark the termination of liberal schooling for all at age sixteen. Then, for at least two years and, perhaps, four, no young person would be allowed to remain in the classrooms of a school. Instead of more compulsory schooling, the young would be subjected to another kind of learning, through compulsory public service of one kind or another, duly compensated. Only after that, only after the incipient ills of adolescence had been cured by some years of activity and involvement in the adult world, would the young person of eighteen or twenty be allowed to opt for such further instruction in specialized, technical, or professional fields of learning as our institutions of higher learning might afford those who manifested the desire and aptitude for it. Whether the young returned to the university for one or another form of post-graduate study, they would all, as ungraded graduates of liberal schooling, have become proficient as learners and habitually disposed to go on with learning, each in his own individual way and each to a degree that fitted his capacity. All would thus be prepared for the duties of citizenship and for the even more arduous effort that every man is morally obliged to make in the pursuit of happiness—the effort to devote as much time and energy as he can to the creative activities of leisure-work, all of which represent the continuation of learning throughout adult life.

2. The society that realized the ideal of effective liberal education for every member of the human race—liberal schooling for all and engagement by all in learning throughout adult life—would truly be, as Robert Hutchins has called it, a "learning society." The thesis that everybody must be educated, he writes, "does not mean that everybody must be educated at the same rate or in the same way or to the same extent. Those who enter an alien culture on their arrival at school are bound to need more time and attention than those who move smoothly from home into the educational system. . . . If the object is to help everybody to become as intelligent as he can be, a variety of methods and even of subjects may be permitted, as long as there is a defensible connection between means and ends" (*The Learning Society*, p. 29). See also *ibid.*, pp. 30–32, 85–103, 122–129. Liberal schooling for all is not enough

to achieve the ideal of the learning society. "In addition to offering part-time adult education to every man and woman at every stage of grown-up life," the learning society must be a society that has succeeded, "in transforming its values in such a way that learning, fulfillment, becoming human, have become its aims and all its institutions are directed to this end. This is what the Athenians did. They did not content themselves with the limited, peripheral effort of providing part-time adult education to everybody at every stage of life. They made their society one designed to bring all its members [i.e., the few who were citizens, not the many who were slaves] to the fullest development of their highest powers. By our standards and in our terms, the Athenians were an uneducated people; the vast, elaborate, expensive, highly organized instructional programs and plants of modern times were unknown to them. They did not have much of an educational system. But they have been the educators of the human race. In Athens, education was not a segregated activity, conducted for certain hours, in certain places, at a certain time of life. It was the aim of the society. The city educated the man. The Athenian was educated by the culture, by *paideia*. This was made possible by slavery. The Athenian citizen had leisure; the Greek word for leisure is the origin of our word for school. The Athenian citizen was expected to turn his free time into leisure, into learning how to govern himself and his community. Slavery gave him the free time; all the traditions, practices, and institutions of the commonwealth were intended to form his mind and character, to induce him, in other words, to transmute his free time into leisure. Machines can do for every modern man what slavery did for the fortunate few in Athens. The vision of the learning society, or, as Sir Julian Huxley has put it, the fulfillment society, can be realized. A world community learning to be civilized, learning to be human, is at last a possibility. Education may come into its own" *(ibid.,* pp. 134–135).

In the Introduction to *The Learning Society*, Mr. Hutchins quotes a passage from *The Great Didactic* by John Amos Comenius, which he says should serve as the epigraph for his book. I requote it here because, written in 1607, it is as extraordinary a prophetic vision of what education should become, as Dante's vision, in 1310, of world government not only for the sake of world peace but also for the development of a world-wide learning society. Remarking that "he gave no bad definition who said that man was a 'teachable animal,' " Comenius declares that "it is only by a proper education that he can become a man. . . . The education that I propose includes all that is proper for a man and is one in which all men who are born into this world should share. . . . Our first wish is that all men should be educated fully to full humanity; not any one individual, nor a few, nor even many, but all men together and singly, young and old, rich and poor, of high and lowly birth, men and women—in a word, all whose fate it is to be born human beings; so that at last the whole of the human race may become educated, men of all ages, all conditions, both sexes, and all nations."

NOTES TO CHAPTER 18

1. As I pointed out earlier, the fact that violent revolutionary action is sometimes justified does not support the mistaken interpretation of the phrase "right of revolution" as meaning that revolutionary action is a natural right. See Chapter 9, Note 6, *supra*. When adequate juridical means are unavailable for the prompt redress of just grievances, violence can be rightfully employed in resistance to injustice or repression, without there being a natural right to the employment of violent measures. Man does not have a natural need to resort to violence, as he has a natural need for, and so a natural right to, a decent minimum of economic goods, individual freedom and political liberty, education, a healthy environment and medical care, etc. The need to resort to violence stems wholly from the injustice and deficiency of political institutions, and consequently the right to resort to violence has a social, not a natural, origin.

2. It is of the utmost importance to preserve the clarity of the distinction between civil dissent by non-violent means and revolutionary dissent by violent means. The distinction has recently been obscured by attempts to assimilate criminal to civil disobedience and by the justification of unlawful action (which is a form of violence) as a means of political protest, and so akin to civil dissent.

   The classic and correct formulation of the doctrine of civil disobedience involves two points: (a) the cause of the disobedience must be a law that is morally repugnant to the conscience of the individual, one that in his view is an unjust law and so is a law in name only and, therefore, not binding on his conscience; (b) the action of the individual in disobeying the prescriptive content of such a law must involve a willingness on his part to submit to the law's punitive content, i.e., to suffer the penalty for disobeying the law's prescription.

One of the best statements of the classic doctrine is to be found in Locke's *Letter Concerning Toleration*. According to Locke, the citizen who is enjoined by an enactment of government to act in a manner that is repugnant to his conscience should "abstain from the action that he judges unlawful and . . . undergo the punishment which it is not unlawful for him to bear. For the private judgment of any person concerning a law enacted in political matters, for the public good, does not take away the obligation of that law, nor deserve a dispensation. But if the law, indeed, be concerning things that lie not within the verge of the magistrate's authority . . . men are not in these cases obliged by that law, against their consciences."

The first departure from this classic doctrine appears in Thoreau's *Civil Disobedience:* to protest the injustice of slavery and the injustice of the war with Mexico, Thoreau disobeyed a tax law that was not in itself unjust, nor thought by him to be unjust; he regarded his disobedience as civil because he willingly submitted to the penalty of being jailed for it. Those who have uncritically adopted Thoreau's mistaken conception of civil disobedience now condone a wide variety of lawless actions in disobedience of ordinances or regulations which are not in themselves unjust, as a way of protesting against injustice in other laws or institutions; and, in addition, they further depart from the classic doctrine by being unwilling to accept the legal penalties for such disobedience. Cf. Sidney Hook, "Points of Confusion," in *Encounter*, Vol. XXXV, No. 3, Sept., 1970, pp. 45–53.

In a recent essay on "Civil Disobedience in a Constitutional Democracy," Marshall Cohen acknowledges the distinction between these two forms of dissent. He points out that what Gandhi called "defensive," and others have called "direct," disobedience is limited to cases in which "the law the dissenter violates is the very law that he regards as immoral. In contrast, what Gandhi called "offensive," and others have called "indirect," disobedience occurs in cases, such as that of Thoreau, in which "the dissenter violates laws (usually traffic laws or the laws of trespass) that he finds unobjectionable in themselves in order to protest still other laws, policies or orders that he thinks immoral or even wicked." Mr. Cohen then criticizes Justice Fortas for his rejection of offensive or indirect disobedience as unjustifiable and unnecessary —as lawlessness or violence that is "nothing less than a form of 'warfare' against society." Against Justice Fortas, Mr. Cohen argues that "indirect disobedience is both justifiable and necessary. It is justified, as all civil disobedience is justified, as a solemn protest against important violations of moral principle. And it is necessary, because there is often no alternative form of protest at a comparable level of depth" (in *The Massachusetts Review*, Vol. X, No. 2, Spring, 1969, pp. 224–225).

I agree with Marshall Cohen that what Gandhi called "indirect" or "offensive" disobedience or unlawful action can be, under certain circumstances, both justified and necessary when, as he points out, "no alternative form of protest at a comparable level of depth" is available to the dissenters as a means of protesting against what they regard as iniquitous, immoral, or unjust policies on the part of their government, or the persistence of unjust institutions. But I disagree with him that such action should be called "civil dissent." It is dissent akin to the violence of criminal or unlawful behavior. Justice Fortas was right in referring to it as "warfare against society," as all revolutionary action is; but calling it that does not support the proposition that it is never necessary and can never be justified. See Note 1, *supra*.

3. Considerations of time have become the most critical considerations in the justification of revolutionary action. How much patience can be expected of those who have been oppressed over a protracted span of time and have suffered a long train of abuses? How much impatience on their part warrants their demand for the immediate rectification of injustices they have long suffered? How quickly can certain evils be remedied, given the will on everyone's part to undertake the needed reforms as well as the ingenuity and imagination required to devise measures that will be effective?

4. In the past, the revolutionary actions that led to the reform of society's institutions and the rectification of long-suffered injustices drew the power that made them effective from the force of numbers—the numerousness of an oppressed majority. As I pointed out earlier (see Chapter 14, Note 1, *supra*.), the most advanced societies in the world today have crossed the threshold of progress with a striking reversal in the relation of the majority and the minority. In these societies, it is now a minority that is oppressed, not the majority. This may not, of course, be true of the world as a whole: of the global population, it may still be a minority that is favored by beneficient conditions, and a majority that is oppressed or underprivileged. The revolutionary actions of the future—those that remain to be taken for the further progress of mankind toward the establishment of the best society that is possible on earth—may, therefore, draw the power they need in order to be effective from a coalition of the oppressed in all quarters of the globe, having the requisite numerousness; or they may involve, either within the boundaries of the more advanced

societies or in the world as a whole, a coalition of the oppressed or underprivileged with men of conscience who, though themselves members of the favored majority, make common cause with their less fortunate fellow-men.

NOTES TO CHAPTER 19

1. Aristotle grades states along a continuum from the least stable and most prone to revolution to the most stable and least prone to revolution. See *Politics*, Bk. V. Injustice is only one of the factors that Aristotle considers in analyzing the causes of revolution; but his view that the polity, or constitutional government with a predominant middle class, is, of all imperfect states, the most stable and least prone to revolution, seems to imply that the classless society under a constitutional government that rendered to each man his due (i.e., secured all natural rights) would be perfectly stable. See *loc. cit.*, 1302^a 9–15, 1307^a 5–27. This does not mean that the best possible society would not be subject to revolution from any causes whatsoever; it means only that in a perfectly just society, there would be no cause of revolution that would justify it.

2. What Dante said of world peace, with the vision of man's whole future on earth before him, might also be said of the dedication of mankind to the pursuits of teaching and learning: it is necessary for the fulfillment of the powers of the human race as a whole. In Dante's view, world peace was the indispensable means to the maturation of the human mind. "The proper work of mankind," he wrote, is "intellectual growth. . . . And since individual men find that they grow in prudence and wisdom when they sit quietly, it is evident that mankind, too, will be most free and easy to carry on its work when it enjoys the quiet and tranquility of peace" (*De Monarchia*, Bk. I, Ch. 4). World peace is a necessary, but not the sufficient, condition for the fullest development of the human mind and spirit, through all forms of creative activity that involve the passions, the will, and the imagination as well as the intellect. Nothing short of the best society that is possible, in which all the external conditions of human life are optimal and stable, will suffice for the attainment of the ultimate goal toward which the human race is by nature inclined.

3. It may be objected that human life would not prosper in a society in which all its external conditions were optimal and stable—that

men need to be confronted with strain and tension, hardships and difficulties, in order to employ their wits and energies to the fullest. In an obstacle-free environment, it may be thought, men would not persist in striving even for a goal that is the fulfillment of their nature. Without adversities to overcome, without urgent problems to solve for animal comfort and convenience, or even for the promotion of human welfare in its highest reaches, men, far from applying all their energies to what is important, would sink into a mental and spiritual lethargy.

If this objection were unanswerable, all the efforts that men have so far made to improve the external conditions of human life, and all the efforts that still remain to be expended on the further improvement of human institutions, would become sound and fury to no significant purpose. When we are ill, health looks like a good that is worth having for its own sake; the same goes for wealth when we are poor, peace when we are at war, freedom when we are enslaved or coerced, equality when we are unjustly discriminated against, and so on. But none of these things is truly an end in itself or good for its own sake. All of them are the indispensable conditions of living well as a human being; but unless, when these conditions are vouchsafed us, we make the strenuous effort required to live humanly well, they are means which have not been used for the end they are intended to serve, and so they have been achieved to no purpose.

Recognizing that advanced technology may put more power at man's disposal than men now know how to use wisely and beneficially should not lead to the recommendation that we stop the development of science or inhibit its technological applications, but rather to the recommendation that men try to acquire the knowledge and wisdom needed to put every increment of power to a good use. Similarly, recognizing that the beneficent conditions of affluence and ease, of freedom and equality, of peace and justice, may weaken the moral fibre of the race and result in human stagnation, torpor, or flaccidity, should not lead to the recommendation that we call a halt to institutional reforms or to revolutionary movements that aim at producing such beneficent conditions. That would be a counsel of despair. We must hope that men can develop the strength of character, the moral virtue, required to make a good use of the very best conditions of human life, even though that would be a more heroic brand of virtue than men have ever exhibited in the past in all their efforts to overcome adversity, to alleviate human suffering, and to promote justice for themselves and for their fellow-men.

References

ADLER, MORTIMER J.: *How To Think About War and Peace*, Simon and Schuster, New York, 1944.
———. *The Idea of Freedom*, Volumes I and II, Doubleday & Company, Garden City, New York, 1958 and 1961.
———. "The Future of Democracy," in *Humanistic Education and Western Civilization*, Essays for Robert M. Hutchins, ed. by Arthur A. Cohen, pp. 30–43.
———. *The Conditions of Philosophy*, Atheneum, New York, 1965.
———. *The Difference of Man and the Difference It Makes*, Holt, Rinehart and Winston, New York, 1967.
———. *The Time of Our Lives*, Holt, Rinehart and Winston, New York, 1970.
ADLER, MORTIMER J., and WALTER FARRELL: "The Theory of Democracy, Parts I–V," in *The Thomist*, Vol. III, pp. 397–449, 588–652; Vol. IV, pp. 121–181, 286–354, 446–522, 692–761; Vol. VI, pp. 49–118, 251–277, 367–407; Vol. VII, pp. 80–131; 1941–1944.
ADLER, MORTIMER J., and PHILIP F. MULHERN: "Footnote to the Theory of Democracy," in *From an Abundant Spring*, P. J. Kenedy & Sons, New York, 1952.
ADLER, MORTIMER J., and CHARLES VAN DOREN (eds.): *The Annals of America*, 20 vols., Encyclopaedia Britannica, Inc., Chicago, 1968.
"An Agreement of the People," in *The People Shall Judge*, University of Chicago Press, Chicago, 1949, Vol. I, pp. 40–48.
AQUINAS, THOMAS: *Summa Theologica*
ARDREY, ROBERT: *The Social Contract*, Atheneum, New York, 1970.
ARISTOTLE: *Nichomachean Ethics*
———. *Politics*
ARENDT, HANNAH: *On Violence*, Harcourt, Brace & World, New York, 1970.

BAKUNIN, MICHAEL: *God and The State.*
BARNETT, S. A.: "On the Hazards of Analogies," in *Man and Aggression*, ed. by M. F. Ashley Montagu, pp. 18–26.
BEATTY, JOHN: "Taking Issue with Lorenz on the Ute," in *Man and Aggression*, ed. by M. F. Ashley Montagu, pp. 111–115.
BERLIN, ISAIAH: "Does Political Theory Still Exist?" in *Philosophy, Politics, and Society*, Second Series, ed. by P. Laslett and W. G. Runciman.
BERNS, LAURENCE: "Thomas Hobbes," in *History of Political Philos-*

ophy, ed. by Leo Strauss and Joseph Cropsey, Rand McNally and Company, Chicago, 1963.

BIRD, OTTO: *The Idea of Justice*, Praeger, New York, 1967.

BLOOM, ALLAN: "Jean-Jacques Rousseau," in *History of Political Philosophy*, ed. by Leo Strauss and Joseph Cropsey, Rand McNally and Company, Chicago, 1963.

BORGESE, G. A.: *Foundations of the World Republic*, University of Chicago Press, Chicago, 1953.

BORGESE, ELIZABETH MANN: *A Constitution for the World*, Center for the Study of Democratic Institutions, Santa Barbara, 1965.

BOUCHER, JONATHAN: "A View of the Causes and Consequences of the American Revolution," in *The Annals of America*, ed. by M. J. Adler and C. Van Doren, Encyclopaedia Britannica, Inc., Chicago, 1969, Vol. 2, pp. 343–352.

BRACTON: *Treatise on the Laws of England*, ed. by George Woodbine, 2 Vols., 1915–1922.

BURKE, JOHN G.: "Technology and Values," in *The Great Ideas Today, 1969*, ed. by R. M. Hutchins and M. J. Adler, Encyclopaedia Britannica, Inc., Chicago, 1969.

CALHOUN, JOHN: *A Disquisition on Government*, in *The Annals of America*, ed. by M. J. Adler and C. Van Doren, Encyclopaedia Britannica, Inc., Chicago, 1968, Vol. 7, pp. 552–562.

CARRITT, E. F.: *Morals and Politics*, Clarendon Press, Oxford, 1935.

CASSIRER, ERNST: *The Question of Jean-Jacques Rousseau*, Columbia University Press, New York, 1954.

CHOMSKY, NOAM: "Notes on Anarchism," in *The New York Review of Books*, Vol. XIV, No. 10, May 21, 1970.

CICERO: *Republic*

COHEN, ARTHUR A. (ed.): *Humanistic Education and Western Civilization*, Essays for Robert M. Hutchins; Holt, Rinehart and Winston, 1964.

COHEN, MARSHALL: "Civil Disobedience in a Constitutional Democracy," in *The Massachusetts Review*, Vol. X, No. 2, Spring, 1969, pp. 211–226.

CROSLAND, C. A. R.: "The Future of the Left," in *Encounter*, Vol. XIV, No. 3, March, 1960.

DANTE: *De Monarchia*, trans. by H. W. Schneider under the title *On World Government*, Liberal Arts Press, New York, 1949.

DEELY, J. N.: "The Emergence of Man," in *The New Scholasticism*, Vol. XL, No. 2, April, 1969, pp. 141–176.

———. "The Philosophical Dimensions of the Origin of Species," in *The Thomist*, Vol. XXX, Nos. 1 and 2, January and April, 1969, pp. 75–149, 251–342.

DJILAS, MILOVAN: *The New Class*, Praeger, New York, 1957.
———. *The Unperfect Society: Beyond The New Class*, Harcourt Brace & World, New York, 1969.
DUNN, JOHN: *The Political Thought of John Locke*, University Press, Cambridge, 1969.
FITZHUGH, GEORGE: *Sociology for the South*, in *The Annals of America*, ed. by M. J. Adler and C. Van Doren, Encyclopaedia Britannica, Inc., April, 1969, Vol. 8, pp. 243–250.
FORTESCUE, SIR JOHN: *The Governance of England*, ed. by Charles Plummer, Clarendon Press, Oxford, 1885.
FOSDICK, RAYMOND: *European Police Systems*, Century, New York, 1915.

GOLDWIN, ROBERT A.: "John Locke," in *History of Political Philosophy*, ed. by Leo Strauss and Joseph Cropsey, Rand McNally and Company, Chicago, 1963.
GOODMAN, PAUL: *Compulsory Mis-Education; Community of Scholars*, Vintage Books, New York, 1968.
———. *People or Personnel*, Vintage Books, New York, 1965.
———. *New Reformation: Notes of A Neolithic Conservative*, Random House, New York, 1970.
GORER, GEOFFREY: "Man Has No 'Killer' Instincts," in *Man and Aggression*, ed. by M. F. Ashley Montagu, pp. 27–36.

HAMILTON, ALEXANDER, JOHN JAY, and JAMES MADISON: *The Federalist*, Modern Library, New York.
HOBBES, THOMAS: *Leviathan*.
HOOK, SIDNEY: "Points of Confusion," in *Encounter*, Vol. XXXV, No. 3, Sept., 1970, pp. 45–53.
HUTCHINS, ROBERT M.: "The Theory of Oligarchy: Edmund Burke," in *The Thomist*, Vol. V, January, 1943, pp. 61–78.
———. *Aquinas and the World State*, Marquette University Press, Milwaukee, 1949.
———. "Doing What Comes Scientifically," in *The Center Magazine*, Vol. II, No. 1, January, 1969, pp. 56–60.
———. *The Learning Society*, Praeger, New York, 1968.
HUTCHINS, RORERT M., and MORTIMER J. ADLER (eds.): *Great Ideas Today, 1969*, Encyclopaedia Britannica, Inc., Chicago, 1969.
———. *Great Ideas Today, 1970*, Encyclopaedia Britannica, Inc., Chicago, 1970.

ILLICH, IVAN: "The Need for a Cultural Revolution," in *The Great Ideas Today, 1970*, ed. by R. M. Hutchins and M. J. Adler, Encyclopaedia Britannica, Inc., Chicago, 1970.

————. "Why We Must Abolish Schooling," in *The New York Review of Books*, Vol. XIV, No. 13, July 2, 1970, pp. 9–15.

JACKSON, JAMES H.: *Marx, Proudhon, and European Socialism*, English University Press, London, 1957.

JAFFA, HARRY V.: "Aristotle," in *History of Political Philosophy*, ed. by Leo Strauss and Joseph Cropsey, Rand McNally and Company, Chicago, 1963.

JOLL, J.: *The Anarchists*, Little Brown and Company, Boston, 1964.

KANT, IMMANUEL: *The Science of Right*.
————. *Perpetual Peace*.

KELSO, LOUIS, and MORTIMER J. ADLER: *The Capitalist Manifesto*, Random House, New York, 1958.

KELSO, LOUIS, and PATRICIA HETTER: *The Economics of Reality*, Random House, New York, 1967.

KRIMERMAN, LEONARD I., and LEWIS PERRY (eds.): *Patterns of Anarchy*, Anchor Books, New York, 1966.

KROPOTKIN, PETER A.: *The State, Its Historic Role*, Freedom Press, London, 1903.
————. *Anarchism: Its Philosophy and Ideal*, Freedom Press, London, 1904.

LASSWELL, HAROLD: *Politics: Who Gets What, When, How*, McGraw–Hill, New York, 1936.

LASLETT, P., and W. G. RUNCIMAN (eds.): *Philosophy, Politics, and Society*, Second Series, Basil Blackwell, Oxford, 1967.

LENIN, V. I.: *State and Revolution*, International Publishers, New York, 1932.
————. *The Emancipation of Women*, as collected from his writings, International Publishers, New York, 1970.

LETWIN, WILLIAM: "Social Science and Practical Problems," in *The Great Ideas Today, 1970*, ed. by R. M. Hutchins and M. J. Adler, Encyclopaedia Britannica, Inc., Chicago, 1970.

LEWIS, JOHN: "On Human Rights," in *UNESCO Symposium on Human Rights*, pp. 54–71.

LICHTHEIM, GEORGE: *The Origins of Socialism*, Praeger, New York, 1969.
————. *A Short History of Socialism*, Praeger, New York, 1970.

LOCKE, JOHN: *Concerning Civil Government*, Second Essay (in the critical edition by Peter Laslett, Cambridge University Press, Cambridge, 1967).
————. *A Letter Concerning Toleration*.

LUBAC, HENRI DE: *The Un-Marxian Socialist: A Study of Proudhon*, Sheed and Ward, New York, 1948.

MABBOTT, J. D.: *The State and the Citizen*, 2nd ed., Hutchinson University Library, London, 1967.

MADISON, JAMES: "A Plurality of Interests and a Balance of Power," in *The Annals of America*, ed. by M. J. Adler and C. Van Doren, Encyclopaedia Britannica, Inc., Chicago, 1968, Vol. 3, pp. 145–149.

MAREK, FRANZ: *Philosophy of World Revolution*, International Publishers, New York, 1969.

MARITAIN, JACQUES: *Scholasticism and Politics*, The Macmillan Company, New York, 1940.

———, *The Rights of Man and Natural Law*, Charles Scribner's Sons, New York, 1943.

———. "On the Philosophy of Human Rights," in *UNESCO Symposium on Human Rights*, pp. 72–77.

———, *Man and the State*, University of Chicago Press, Chicago, 1951.

———. *The Range of Reason*, Charles Scribner's Sons, New York, 1952.

———. *On the Philosophy of History*, Charles Scribner's Sons, New York, 1957.

MARX, KARL, and FREDERICK ENGELS: *The Communist Manifesto*.

MAXIMOFF, G. P. (ed.): *The Political Philosophy of Bakunin: Scientific Anarchism*, The Free Press, Glencoe, 1953.

MAYER, MILTON: *Man v. the State*, Center for the Study of Democratic Institutions, Santa Barbara, 1969.

McDERMOTT, JOHN: "Technology: The Opiate of the Intellectuals," in *The New York Review of Books*, Vol. XII, No. 2, July 1, 1969.

McILWAIN, CHARLES HOWARD: *The Growth of Political Thought in the West*, The Macmillan Company, New York, 1932.

———. *Constitutionalism Ancient and Modern*, Cornell University Press, Ithaca, 1940.

MEAD, MARGARET: *Culture and Commitment: A Study of the Generation Gap*, Doubleday, New York, 1970.

MILL, JOHN STUART: *On Liberty*

———. *Representative Government*

———. *The Subjection of Women*.

MONTAGU, M. F. ASHLEY (ed.): *Man and Aggression*, Oxford University Press, New York, 1968.

MONTESQUIEU: *The Spirit of Laws*

MORGENTHAU, HANS: *The Purpose of American Politics*, Alfred A. Knopf, New York, 1960.

MYRDAL, GUNNAR: *Beyond the Welfare State*, Yale University Press, New Haven, 1960.

NOVAK, D.: "The Sources and Varieties of Anarchism," in *Patterns of Anarchy*, ed. by Leonard I. Krimerman and Lewis Perry, Anchor Books, New York, 1966.

OPPENHEIMER, FRANZ: *The State*, Huebsch, New York, 1922.

PETERS, R. S., and P. WINCH: "Authority," in *Political Philosophy*, ed. by Anthony Quinton, Oxford University Press, New York, 1961.

PLAMENATZ, JOHN: "The Use of Political Theory," in *Political Philosophy*, ed. by Anthony Quinton, Oxford University Press, New York, 1961.

———. *Man and Society*, McGraw-Hill Book Company, New York, 1963.

———. *Consent, Freedom and Political Obligation*, Oxford University Press, New York, 1968.

PLATO: *The Statesman*.

———. *The Republic*.

PLEKHANOV, G.: *Anarchism and Socialism*, Twentieth Century Press, London, 1895.

PLUMB, J. H.: *The Death of the Past*, Houghton Mifflin Company, Boston, 1969.

Preliminary Draft of a World Constitution, University of Chicago Press, 1948.

PROUDHON, P. J.: *General Idea of the Revolution in the Nineteenth Century*, Vanguard Press, New York, 1923.

———. *What is Property: An Inquiry into the Principle of Right and Government*, W. Reeves, London, 1902.

QUINTON, ANTHONY (ed.): *Political Philosophy*, Oxford University Press, New York, 1961.

REITH, CHARLES: *A New Study of Police History*, Oliver and Boyd, Edinburgh, 1956.

RICHARDSON, JAMES F.: *The New York Police*, Oxford University Press, New York, 1970.

ROUSSEAU, JEAN-JACQUES: *The Social Contract*.

RUSSELL, BERTRAND: *Roads to Freedom*, Allen and Unwin, London, 1918.

SCHEIRLA, T. C.: "Instincts and Aggression," in *Man and Aggression*, ed. by M. F. Ashley Montagu, Oxford University Press, New York, 1968, pp. 59–64.

SCHUMPETER, JOSEPH: *Capitalism, Socialism, and Democracy*, Harper Bros., New York, 1950.

SIMON, YVES: *Nature and Functions of Authority*, Marquette University Press, Milwaukee, 1940.

———. *Community of the Free*, Henry Holt and Company, New York, 1947.

———. *The Philosophy of Democratic Government*, University of Chicago Press, Chicago, 1951.

———. *A General Theory of Authority*, University of Notre Dame Press, Notre Dame, 1962.

———. *Freedom and Community*, Fordham University Press, New York, 1968.

SOREL, GEORGES: *Reflections on Violence*, Collier Books, New York, 1950.

SPENCER, HERBERT: *The Man Versus The State*, with an introduction by Albert Jay Nock, Caxton Printers, Caldwell, Idaho, 1954.

STIRNER, MAX: *The Ego and His Own*, The Modern Library, New York.

STRACHEY, JOHN: *The Challenge of Democracy*, Encounter Pamphlet No. 10, London, 1963.

STRAUSS, LEO: *What Is Political Philosophy*, Free Press, New York, 1959.

———. "Plato," in *History of Political Philosophy*, ed. by Leo Strauss and Joseph Cropsey, Rand McNally and Company, Chicago, 1963.

STRAUSS, LEO, and JOSEPH CROPSEY (eds.): *History of Political Philosophy*, Rand McNally and Company, Chicago, 1963.

SWIFT, JONATHAN: *Gulliver's Travels*

TAWNEY, R. H.: *Equality*, Barnes and Noble, New York, 1964.

The People Shall Judge: University of Chicago Press, Chicago, 1949.

"The Progressive Party Platform of 1912," in *The Annals of America*, ed. by M. J. Adler and C. Van Doren, Encyclopaedia Britannica, Inc., Chicago, 1968. Vol. 13, pp. 250–254.

TOCQUEVILLE, ALEXIS DE: *Democracy in America*, 2 vols., ed. by P. Bradley, Alfred A. Knopf, New York, 1945.

THOREAU, HENRY DAVID: *Civil Disobedience*, in *The Works of Thoreau*, ed. by Henry Seidel Canby, Houghton Mifflin, Boston, 1937, pp. 789–805.

TOYNBEE, ARNOLD J.: *Civilization on Trial*, Oxford University Press, New York, 1948.

TUGWELL, REXFORD G.: "Constitution for a United Republics of America," in *The Center Magazine*, Vol. III, No. 5, September/October, 1970, pp. 24–45.

UNESCO Symposium on Human Rights: Comments and Interpretations; Allan Wingate, London, 1949.

VAN DOREN, CHARLES: *The Idea of Progress*, Praeger, New York, 1967.

WHEELER, HARVEY: *The Political Order: Democracy in a Revolutionary Era*, Praeger, New York, 1968.

———. "The Politics of Revolution," in *The Center Magazine*, Vol. I, No. 3, pp. 49–65, March, 1968.

WOLIN, SHELDON S.: *Politics and Vision*, Little Brown and Company, Boston, 1960.

WOODCOCK, G.: *Anarchism*, World Publishing Company, Cleveland, 1962.

ZUCKERMAN, SIR SOLLY: "The Human Beast," in *Man and Aggression*, ed. by M. F. Ashley Montagu, Oxford University Press, New York, 1968, pp. 91–95.

Index of Proper Names

Index of Proper Names